The People vs. the Golden State Killer

THIRD
STATE
BOOKS

SAN FRANCISCO

The People vs. the Golden State Killer

Thien Ho
Sacramento District Attorney

The People vs. the Golden State Killer
by Thien Ho

Published by Third State Books
93 Cumberland Street
San Francisco, CA 94110
Visit us at: www.thirdstatebooks.com.

Edited by Charles Kim
First edition: November 2025

ISBNs:
979-8-89013-035-8 (hardcover)
979-8-89013-037-2 (e-book)

References of Thien Ho as District Attorney are for identification purposes only.

The author and the publisher have made every effort to ensure that the information in this book is as accurate and thoroughly researched as possible. We regret any errors, inaccuracies, omissions, or other inconsistencies and will correct them in any future printings.

Printed in the United States by Thomson Reuters

I dedicate this book to my family, for they are the compass that guides me, the path on which I walk, the wind that pushes me forward, and the inspiration that lifts me to the stars.

Thien Ho

Introduction

Visalia, California, is located in the Central Valley, a region whose abundant agricultural industries have long fed the Golden State and America. In the 1970s, it was a farming community in which neighbors knew one another and no one locked their doors. During long, hot summers, kids went swimming and fishing in cool, gurgling local creeks and rode their bikes late into the warm evenings. In autumn, the leaves turned bright red and golden hues as the air filled with the bustle and noise of children and school buses.

But underneath its bucolic, small-town veneer, a sinister series of crimes spread like an uncontrolled infection. From 1974 to 1975, Visalia experienced over 120 burglaries in a three-square-mile radius. The local authorities were at a total loss to find the masked bogeyman and stop the spree. The local media dubbed him the Visalia Ransacker, or simply the Ransacker. The criminal often attacked multiple times in one night; on November 20, 1974, he burglarized eleven homes in just one evening.

The Visalia Ransacker's modus operandi was fairly consistent: He would break into an unoccupied home and place small glasses or plates by the front door as a makeshift alarm. He turned off the air-conditioning unit so he could hear if someone was approaching. Although the victims were not physically present during the break-ins, everything he did was tied to violating their sense of safety and control. He walked around their homes, as they would. He ate their food and drank their beer, as they would. He went through their closets and picked out their clothes. He also demonstrated a fetish for ritual: He would place women's clothing carefully on the bed, sometimes in the pattern of a body, as if he were dressing them himself. If he found a pornographic magazine, he would use lotion to masturbate inside the house, leaving his semen behind to mark his newly conquered territory like an animal. He would occasionally take one earring, leaving the other in the pair behind as a reminder of how he had violated their home, their possessions, and their sense of safety.

The local newspapers reported every home invasion with front-page stories detailing the spine-chilling and salacious facts of each incident. As panic spread in the community, fueled by the evening news coverage, people bombarded the police with calls of Peeping Toms, prowlers, and burglaries, demanding that something—anything—be done. Pressure mounted on the police, and it seemed every roll call of every shift led with an update on yet another burglary. The Ransacker struck with utter impunity. While most burglaries were economic crimes motivated by greed, his motives were different. Something more sinister compelled him: power and perversion. So far, no one had been hurt—yet.

Forty-five-year-old Claude Snelling was a professor of journalism at the College of the Sequoias. Often sporting black, horn-rimmed glasses and neatly slicked hair that framed his square jaw, he was popular among students for his warm smile and demeanor. He was adored by his wife and children, two boys and a daughter, who described him as a "big softie," kind-hearted and supportive. He was particularly close to sixteen-year-old Beth. The two often hiked in the mountains together. Claude would listen to her talk about school, friends, or boys and gently offer his advice.

On Sept. 11, 1975, the Ransacker broke into the Snelling home, on the 500 block of Whitney Lane in Visalia. No one knows how the Ransacker came to choose Beth as his next victim, but in the months leading up to that night, she had become an object of his obsession. She saw him several times prowling outside their home, peeking through her bedroom and bathroom windows. She discovered shoeprints he had left underneath her window. Just before 2 a.m., Beth awoke from a dream and felt a hand covering her nose and mouth. In the dark, a masked stranger hovered over her. He pressed his weight against her body and whispered in a low raspy voice, "You are coming with me. Don't scream, or I'll stab you."

With his right hand, he dragged Beth from her bedroom; with his left hand, he pulled a revolver from behind his back. Beth described him as a stocky white male. As he pulled her into the family room, he aimed the gun at her head. "Don't scream, or I'll shoot you." As she was dragged from the house through the rear door, located between the kitchen and the family room, Beth began crying and tried to pull away.

Hearing Beth's shrieks, her father leaped out of bed and ran toward the sound. By that point, the intruder had forced her out the back door and through a gate that separated the backyard from the carport. Crumpled on the ground at her attacker's feet, Beth heard her father yell, "Hey!" and saw him charge out the back door to her rescue. The Ransacker turned and fired his gun twice, killing Snelling instantly. He then looked down at Beth and turned his gun back at her head. Having seen her father killed mere feet away, she thought, *This is it*. She lowered her head, expecting to be executed. Instead, the Ransacker kicked her in the face three times before he turned and ran off in the dark.

During the autopsy, the coroner recovered one bullet from Claude Snelling's body. Testing showed it was fired from a .38 Miroku revolver, an uncommon handgun. A Miroku had been stolen by the Ransacker in a burglary on August 31, 1975. Snelling's murder was inevitable; the escalating pace of lurking and burglaries had led to this. Peeping Toms and prowlers become aroused by invading the privacy of others. With each incident, the Ransacker needed more stimuli to reach the same level of titillation. The burglaries he committed, the playing with women's undergarments, the masturbating—they only heightened his excitement and fed his insatiable lust. The attempted kidnapping of a sixteen-year-old girl in the middle of the night was a step in the unnatural progression and evolution of a budding serial rapist and killer. The Visalia Ransacker had graduated from prowling to voyeurism to burglaries, and now to committing a murder. There was no turning back.

Alarmed by the escalating violence, the public demanded answers and action. Visalia police established a task force that pulled in officers from local and regional law enforcement and the California Highway Patrol. What no one knew was that the bogeyman they were hunting was a cop. In the ultimate irony, the Ransacker, a member of the Exeter police force, periodically assisted the very group assigned to find him.

On the evening of December 10, 1975, the Visalia Ransacker Task Force conducted a series of sting operations focused on areas where the assailant had previously hit. At one site, veteran Visalia Police Officer Bill McGowen stationed himself in a dark garage with the door opened, hoping for fate to bring the burglar-murderer to him. With a wife and a family of his own, McGowen lived in the community he served and felt the same fear his neighbors did—police were not immune from the Ransacker's seemingly random attacks. Sitting in the dark, all he could do was wait.

Suddenly, the policeman heard the faint sound of footsteps. Peering outside, he saw a masked man in a crouched position along the shrubbery, creeping toward the open garage. When the prowler was close enough to confront, McGowen jumped out with his firearm and flashlight. "Police! What are you doing here?" Under the faint white glow of the streetlamp, the two men stood facing each other. Neither moved a muscle nor uttered a word, the moment frozen in time. Then, like a lightning bolt tears apart a dark sky, the Ransacker pulled his mask off with his right hand, revealing his round baby face and light brown hair to his challenger. And with a subtle shift of his body, he took off running and hopped a fence.

Officer McGowen gave chase, but the Ransacker was lighter on his feet, hurdling fences with the ease and quickness of a black cat. Struggling to stay with him, McGowen, his heart pounding in his chest, pulled out his weapon and fired a warning shot into the ground. The suspect froze again, a few feet away, with his back to the officer. McGowen ordered the Ransacker to put his hands up. Slowly raising his arms, he yelped in a high-pitched, effeminate voice, "Oh my God! Don't hurt me! Oh my God, don't hurt me!"

Standing in the backyard of a home on the 1500 block of West Kaweah Street, the hunter became the hunted, trapped among lawn furniture. McGowen was the first police officer to meet the shadowy villain face-to-face. Finally, someone had seen the monster behind the mask. The

Ransacker squealed, "I give up! See, see, I've got my hands up." But McGowen could only see his right arm; he demanded to see the other arm, which was out of view. As the culprit turned around, his hidden hand drew a gun from his jacket pocket and fired point-blank at McGowen. But the heavens were with him that night: The bullet struck the officer's flashlight, saving his life. Glass from the shattered lens ricocheted into his face and cut the skin around his eye, and the bullet's impact knocked him to the ground. But he was otherwise unscathed. By the time he recovered from the blow and looked up, the shooter was gone in the night. No other member of law enforcement would come this close to the Ransacker for four decades.

Other officers soon arrived on scene, and when McGowen told them what had happened, they asked him, "Bill, what did the Ransacker look like? You're the only person to have ever seen his face up close like that! What did he look like?"

He replied, "You know, I can't put a name on it, but I have seen him somewhere before."

After that night, the Ransacker never returned to Visalia, leaving over 120 unsolved home invasions in his wake. Police officer Joseph James DeAngelo Jr. transferred to the Auburn Police Department, about a half-hour drive from Sacramento. Within months of his arrival, a serial rapist began brutalizing women and girls in the eastern part of Sacramento County. The media called him the East Area Rapist. He would eventually sexually assault over fifty women and kill thirteen people in perhaps the greatest crime spree by a single individual in California history. Then, he disappeared without a trace for more than thirty years. He became the obsession of detectives, criminalists, victims and survivors, true-crime enthusiasts, journalists, writers, filmmakers, and more. As the years passed, his specter only became grander. He was the Visalia Ransacker, the East Area Rapist, the Original Night Stalker, and the Golden State Killer. The bogeyman who couldn't be found—until we found him.

— — —

As the Ransacker was moving to Sacramento to continue his predatory evolution, halfway around the world, in a country traumatized by war and dying under the yoke of a communist dictatorship, my family was getting ready for our own journey.

I was born during the Vietnam War. I came into the world six weeks premature; the doctors told my parents that I would likely not survive. With limited wartime resources, the hospital had only one incubator. The doctors placed me in it alongside two other premature infants. After a month, I was the only one still alive. My father claimed proudly that I had sucked up all the oxygen in the incubator.

We then moved to a little house in the mountains of Da Lat, renowned for its spectacular waterfalls and pine forests. But when the Communist North Vietnamese began their advance down the peninsula, we headed farther south, to Saigon. The faded tapestry of my childhood memories leaves me with more emotions than distinct images. My father was a teacher, and my mom stayed at home to raise me. I was the eldest child, and male, which carried a heavy significance and responsibility in Asian families. According to my mother, I spoke in full sentences by nine months and never stopped talking from then on. I was a curious kid who asked a million questions and never once paused for breath except to hear the answers—a trial lawyer in training. My father was thin with an angular jawline that framed a wide nose upon which sat black horn-rimmed glasses. He had a thick head of black hair and spoke fluent French and Vietnamese along with some English he'd learned in school. My mother had an oval face and warm brown eyes. Like many Vietnamese women of the time, she had straight black hair that came down to her hips. She grew up in the countryside, where her father was a rice farmer. She tended water buffaloes and lived in a house with a dirt floor. Her difficult childhood hardened my mother underneath her soft exterior.

My parents were like fire and ice. I have never seen my father get angry or heard him raise his voice in my entire life—calm and calculating, he always thought several moves ahead, traits that would later save our lives. My mother had a fiery temper that would flare up in an instant, her volcanic explosions consuming everything before them, including me.

As their son, I inherited my father's intellect and my mother's passion. We were neither rich nor poor. I never once felt hungry, or as if I were missing out or out of place. I recall being sandwiched between my parents on our moped—the number one means of transportation in 1970s Saigon, as it is today—as we weaved through the winding city streets, driving past the French-inspired architecture and cafés and along the Saigon River and canals.

On April 30, 1975, South Vietnam fell to the Communist regime of the North, and Saigon was eponymously renamed Ho Chi Minh City after its leader. (Like many South Vietnam expatriates, my family refers to the city only as Saigon.) When the Communists came into power, we saw our friends, families, and neighbors disappear or be taken away to "reeducation" camps in the jungle. My uncle, a South Vietnamese government worker, was arrested and sent to one of the camps without charge, a trial, or due process of any kind. He returned several years later, having endured torture and starvation. My father, who taught at a local school, and my mother worried constantly about being arrested, terrified that the same injustice could happen to them. A knock at the door or a uniformed officer appearing unexpectedly at the school induced anxiety and panic. But life continued. My younger brother was born in March 1976.

Many South Vietnamese, especially those with money or connections to the US military, left in the final hours before the South Vietnamese government collapsed on April 30, 1975. We had neither; and so, we were trapped. Even after the fall of Saigon, people continued to escape from Vietnam, with its coastline of nearly two thousand miles and trails across the border to Cambodia and eventually to Thailand. But there were no good options. Leave, and risk getting caught and imprisoned. Make it out to sea, and risk getting pillaged by marauding Thai pirates or lost on a vast, endless ocean. Stay, and risk getting arrested and killed or sent to a camp. Stay, and live on your knees, unable to speak, to vote, to believe in your God, or to pursue a dream of a brighter future for your children.

I once read a Zen koan about a student who decides that, when the situation is untenable, break the situation. Imagine being faced with the decision to leave the only country you've ever known, abandon the house you own, walk away from your career, leave your friends behind, and say goodbye, perhaps forever, to your whole family. And you'd risk death in the process. All to start a new life in a country where, in the best of circumstances, you don't speak the language and have nothing but the clothes on your back. My parents resolved to break free and leave, and they paid a cost that cannot be fully measured.

The escape plan needed to be meticulous, with contingencies in place. For months, my parents and several friends pooled their money to buy a fishing boat and hire a captain to take us across the South China Sea. Their hope was to reach the Philippines where, they'd heard, Americans were accepting refugees at the Subic Bay military base. To get past checkpoints in the Mekong River delta before heading to sea, my father stole a uniform from a Communist military officer. He would stand on the boat's deck along with the fishing boat captain, and we would get waved through.

As a child, I loved toy guns, little soldiers, and airplanes. I would crawl around the house with a small play rifle, pretending I was fighting in the jungle or jumping out of a fort made of chairs and blankets with my plastic pistol, mimicking the *pew pew* sound of gunfire. A few nights before we were scheduled to leave, I couldn't find my favorite toy pistol. As I went through the house searching for it, I saw my father sitting at the dining table, painting it black. "What are you doing with my gun?" I asked. He told me, laughing, "I want to play too. I'll buy you another one."

As we snuck aboard the tiny fishing boat, my parents hid my two-month-old brother in a cardboard box with holes for ventilation. He was mild-mannered and rarely cried. Sometimes, I would forget he was even there. Inside that ventilated cardboard box, he lay completely still and quiet. There were more than thirty men, women, and children crammed below deck. In the darkness, I could see the whites of their eyes. My parents told me we were going on a trip across the ocean and asked me to not say a single word, which was really difficult for me to do. "Don't talk, don't even cough," my mother told me. I didn't fully realize what was happening but sensed the fear in the air—the whispering, the tense looks, families huddling together.

Up on deck, my father stood in his stolen uniform, my painted handgun in his holster. Under a full moon, we made our way out to sea. We were waved through several checkpoints without being stopped. The uniform was working. At the last checkpoint before hitting the open water, a guard motioned us to stop for inspection. Why were we slowing down? Worried looks spread across the crowd. Everyone remained silent. I moved slightly so I could see my father through a crack in the floor.

A young military guard looked him up and down. "Why are you out here?"

"I just bought this boat from this captain, and we are going for a cruise with my wife and two young boys who are below deck."

Skeptical, the guard turned his head to the side and said, "I don't believe you. I think you have a bunch of refugees below deck, and I want to search right here, right now!"

My father had never gambled in his entire life, but in that moment, he pushed all the poker chips to the middle of the table. "Go ahead and look below deck if you want." His voice got deeper and louder, and he put a hand on his holster. "But if all you see is my wife and two boys, I will take this gun and blow your fucking brains out. How dare you question me? I outrank you!" he yelled and pointed to his uniform.

The guard paused, and after an uncomfortable silence, he stammered, "Um, I'm sorry. I didn't mean to question you. I don't need to look. But let's come back to the guard shack for a drink before you go." The gamble had paid off. They walked off the boat and headed back to the guardhouse. In the meantime, my mother feared the worst. Never one to hold her tongue, she started chiding the other men for hiding while my father was up there alone. The men could only whisper among themselves, debating what to do. After a few minutes, my father returned to the boat, to my mother's great relief. He came below deck to explain what was happening. The Vietnamese love their cognac, and he and the young guard had shared a glass together before the guard allowed us to depart. Just then, the boat started moving again.

We had passed all the barriers and could see the sea ahead. My father was a schoolteacher and his friends on the boat were all city folks. Knowing nothing about navigating a boat in open water, they had hired a captain to navigate us across the ocean to freedom. His family was to join us, but for some reason, they missed the rendezvous time, and we had to leave without them. Unwilling to forsake his wife and children, the captain jumped off the boat and swam to shore, abandoning us to find our own way across the South China Sea.

Robert Burns wrote, "The best-laid schemes of mice and men / Go oft awry." We faced an agonizing decision: proceed out to sea, with no one onboard able to steer the ship competently; or turn back and risk capture. There was, really, no choice. My parents and the other adults decided to take our chances at sea. I could feel the salty sea breeze against my face. There were a few other kids on the boat, and we excitedly ran around the deck as dolphins swam around us and leaped in the air. We were free.

The euphoria and excitement faded quickly as we headed east with no sense of direction. Approximately 900 miles separate Vietnam from the Philippines. My father thought it would take several days, but the days turned into weeks. The nights were the worst as we sailed through total darkness. We ran out of gas, food, and water. Hunger pains gave way to thirst, fatigue, and lethargy. No more running or screaming in excitement. I just lay in my mother's lap, exhausted. I asked for food and a sip of water, but there were none. All she could do was brush my hair with her fingers and hold me.

There was nothing to do but drift along, carried by the ocean. My father kept watch on deck, but all he could see was clear blue sky and an endless horizon. With the sun beating down, he felt despair overwhelming him. He didn't believe in God; unless he could see something, touch it, and talk to it, he wasn't going to believe in it. But as he stood there helplessly, he began to pray. "I know that I have denied that You even exist. But if You save my family, I will never question You again." As my parents tell it, within a half hour, a merchant ship sailed by. All the adults came up, screaming and hollering to get its attention. The crew took us all onboard; they were headed to Malaysia.

While we languished in a refugee camp, my uncle, who lived in Stockton, worked furiously to obtain the paperwork to bring us to California. Months later, in fall 1976, we landed at the airport in San Francisco with nothing but the clothes on our backs and each other. My father quickly found a job driving trucks during the day and attended community college at night. My mother would tuck my brother and me into bed and then work the graveyard shift at a local food factory. She would return in the morning smelling like the peaches she had been canning all night long.

On my first day of school, I didn't understand a single word anyone said. The teachers introduced me to another Vietnamese boy, but he refused to play with me because I couldn't understand English. I stopped talking. Left alone after school, while my parents went to work, I learned the language by watching Bugs Bunny cartoons. In 1980, we moved to San Jose, the heart of the Vietnamese community in Northern California. In 1991, I was accepted into the University of California, Davis, where I majored in political science and studied communications. In 1998, twenty-two years after arriving in the United States, I graduated from law school and became a prosecutor.

— — —

Before her untimely death, journalist Michelle McNamara wrote the hugely popular *I'll Be Gone in the Dark* and coined the "Golden State Killer" moniker. My colleague, criminalist Paul Holes, wrote *Unmasked*, a harrowing account of his life spent chasing the East Area Rapist/Golden State Killer and myriad other serial killers. These and other books and documentaries have brought the Golden State Killer into the mainstream. His crimes have been obsessed over by countless amateur sleuths, and like John Wayne Gacy and Ted Bundy, his legend has, to a certain extent, been romanticized. His spree of terror has softened in the public's mind after four decades.

Until now, no one has written about the entire investigation, capture, and prosecution of this notorious serial killer. As the lead prosecutor of the Golden State Killer case, I devoted almost three years of my life to making sure that DeAngelo would never spend another minute as a free man. Now that he is serving eleven consecutive terms of life without the possibility of parole and one additional term of life behind bars, I want to strip away the mystery of the monster behind the mask and peel away the myths shrouding his deeds. I want to fill the space left behind with stories of the intrepid women and men of law enforcement who never gave up their pursuit of the EAR/GSK, who wanted to bring justice and closure to this criminal's victims. I want to give voice like never before to the heroic survivors and their loved ones, who waited so long to claim back their lives. We have all fought together not to vilify and punish an evil human being, but for our own healing, redemption, and human right to be heard. A portion of the proceeds from this book will fund a nonprofit created by several GSK survivors.

The People vs. the Golden State Killer takes place principally in two time periods: 1974 to 1986, the years during which Joseph DeAngelo committed his known crimes; and 2018 to 2020, when DeAngelo's identity was discovered, and we conceived and executed our plan to arrest and prosecute him. In this official account, you will learn for the first time the entire story behind the investigation, pursuit, and prosecution of the Golden State Killer. You will accompany the "Body Snatchers" as they stalk and arrest DeAngelo. You will follow us as we search every inch of his house. You will sit in the interview room as detectives interrogate him and learn firsthand exactly what incriminating things he says when they leave him alone. You will watch the contentious behind-the-scenes fight among the counties to host the case of the century. You will study the legal strategy we use to hold him accountable for his crimes. You will attend court with the prosecutors as we seek to deliver justice for victims and survivors. You will stand behind the victims as they fight to be heard. And finally, you will go behind the curtain as DeAngelo stands and admits to all his crimes and receives his punishment.

On the trail of this remarkable cold case, everything starts and ends in Rancho Cordova.

1
The “Cho”

Summer 1976

In the 1970s, Rancho Cordova, known by locals as the "Cho," was a quiet community full of ranch-style homes on the eastern edge of Sacramento County. Many of its residents were service members at nearby Mather Air Force Base. The Cho was a place where people could raise a family. Kids rode their bikes in the concrete canals that crisscrossed the neighborhoods or floated lazily on rafts down the American River. On hot Sacramento summer nights, people left their windows open to let in the cool Delta Breeze.

Like Visalia, Rancho Cordova was a tight-knit community, where few locked their doors and windows or looked over their shoulders—until the East Area Rapist came to town. From 1976 to 1978, he committed six assaults in the Cho and nearly fifty rapes in Sacramento County alone. His first victim, a twenty-three-year-old resident named Phyllis, was assaulted while her dad was out of town. Subsequent attacks occurred mostly in neighborhoods that bordered the American River. A long parkway running along the water provided the offender with quick access to homes and easy escape routes.

Since the sexual assaults first occurred in the eastern part of the county, the media called him the East Area Rapist, or EAR. Once it became clear to the public that a serial rapist was on the loose in their town, residents turned their lives upside down to protect themselves. People slept with guns under their pillows. Entire families slept in one room and pushed furniture up against the door to barricade themselves against intruders. Gun shops and hardware stores couldn't keep security products such as deadbolt locks, alarm systems, and weapons in stock. Some bought large guard dogs to protect them. A few even resorted to sleeping on the roof. Neighbors formed watch groups, and men organized mini militias that patrolled their neighborhoods at night. Police helicopters began flying regular rounds over the town, their spotlights scanning the streets for predators. The constant whir of their rotor blades added to the feelings of anxiety.

On the night of February 2, 1978, in a subdivision of the town called Cordova Meadows, Katie and Brian Maggiore were out for a stroll with their poodle. Brian was a staff sergeant over at Mather, and with his mop of light brown hair and square jaw, the twenty-one-year-old looked every bit the part of a military man. He had just married twenty-year-old Katie, whose brown hair flowed past her shoulders and framed her blue eyes and slender face. They had both grown up in the Central Valley before marrying and moving to Sacramento when Brian was stationed at Mather. The young and attractive couple talked about starting a family.

It was shortly after 9 p.m. on a particularly dark evening, the faint glow of a quarter moon and an occasional streetlamp the only light. Winters in Sacramento could be surprisingly cold, particularly by California standards. It had rained the night before, and the grass and barren trees and sidewalks smelled fresh and damp. As the Maggiores walked, they noticed that many homes had installed metal bars on all exterior points of entry. It had been two years since the EAR first struck a few blocks away from where they were walking, and his attacks had intensified and spread across Sacramento. There had been recent reports of burglars and prowlers in this working-class neighborhood. People came home to find a window or sliding glass door unlocked, but nothing missing. Investigators knew the EAR was known to stalk his prey, obsessively watching his future victims. He noted their schedules meticulously, biding his time until, when least expected, he would strike in the middle of the night. He would break into a house, but not for the purpose of stealing; instead, he would take a family photograph, an earring, or some other small object and hide it under a sofa cushion or in a drawer before leaving. Then, a few days later, he would return to check whether the homeowners had noticed the hidden item.

While jogging southbound on West La Loma Drive, Benny Pickett looked to his left and saw Brian and Katie farther up the street on La Alegria Drive, walking their dog toward him. As he crossed the street, he saw to his immediate left a white male standing behind some bushes, peeping into the living-room window of the house on the corner. The prowler was wearing a long, light brown jacket, and a knit mask covered his head. Benny, who had just graduated from high school, was engrossed in his jog and didn't give much thought to the man next to the window. He kept running. As the Maggiores continued to walk on La Alegria Drive toward West La Loma, they were about to encounter the masked man.

That initial interaction between Brian, Katie, and the intruder will forever be lost to the darkness of time. Perhaps Brian confronted him for peeping into a window. He was the sort of person that, if he saw something out of place, wouldn't just let it go. He would step in and speak out if he perceived an injustice or wrong. Whatever happened, the killer pulled a gun, precipitating a horrifying chain reaction of events. He chased the Maggiores into the backyard of a house on La Gloria Way, a block away.

Thirteen-year-old David* was doing homework upstairs in his bedroom, which overlooked the backyard. He heard the wooden side gate open, followed by loud, frantic voices. Jumping up from his desk, David looked out his window to see the young couple run through his yard toward a hole in his neighbor's fence, a section of which had fallen down in a storm the night before. Then, he saw the outline of a man wearing a mask running after them. He raised a gun and fired several shots near the neighbor's patio area. Sheriff's deputies later found Brian lying on the ground near the patio with gunshot wounds to his chest and head.

Seeing her husband gunned down in cold blood, Katie ran along the side of the house, screaming frantically for help as she tried to escape to the street. She reached the end of the yard and tried to open the gate, but it was locked. She was trapped, with nowhere to run, alone with the masked killer. All she could do was cry out for help, but no one came to her

* Names with asterisks are aliases to protect the individuals' identities.

aid. The EAR ran up behind her, raised his weapon, and shot Katie in the back of the head. She was still alive when the police arrived but lost her fight for life on the way to the hospital.

Karl* lived two houses from where the Maggiores were murdered. He had just started his junior year at Cordova High. Most seventeen-year-olds have no sense of fear or danger, wrapped in an armor of invincibility, and Karl was no different. When he heard the shots, he leaped off his couch and ran out the front door toward the sound of gunfire. Coming to a stop a few feet from the bottom of his neighbor's driveway, he heard rustling in the bushes and the rattling of the wooden gate to his neighbor's yard. Suddenly, a man jumped over the fence and landed softly on the ground, like a cat falling from a tree. Wearing a light brown jacket and a mask over his face, the man held a gun in his left hand. In one smooth motion, the man stood up, straightened his body, and ran straight at the teen. As Karl froze in place, unable to move or utter a sound, the two strangers locked eyes. Karl was face to face-to-face with the East Area Rapist. Before the boy could do or say anything, the EAR pivoted to his left and ran across the street, jumped over another fence, and disappeared in the dark.

After encountering Karl, the EAR continued leaping over fences and running between homes and alleyways. Minutes later, the blaring sirens of police cars and ambulances filled the air. He knew from his prior assaults that authorities would quickly erect checkpoints at all major points of ingress and egress. Soon, helicopters would hover, their spotlights searching for him. Armies of law enforcement would descend upon the neighborhood with bloodhounds, fanning out in all directions. The hunter now became the hunted. He was running out of time.

Not wanting to be seen holding a firearm, he took the knit mask off and wrapped the gun in it as he ran through the neighborhood. Sharon,* who lived in a small duplex a few streets away from where the killings happened, was washing dishes when her dog started barking furiously. She heard police sirens and the pulsating noise of helicopter blades. Stepping outside to see what the commotion was about, she encountered a white male wearing a brown jacket, holding in his hands what looked like a mask with the butt of a handgun protruding from it.

Sharon was able to get a clear look at the EAR's face as he ran by her. Later, she helped a police artist draw a sketch portrait, which was published in all the local newspapers and shown on television newscasts. Some have referred to it as the "Robin Williams sketch" due to the drawing's curious likeness to the young TV actor, who would go on to star in the hit show *Mork & Mindy* later that year. Once the sketch was released to the media, the EAR never returned to Sacramento. Instead, he shifted his reign of terror to other parts of the Bay Area and then to Southern California. Although he never returned to Rancho Cordova after that night, the EAR did leave something behind in the backyard next to Brian's body. Deputies found a pretied shoelace at the crime scene, which would later connect him to many of his other crimes.

— — — — —

Spring 2018

In the forty-two years since the East Area Rapist started his crime spree and terrorized Rancho Cordova in 1976, the Sacramento County DA's Office had grown from a handful of attorneys to over 160 prosecutors and nearly 400 employees. With a reputation for having some of the best trial lawyers in the state, the office thrived under the steady leadership of Jan Scully, the first woman in the county's history to serve as district attorney (1995–2014). Her successor, Anne Marie Schubert, displayed a leadership style that some described as unfocused and erratic. Facing a tough internal challenger in her first bid for reelection, she jumped from one crisis to the next. But neither she nor anyone else could have predicted the spark that spread like a wildfire through parched, drought-stricken timber. A racial reckoning engulfed Sacramento in the spring of 2018.

On March 18, police received a call about a suspicious individual breaking into cars and homes. When they arrived at the scene, they encountered an African American man, twenty-two-year-old Stephon Clark, who advanced toward them, holding his hands up in front of him as if holding a gun. Officers shot and killed him. Although subsequent independent investigations found the police's response was justified, the Sacramento community was outraged at what it felt was excessive force. For weeks, Black Lives Matter protesters surrounded the Sacramento DA's Office every day, marching and calling for Schubert to be recalled.

On April 24, as protesters occupied the sidewalk in front of the building, beating drums and hanging effigies of the DA on a pole, Schubert was hunkered down in her corner office, paralyzed. On the other side of the building, sitting in my office within the Homicide Bureau, I kept my head down and worked on my cases. I had been a prosecutor for nearly twenty years and felt I was just hitting my prime as a trial lawyer. I had tried nearly every type of case one could and successfully obtained the convictions of serial rapists, child molesters, and other deviant monsters who preyed upon the most vulnerable among us. I had racked up conviction after conviction against coldblooded killers. I went after hardened gangbangers from the Meadowview Bloods, the Strawberry Manors, and every subset of Norteños and Sureños in the county.

Homicide was led by Chief Rod Norgaard, a short, barrel-chested man who exuded a frenetic, Tasmanian devil cartoon energy. In his mid-fifties, Rod sported a white goatee and a wicked sense of humor. The cops loved him because he would entertain them in his office with war stories, but more important, he was a brilliant tactician willing to give advice on how to investigate a murder, interrogate a suspect, or build a case. Rod filed all homicide cases handled by the bureau, and each one had to satisfy his strict standards of proof. People knew that food was the way to Rod's heart, and they came bearing donuts, carnitas tacos, or halibut ceviche. Although food got your foot in the door with Rod, you still had to prove your case. I considered Rod a friend and mentor. He often gave me the toughest and most challenging cases. When he was on vacation or out of town, he had me review all the search warrants and delegated the responsibility of filing homicide cases to me.

I like to go into the office early and get work done before things get busy and people knock on my door. That morning, I arrived around seven, brewed myself a pot of green tea, and started to review a homicide case. Seventeen-year-old J. J. Clavo had been shot and killed while driving to a football game at Grant High School—a senseless gang-motivated shooting by a fifteen-year-old. Clavo was a star player who was beloved by his teammates. His friend in the passenger seat was also shot multiple times but survived. In the days following his murder, I met with his mother, Nicole Clavo. No words can ever console a grieving parent who has lost a child. All I could do as a law-enforcement official was to be present, hold her hand, and promise to help her obtain justice for her son.

Since my office was located right next to Rod's, I witnessed a constant parade of police officers, attorneys, and people wanting his advice and counsel. At 10 a.m., I was standing right outside my office talking to my secretary, Noemi Rosado. Noems, as I often called her, had been with the Homicide Unit for years and worked for the legendary John O'Mara, who ran Homicide for over three decades. Noems is half Mexican American, half Puerto Rican, and all attitude. She never hesitates to offer her opinions and is fiercely loyal. She can also keep a secret, as I soon learned.

Standing there talking to Noems, I saw Chief Deputy Steve Grippi walk in with Rod. As the second-in-command, Steve ran the day-to-day operations of the office. He was the man behind the curtain, pulling the strings and making the tough calls. An Italian American with dark olive skin and thinning silver hair, he had a knack for taking complex problems and boiling them to their essence, like a fine red wine sauce. His deep sense of fairness was at times punctuated by streaks of anger. We were always worried about making Steve angry for fear that his temper might go "full Grip" on you. Like many of his generation in our office, Steve was an amazing trial lawyer who excelled in the courtroom.

Several times that morning, Steve popped his head into Rod's office, speaking in hushed tones and then hurrying off somewhere else before coming back. The way they moved and talked, their hands cutting and stabbing the air, conveyed an urgency and purpose shrouded in secrecy. Something was up. I looked over at Noems and asked, "What the hell is going on? They seem up to something. Do you know?" Without skipping a beat or even looking at me, she replied nonchalantly, "I'm not sure what's going on," and quickly changed the subject.

Rod and Steve went into Rod's office a final time and slammed the door shut behind them. My curiosity was piqued beyond measure. I went into my office, which shared a wall with Rod's, and closed the door. In our four-story building constructed over fifty years ago, the walls were paper thin and poorly made, and you could sometimes make out what was being said on the other side. So I put my ear up against the wall and listened. Initially, I could only hear unintelligible murmurs, not unlike the "sound" of ocean waves when you hold a seashell to your ear. Squeezing in between a wooden credenza and a metal file cabinet, I yanked my left arm behind my back and twisted my neck so the side of my head lay flat against the wall surface. In painful discomfort, I held my breath and closed my eyes to concentrate on every syllable and sound. Then, I heard Rod utter, "The lab report showed a one-in-sixteen-septillion DNA match to the EAR!"

In Sacramento, the term EAR meant one thing, and one thing only: the East Area Rapist. After forty years, he was still alive, and we had found him. I sat down in my chair and stared at the wall, trying to absorb what I had just heard. A mixture of shock and adrenaline coursed through my veins. I tried to contain my emotions and not make noise in case they heard me from the other room. But I couldn't do it. I jumped up out of my chair, threw my arms in the air, and screamed as quietly as I could, "Yes!" We had just broken through in the biggest case not only in the history of our county, but arguably in the entire state of California. We had finally located one of the most notorious serial killers to ever roam our streets. And we were not going to let him get away.

In fact, law enforcement never gave up on bringing him to justice as each new generation of officers continued to look for him. I had first heard of the EAR six years earlier as I was getting ready to try my first homicide case. The body of Rajneet Singh was discovered behind a brick wall in Rancho Cordova on New Year's Day. She was naked from the waist down with her bra pulled up to her neck and her underwear tossed to the side of her body.

As the trial approached, I visited the crime scene with the lead detective, Sheriff's Homicide Sergeant Jim Barnes. He was a bear of a man, standing nearly six-foot-four and filling every inch of the driver's seat of the full-size F-150 pickup truck in which he picked me up. I asked Billy Satchell, a friend in my office, to come with me. Billy had grown up in Rancho Cordova and gone to high school with the victim. Having grown up in the Cho since the late 1970s, he knew the local landscape as well as anyone. His parents had met while his dad was serving in the armed forces. As a biracial couple—she was white, he was Black—living in a trailer park, they faced dirty looks, long stares, and outright racism while stationed in the South.

After his parents divorced, Billy grew up with his mother in a tiny public-housing apartment along Coloma Road in Rancho Cordova. He played football in high school and was a social chameleon of sorts. Looking at him, people thought he could be Mexican or Persian or Indian or any other number of ethnicities. He loved studying languages and had a keen sense for dialect and tone, becoming proficient at multiple accents. He stood almost six feet tall, with a receding hairline and the stocky build of a former high school middle linebacker. Billy knew the streets and possessed a deep reservoir of common sense. He had a quick temper and a quicker wit, mixed with an everyman's approach to the world. He and I had met a decade earlier as young prosecutors assigned to handle preliminary hearings.

Billy spent his summers in South Sacramento with his grandfather, a property manager for an apartment complex where most of the residents were Vietnamese Americans. He recalls endless summer days running along the creeks and playing with immigrant boys. They traded bottle caps that had been hammered and polished smooth, caught frogs, and played hide-and-seek. To play, he had to learn how to count in Vietnamese; when we first met, Billy proudly demonstrated that he could recite the numbers from one to ten. We quickly formed a deep friendship and a friendly rivalry. Moving up the ranks together, we always competed as to who could try more cases or handle the most challenging trials.

As we drove to the crime scene, we passed by rows of ranch homes, all of them with metal bars on their windows and doors. I commented to

Sergeant Barnes, "It looks like people are locking themselves up in their own homes. Prisoners in their own castles."

"It wasn't always this way," he replied. "The EAR changed everything."

My curiosity was piqued. "What are you talking about?" Growing up in San Jose, I had never heard of the EAR. "Is that his name? Who the fuck is the EAR?"

Before Sergeant Barnes could answer, Billy interrupted. "The East Area Rapist. Back in the 1970s, the EAR started committing rapes all throughout this area, breaking into people's homes, tying them up with shoelaces, and ransacking their houses. After eating their food and drinking their beer, he would return to the bedroom and take the wife to another room. He would return to the bedroom, force the husband onto all fours before draping a bedsheet over his body and placing plates and glasses on his back. He would warn the husband, 'If I hear anything break, I'll kill your whole family.' He would rape the wife before escaping in the night."

I had spent years prosecuting every type of sexual-assault case imaginable, from a sadistic predator who zip-tied and assaulted his victim in a bamboo grove on the winter solstice to a serial rapist who preyed upon sex workers in alleyways and parking lots. To mentally cope with years of being embedded in the sex-crime unit, I developed ways to block and compartmentalize the emotional toll, to the point where human depravity no longer shocked or surprised me. But Billy's account of the EAR jolted me like a defibrillator. I sat straight up in my seat and felt the pounding drumbeat of my heart get stronger and louder. I was hooked. I wanted to learn more.

Sergeant Barnes added, "The EAR would later kill a young couple walking their dog just a few blocks from where we are right here. He also killed ten other people in Southern California and committed rapes across the entire state. We are still looking for him."

"I grew up here where it all started," Billy said. Then his voice got really low. "For us, he was the bogeyman. All the kids talked about him, wondering if he would ever come back."

"Do you think he's alive or dead?" I asked.

Billy guessed he was dead, theorizing that he may have been shot and killed while breaking into someone's home. Barnes told me that he was part of a group of investigators from across the state working to solve this case. He had just returned from Santa Barbara, where investigators had shared evidence and pored over suspect lists. He thought the EAR was dead but wouldn't give up his search for the monster. He wanted the victims to get answers after forty years of questions and anguish.

I turned to Barnes and said, "I'm a blue-collar type of prosecutor who takes whatever case I am assigned. I just handle whatever file shows up on my desk. I've never asked to be assigned to a case. But if you ever catch the EAR, I'll make an exception. I hope one day you will find him, because the victims deserve justice."

2
The East Area Rapist

June 1976

The East Area Rapist's first known attack occurred at approximately 4 a.m. on June 18, 1976, in Rancho Cordova.

Twenty-three-year-old Phyllis Zitka exuded a warmth and natural friendliness. Not particularly tall or athletic or boisterous, she spoke with a soft voice and gentle gestures. She had a protective, almost motherly quality, especially toward her little sister, Karen, who lived with her husband in San Diego, 500 miles to the south. Phyllis and her father had moved to Rancho Cordova in late 1974—he was a longtime military man who had been assigned to Mather Air Force Base—and the sisters missed each other dearly and talked often.

For Phyllis, life had been happy and carefree. But on Christmas Eve of 1974, she lost her mother to cancer. She had been the anchor and heart of their family, grounding every aspect of their lives as they lived the transitory childhood of military brats. But now she was gone, and the girls were separated. The subsequent year and a half was tough for both women as they struggled with their mother's passing and watched their father grieve his beloved wife.

When Phyllis went to bed on the evening of June 17, she was alone in the house; her father was on the East Coast visiting his sister. She was tired and looking forward to a restful night's sleep, but something woke her up in the middle of the night. Groggy and disoriented from being pulled out of a deep sleep, she initially thought her dad had come home early from vacation. In the dark, she saw a man standing at the foot of her bed, wearing only a mask over his face and a T-shirt. He was naked from the waist down and had an erection.

As her eyes came into focus and she realized it was not a bad dream but a real-life nightmare, Phyllis felt her heart jump into her throat. When her attacker saw she was awake, he jumped on top of the bed and waved a knife in the air. She immediately pulled the covers up over her head, as if somehow the bedsheet would shield her against this monster, but he yanked the cover down and ripped it off the bed. Then he pressed a sharp kitchen knife against her throat. Speaking in guttural spurts through clenched teeth, the assailant warned Phyllis, "If you make one move or sound, I'll stick this knife in you! I wanna fuck you!" Pointing the tip of the knife at her and flicking it several times to the side, he ordered Phyllis to take her clothes off. Trapped in her dark room alone with this monster, the only thought that kept running through her mind was, *Stay alive.*

Phyllis told her attacker that she was menstruating. He ordered her to remove the tampon and throw it on the ground. He then flipped her over onto her stomach and tied her hands behind her back with a small rope that he had brought with him. He ransacked her closet, nightstand, and drawers before returning with a piece of cloth he used to further bind Phyllis's wrists. He turned Phyllis onto her back and sexually assaulted her for several minutes before he got up and rummaged through the house. At one point, Phyllis heard him in the living room whisper loudly, "I told you to shut up!" Although she never saw or felt anyone else's presence, it sounded like two people whispering to each other, or someone simply talking to themselves.

Then, the house fell eerily silent. Hoping the man was gone, Phyllis loosened the bindings and removed her blindfold. She ran to her father's bedroom and called the police for help. When her father found out his daughter had been raped while he was out of town, the proud, grizzled veteran immediately got in his car and drove nearly nonstop across the country to comfort her.

During her interview with the patrol deputies and the detective, Phyllis described her assailant as a white male with broad shoulders. He wore a tight-fitting white ski mask over his head, with two slits cut out at the eyes; strands of blond hair stuck out from underneath the mask. The rapist also wore light canvas gloves with elastic cuffs. As he groped and fondled her body, the rough material felt like sandpaper. He never took them off. She described his penis as particularly small. After four similar attacks occurred in Sacramento County by Labor Day, the Sheriff's Department realized it was dealing with a serial rapist and assigned one of its top detectives to investigate.

— — —

In the fall of 1976, my family and I were living in Stockton, an hour south of Sacramento, in a tiny one-bedroom apartment on Hammer Lane. Stockton was, and is, a gritty town, and Hammer Lane was in its grittiest area, where most of the immigrants and refugees from Vietnam lived. We had just arrived in the United States that summer. I loved watching American television, especially crime shows. My favorite was *The Streets of San Francisco*. Every Thursday night, I rushed through my homework and scarfed down the dinner my mother made for us—usually a bowl of rice with pickled vegetables and cheap protein like eggs or pork—and sat down in front of the television. Law enforcement back then was male-dominated and lacked diversity. Hollywood and the media almost always portrayed the police as white, and *The Streets of San Francisco* was no different. It starred Michael Douglas as Inspector Steve Keller, who fought the city's criminals wearing a corduroy bell-bottom suit, his flowing brown hair perfectly coiffed. His partner, Lt. Detective Mike Stone, played by Karl Malden, was a gruff and snarly character who had the red, bulbous nose of an alcoholic cop who had seen too many crime scenes, chased too many bad guys, and arrested too many perps. While I was learning police procedures watching Hollywood's fictional version on TV, a trailblazing detective was rising quickly through the ranks in Sacramento.

Only a few women served in the Sacramento Sheriff's Department, and many wore skirts and high heels and carried their service revolvers in their purses while on duty. Detective Carol Daly struck quite the contrasting image in public. In 1968, while working as a clerk/typist for the coroner, she applied for a deputy position with the Sheriff's Department. After she and a handful of other women graduated from the Academy, the sheriff told the media, "We hired some good-looking broads." Tall and thin, she had shoulder-length platinum blonde hair that she wore in a 1960s-style bob haircut with a high crown and long bangs. Anyone who perceived the detective as soft and weak because of her gender was sorely mistaken. Her colleagues knew she was tough as nails and one hell of a detective. Yet Daly was also incredibly compassionate, especially toward those who were suffering. Again and again, she would listen with quiet empathy as victims recalled their horrific experience. She treated them not as evidence, but rather as injured patients who needed care and treatment. During her three-decade-long career with the Sheriff's Department, Daly became the first and only woman ever to be named undersheriff, the department's second-in-command.

At the height of the East Area Rapist investigation, Detective Daly became one of the public faces of law enforcement. She appeared at town-hall meetings and in television interviews, exuding strength and competence. In fact, she occasionally posed wearing a pearl necklace and holding a revolver in her hands. One local news station recorded her giving forward-thinking advice to women gathered at a town-hall meeting: "One thing I want to emphasize, ladies, is for you not to be polite. We've all been raised not to hurt anybody, to be polite, and don't do this or that. But the important thing to remember is, if you are going to protect yourself and if you are going to defend yourself, you must injure your attacker. And I don't mean just hurt him, because by hurting him, you're only going to make him angrier. But you must injure him enough to incapacitate him, in any way that you can."

Over the Labor Day weekend, Daly received a phone call at home about a rape reported on Crestview Drive in Carmichael, a suburb located in the unincorporated area of Sacramento County. It was one of the more affluent areas of Sacramento, where ranch-style homes nestled among old oak trees on large lots abutting the American River. Detective Daly said goodbye to her husband and children and headed off to the crime scene.

The victim, Trish,* had been interviewed several hours earlier by patrol deputies, who typically have the least experience and the shortest amount of time to investigate a crime. Their main duty is to secure the scene, apprehend the suspect if they are still there, and gather preliminary information. If it's a serious case such as a rape, they hand things off to a detective, who has the experience and the time to investigate and build a case. "Just the facts, ma'am," the famous line from the police drama *Dragnet*, may have been the mantra of law enforcement, but investigating rape cases was different, and Detective Daly instinctively knew that. As she walked over to Trish, Daly felt her pain and her plight. A few hours before, she had had the very fabric of her life torn to shreds.

Trish was twenty-nine years old and recently separated from her husband. She was just getting used to her new life and raising her daughter and two adolescent sons on her own. She worked at the local community college, a new job that offered her an opportunity to be independent and to enjoy her newfound freedom. Living with three kids in a tiny apartment, Trish came on her own to her parents' house on Crestview Drive to do some laundry. Her parents went out for the evening, leaving Trish alone in the house.

When Daly knelt face-to-face with Trish and put her hand on her shoulder, Trish began to cry. With long, painful pauses wracked with emotion, Trish told the detective what happened. She had arrived at her parents' home around 6 p.m. and parked her car in the driveway. She moved back and forth all evening between the house and the garage, where the washer and dryer were kept. She watched television until about 11:15 p.m., then went to load the clean laundry into the car. This is what happened next, in her own words:

> I didn't hear or see anyone, but I did feel as if someone was around me. Maybe I heard or felt his breath. I don't know. . . . Before I could react or turn around or look around, he came up from behind, put

> his hands on my shoulder, and flipped me around. I was crouching down putting the laundry basket into the back seat, and so I was bent halfway in the car and halfway out when he attacked me. After flipping me up and around, he punched me in the nose. Blood came gushing out. I fell to the ground and could barely move or barely see. When he punched me, I flew backwards and hit my head on the driveway. After hitting my head on the ground, I blacked out for a moment. He kept shaking me to wake me back up. As I opened my eyes, I felt a knife up against my neck. I was still seeing stars.
>
> While holding the knife up against my neck, he kept yelling "Get up! Get up!" He dragged me to the side yard and made me lay on the ground. He flipped me onto my stomach and tied my hands behind my back. . . . I was totally afraid. I can't put it into words. It was totally dark, it's like your worst nightmare happening. I figured it was dangerous when he punched me to begin with. I knew something was going to happen.

The East Area Rapist dragged Trish through the screened porch and sliding glass door into the family room. Leaving her on the floor, he ransacked the house. She heard him open the refrigerator and drink her father's beer. Then, over the next several hours, he assaulted her repeatedly. He also taunted her, saying, "Oh, your dad's a flyboy. I was in the Army." He had noticed pictures and memorabilia throughout the house indicating her father's service. Trish's parents had an organ in the family room, where she had had music lessons growing up. After he raped her, the EAR left her naked and tied to the organ bench. As in the Maggiore murder scene, investigators found shoelaces in a granny knot on the ground. He had brought the bindings with him. Blindfolded and bound, she lay on the floor crying and wondering when the nightmare would end. Just like Phyllis, Trish eventually heard the house go silent. After what seemed like hours, she loosened the bindings and grabbed the phone to call for help.

Trish told Detective Daly that her attacker was a white male who had a small penis and wore a ski mask made from flannel or canvas with slits cut out for the eyes and mouth. Early in the attack, he opened the air conditioning closet and shut it off, ostensibly so he could hear if anyone came home unexpectedly. The Visalia Ransacker had taken the same precaution, but back in the 1970s, none of the law-enforcement agencies shared information or collaborated in their investigations. They stayed siloed in their own cases and jurisdictions, allowing criminals like the EAR to move freely among counties without fear of coordinated investigations.

Trish's ordeal happened over the Labor Day weekend, and she had to return to work the following Tuesday. She had a black eye and a swollen nose. When her coworkers asked what had happened, she replied she had been mugged. She told her children the same story, keeping her terrible secret buried deep within her heart. A bump remained where the EAR broke her nose. Every time she looked in the mirror and saw it, she thought of the assault and wondered how the EAR had picked her to be one of his victims. "I never knew if he came up upon me by accident or if he carefully planned his attack beforehand. Who was he? Did he know me? Did he know I would be at my parents' house that night? He took my driver's license. Will he follow me from now on?" Despite her daughter's horrific experience, Trish's mother didn't want to sell the house or move. Thus, every dinner, every holiday, and every family gathering occurred just a few feet from where she had been brutally raped and left bound to a bench like an animal. Many times over the years, Trish wondered whether she would ever see the EAR brought to justice. Would she ever get to see the face behind the mask?

— — —

On the morning of October 5, 1976, thirty-year-old Jane Carson was lounging on her bed, snuggling with her three-year-old son, JP. Both Jane and her husband served our country in the United States Air Force, Jane as a reserve captain and John as a captain. Pictures on the walls of their home showed them in uniform and attending events at the Officer's Club on base. At the time, Jane attended nursing school. They lived in a ranch home in Citrus Heights, a town northeast of Sacramento. John had left for the base before the sunrise; Jane was cherishing a quiet moment with her son, who shared her blue eyes, when she heard someone flip the light switch in the hallway. When the patter of heavy footsteps rushed down the hall towards her bedroom, she thought her husband had returned to grab something he had forgotten.

A masked figure appeared in the doorway. Stunned, Jane, a military officer used to giving orders and getting answers, barked, "What's going on?"

"Shut up! I want your money and I won't hurt you. Shut up and stay there!" the man growled in response. Worried about JP's safety, she pleaded, "Take whatever you want, but please don't hurt us." She pulled JP close to her chest and held onto him tightly. She was ready to fight if need be.

"Shut up, shut up, I said. I have a knife!" he screamed. Moving quickly toward her, the EAR tied Jane's hands behind her back with shoelaces, then ran his blade along her body to prove he wasn't bluffing. He blindfolded her with a towel to further exert his power and control over her. Jane begged several times for him not to hurt her son, but the attacker only repeated his threats. "I swear, I'll use this knife. Shut up!" Blindfolded, her hands tied behind her back, Jane heard the sound of sheets and towels being ripped. The sound of every fiber of fabric ripping terrified her. *What's going to happen next? Is he going to hurt my son?*

The EAR knotted her hands and her ankles together using the torn fabric while JP lay in the bed next to her. At the complete mercy of this monster, Jane strained to hear every word and movement to figure out what was happening. She heard him rummage in the drawers and cabinets and walk through the other rooms. Upon his return, he leaned next to Jane's ear and whispered, "I've got your money and I'm going to leave in a few minutes." Her sense of relief evaporated when she heard more ripping and felt JP being moved away from her. In a panic, she asked, "Where's my son? Where did you move him to? Please don't hurt him."

"Shut up, shut up!" the EAR responded. He took strips of torn sheets and tied JP's hands and feet. He then stuffed a washcloth into Jane's mouth. After walking around the house again for several minutes, he returned and stood on the side of the bed next to Jane. She could hear his heavy breathing, and even blindfolded, she sensed him staring at her body. He ordered her, "Play with my penis!" When she refused, he yelled, "Do as

I say, or I'll use this knife!" and forced her to fondle him for several minutes. Like other victims, Jane later described his penis as being abnormally small.

The EAR then rolled Jane onto her back, untied the bindings and sexually assaulted her. But that was not enough for him. He was a sadist who enjoyed psychologically torturing his victims and robbing them of their dignity. He taunted Jane, asking, "How does this feel? How does this fucking feel? Is it like the captain's? Boy, you really looked good at the club. Come on, come on, move. Put some emotion in that. Come on, do it, or I'll use my knife."

After he was done, he declared, "I'm going to make myself something to eat now." This was his way of showing Jane that her house, her home, and her body all belonged to him. He would take and do whatever he wanted. Before heading to the kitchen, he warned, "If I hear this bed move, I'll come back and use my knife. I don't want to hear anything move in this bed. I'll come back here and use this." He pressed the tip of the knife against Jane's body.

Throughout the entire sexual assault, JP was kept off the bed but nearby, his hands still tied. When the EAR was in the kitchen preparing and eating his snack, JP asked his mom, "Mommy, is the doctor still here?" Jane calmly told him the doctor was in the kitchen. Eventually, JP fell asleep. After several minutes passed, Jane no longer heard sounds coming from the kitchen. She got out of bed, removed the blindfold, and hopped to the rear patio door. She managed to open the door and yell out to her neighbor for help. Hearing her cries, the neighbor came over and cut Jane and JP from their bindings.

When the deputies arrived, they used a tracking dog that found a scent trail that led from the rear of the residence through the backyard, over the fence, and across an open field, ending on the street. The EAR had gotten into a car and driven off. Just like that, he was gone.

— — —

Some people may think we Californians are soft, thanks to the plentiful and warm sunshine we have in the Golden State, but winters in Sacramento alternate between stretches of sunshine against the backdrop of barren trees, nights with suffocating tule fog thick as cotton balls swallowing every living and breathing thing, and unrelenting downpours of cold, bone-chilling rain. It was one week before Christmas of 1976. Fifteen-year-old Kris Pedretti lived with her parents and older sister. The baby of the family, she enjoyed school, sleepovers, and Sunday morning church. Life was simple and carefree. Strings of Christmas lights and festive decorations brought a warm sparkle and sense of joy to her home. The smell of pinecones and a freshly cut Christmas tree in the family room filled the air with holiday spirit. Shiny ornaments, stockings, and wrapped presents ushered in Kris's favorite time of the year.

The one-story ranch house sat on a quiet street close to a nature reserve in Fair Oaks, a suburb of Sacramento that ran along the American River. At 6:15 p.m. on December 18, 1976, Kris's parents left to attend a Christmas party while her older sister went to a friend's house. Kris stayed home most of that day nursing a cold she couldn't quite shake. She decided to practice piano in the family room. She enjoyed playing and filling the house with music, especially during the holidays. Feeling hungry, Kris went to make herself a pizza. As she placed it in the oven, she heard strange noises inside her home. Knowing that old houses creak and rattle, especially in winter, she thought nothing of it. Suddenly, Kris looked up to see a strange man in front of her; he was pointing a knife at her throat. She froze. Was it a dream, a figment of her imagination? This couldn't be happening, not now, not in her own home. As he moved closer, the masked man threatened the girl. "Make a move and I'll kill you! Do you have any money in the house?"

Kris told the intruder that she didn't have any money. Through clenched teeth, he spat out, "Are you lying to me? When are your parents coming back? You better tell me, so I know how much time I have!" He ordered her to stand up and led her down the hallway, pressing the knife up against her skin. He paused in the hallway to pull shoestrings from his pockets. Tying Kris's hands tightly behind her back, he warned her, "Get moving! If you say anything, or flinch, I'll push this knife all the way in, and I'll be gone in the dark of night." After forcing her out the patio door into the backyard, he made her sit on a picnic table. Kris sat shivering in the winter cold. He then pulled more strings from his pocket before looping them around her legs, cinching them tightly enough to make them numb. He stuffed a piece of cloth in her mouth and blindfolded her.

Robbed of her sight, her voice, and her ability to move, she could still hear him heavily breathing behind her. His voice seemed disembodied, as if it emanated from a godlike presence. "If you move, I'll kill you. I'll be watching you every ten seconds from the window." Kris heard the EAR go back and forth into the house, where he opened and shut cabinets loudly. He came back periodically and stood next to her so she could hear his panting and feel his breath on her neck, only to go back inside. It was disorienting and terrifying.

Shivering in the cold, she lost track of time. After what seemed like a long period, he came back and leaned in against her face. "Have you ever fucked a guy?" he whispered. When the teenager responded no, he growled, "You better not be lying to me. I'll kill you!" He wanted her to fear what was coming. "Have you ever felt a dick? Well, I want you to play with mine."

The EAR then forced Kris back into the house and into her parents' room. He pushed the fifteen-year-old onto her parents' bed and assaulted her, stealing her innocence, dignity, and security. He then left her on her parents' bed as he walked around the house, rummaging through the silverware in the dining room. She heard him open the refrigerator and drink her father's beer—the EAR's usual MO. After a few minutes, he returned and moved her by the fireplace in the family room. He forced her to the floor and raped her again. When he was done, he left her blindfolded and naked next to the piano she loved playing.

When would her nightmare end? Where was her assailant? These questions raced through Kris's mind as she lay on the floor, fearing what might come next. After several minutes of silence, she realized that her attacker had left. She managed to free herself and called the police.

The EAR was gone, but Kris's nightmare was only just beginning. This was the 1970s, and law enforcement didn't have the wherewithal to help victims empathically. Detective Carol Daly was not yet assigned to investigate the case. When the deputies arrived, they interviewed Kris as she sat next to the fireplace and piano where she had just been brutally raped. Barely dressed and crying, still in shock, she felt like a piece of evidence being questioned. While the deputies may have been well intentioned, their methods of questioning made her feel less than dignified. The EAR had treated her like an object, and now the police were making her feel demoralized. She retreated into a shell, shutting down all her emotions. It was her way of coping and surviving. There was no victim advocate, counselor, or therapist to hold her hand. She felt utterly alone.

When Kris's parents came home, her father told her to never talk about the assault again. All the shame came crashing down upon her shoulders, and no amount of washing or showering could remove this stain from her soul. She bore the emotional abandonment alone since no one understood her pain. She was only fifteen years old, and the long road ahead would lead her to dark places—drugs, despair, and abusive relationships. On that cold winter's night, the East Area Rapist took more than just her innocence, he took her voice. It would be many years before she would find it again.

— — — — —

April 2018

After pressing my ear up against Rod's office wall and hearing the word "EAR," I quickly went to see Billy Satchell. I never forgot the conversation we had in Sergeant Barnes's truck six years earlier. I walked over to his office, and as I recounted what I'd heard through the wall, his eyes got bigger and bigger, and he held both palms to his head, saying, "No fucking way, no fucking way . . ." as he rocked back and forth in his chair. I had always held out hope that the EAR was still alive and that we would catch him. We had to keep this secret since we weren't supposed to know about it. I looked online for any announcement or report about his capture. Nothing. We walked out to get coffee. Leaving the building, we passed the phalanx of police and protestors. The atmosphere was electric.

Before going to bed that night, I scoured every single news outlet I could think of—the *Sacramento Bee*, local news stations, CNN, Fox News, et al.—for any mention of the East Area Rapist. Nothing. I tossed and turned and dreamed about the EAR all night long. I woke up every hour, grabbing my cell phone and checking the news for an update. Still nothing. Finally, at 4:30 a.m., a *Sacramento Bee* news flash: Our office had announced a major development in the East Area Rapist case and would be holding a press conference later that morning at the Sacramento DA's Crime Lab. My whole body was abuzz. I couldn't go back to sleep.

I came into the office early the morning of April 25 to an office-wide email about the press conference with a link to a live feed. At 10 a.m., I logged on, closed the door, and turned up the volume. I felt giddy, like a kid opening their presents on Christmas morning. When the press conference began, Sacramento DA Anne Marie Schubert stepped up to the podium to speak.

> For over 40 years, countless victims have waited for justice. Over these years, hundreds of individuals have sought justice for these victims and their families. Many have dedicated their virtual entire professions to seeking this answer. For many of us, it was more than a professional commitment. It became personal for many of us. . . . The answer was, and will always be, in the DNA. We knew

> that we should, and could, solve it using the most innovative DNA technology. . . . We all knew that we were looking for a needle there in the haystack, but we also knew that the needle was there. In the last six days, the passion, the persistence, and the knowledge finally came to give us an answer in this building behind us, our Crime Lab. The Crime Lab employees and the DNA analysts who worked tirelessly in the last few days to find that answer. Yesterday, an arrest warrant was issued, a complaint was filed, charging that individual with two counts of murder with special circumstance for the murder Brian and Katie Maggiore here in Sacramento in February 1978. It is fitting that today is "National DNA Day." We found the needle in the haystack. And it was right here in Sacramento.

As I listened to DA Schubert, I thought about the generations of officers who had refused to give up pursuing the East Area Rapist/Golden State Killer. Law enforcement is often demonized, especially for the actions of a few. At the same time, during my career, I have seen in my colleagues an unwavering dedication to pursuing and obtaining justice for victims. Dogged determination and passionate persistence brought Joseph DeAngelo to a jail cell and the courtroom. The police completed its mission and would now hand the case over to the District Attorney's Office to prosecute him.

Prior to my assignment to the Homicide Unit, I had prosecuted sex crimes for many years. It was the most impactful work of my long career as a prosecutor, but it took an emotional toll. After prosecuting child molesters and serial rapists, a part of me grew jaded and paranoid. In England, "sin-eaters" eat food, such as a piece of bread, at a funeral to spiritually accept the sins of the deceased, allowing their soul to pass on to the afterlife with their sins absolved. In a way, prosecutors serve that role in society. That doesn't mean we absolve a sexual predator of their sins. Rather, we take in and absorb the sins of the worst among us. We shine a light on the destruction they wreak and bring them to justice. Every day, we read the grotesque details of crimes in the police reports, we look at the pictures of violated bodies, we talk to shattered victims as they whisper in hushed voices and look at the ground in shame—an emotion they should have never had to feel. We see people at their lowest. We see humanity at its worst. We see and absorb all the sins of the world.

I tried twelve sexual-assault cases in less than two years; a prosecutor with a regular workload might take four to five years to see that many trials. After prosecuting a molester who raped five girls under the age of eight, I couldn't help but see every man playing with a child at the park as a potential child abuser. I wouldn't let my daughters have sleepovers at their friends' homes. I slept little, and when I did, I dreamed about my cases. I woke up thinking about the trial I was working on. Watching the press conference, I knew that whoever was assigned to prosecute the Golden State Killer would have to absorb a tremendous amount of sin.

As I listened to DA Schubert, my thoughts kept cycling back to the GSK's victims. For forty years they had waited to find the truth, to see the face of their rapist or the killer of their loved one, to know his name, to finally receive a measure of closure, to feel that the world was a fair and righteous place. The victims' once-young faces were now wrinkled, their hair turned gray. Some had passed away waiting for justice. The trauma they all suffered exacted a heavy toll, leaving behind broken marriages, abusive relationships, and alcohol and drug abuse to numb the pain.

The capture of Joseph DeAngelo answered some of their vital questions, but it led to still many more: Why did he choose me? What did he do with my wedding band or earring? Where was he all these years? Did he ever stop raping and killing? As a prosecutor, I knew the victims faced a long, winding road ahead. But at least the bogeyman could no longer hide.

For several weeks after the arraignment, the GSK case sat without a prosecutor assigned to it. My money was on Rod getting assigned the case since he was the chief of Homicide. But he was in his mid-fifties and only a couple years from retirement; he knew that time was his enemy. A case of this magnitude could not be completed in the time he had left. Thirteen known murders, upwards of fifty rapes, and over 120 burglaries in twelve years, in eleven different jurisdictions up and down the State of California. Upwards of a thousand witnesses from all corners of the state would be called and asked to remember, recreate, reenact, and retell the horrors that occurred nearly forty years before. Moreover, discovery, or evidence that we must share with the defense—police and lab reports, transcripts, photographs, videos, and other records—numbered several million pages. In each county, multiple law-enforcement agencies needed to dust off cabinets and cardboard boxes in evidence storerooms, scour documents on microfiche and microfilm, and collate and organize them before sending them to Sacramento for organization and dissemination to the defense.

DA Schubert's complaint charged DeAngelo only with Brian and Katie Maggiore's murders. What about the countless rapes he committed? The statute of limitations had run out on those cases long ago. With what else could he be charged? Other counties had murder charges that needed to be consolidated or combined with the Sacramento allegations. And where would the case be tried? Ventura, Santa Barbara, Orange, or Sacramento County? A prosecutor was needed to coordinate and answer all these questions. Against this backdrop, I remembered the prediction I'd made to Sergeant Barnes and Billy six years earlier. But first, I needed a question answered.

I met my wife, Jenny, many years ago while attending the University of California, Davis. The first time I saw her on the quad, I literally stopped and said to myself, *I would love to meet her*. So I did. We instantly hit it off and found out we had so much in common—she'd also escaped Vietnam; her family fled the day Saigon fell—and we've been together ever since. As the rock and foundation of our family of five, she needed to be okay with the prospect of my spending the next several years prosecuting the Golden State Killer. I might have to live in Ventura or Orange County for up to a year if the case were tried in Southern California. With three young children, she already bore the brunt of family responsibilities while I tried nearly a hundred cases during my career.

When I am in trial, my family has to share me with my job. Whether I'm at the kids' soccer practice, at the dinner table, or on vacation at Disneyland, my mind is never far from my cases. I can't just flip a light switch, turn off my brain, and leave them at the office or in the courtroom. I keep a notebook on me to write down random thoughts and strategies.

Driving in the car, taking a shower, or going on a walk, I will pause whatever I'm doing to record notes and to-do lists. Being in trial is an obsession, where I most feel alive. The GSK case promised to be the granddaddy of them all, an all-consuming obsession with which my wife would have to share her husband.

Jenny and I had a long discussion during which I shared with her the salient facts of the case. She listened intently, her eyes focused on me, her mind deep in thought. "Those victims deserve justice, and they deserve to have someone like you fighting for them," she concluded. With those words of affirmation, I knew what I had to do Monday morning.

Rod was a quintessential morning guy, waking up every day at 4:30 a.m. to walk his dog, work out, and share breakfast with his wife before arriving at work before 7:00. I wanted to catch him early, before all the detectives and attorneys came knocking at his door and pulled him in a million different directions. His door was closed when I got to my office at 7:00. Noemi was already in her cubicle. As Rod's longtime secretary, she always had a good pulse on Rod's mood. I had been rehearsing my pitch. "How's the old man doing this morning?" I asked Noems. "Oh, he's in a good mood," she responded and gave me a little wink.

I knocked on Rod's door and walked in. He was sitting on the big, red leather chair in the corner of his office, the same chair that the legendary John O'Mara had sat in for over thirty years as head of the Homicide Unit. It was worn and cracked and creaked loudly when you sat in it, but it was O'Mara's chair; it connected us to our past. Rod motioned me to sit down across from him.

"Rod," I began, looking him straight in the eyes. "If you were on SEAL Team Six, and they told you they had found Osama bin Laden in Pakistan, what would you say to your commander?"

Rod chuckled, his eyes twinkling as a wide grin wrapped around his face. "What would *you* tell the commander?"

Without skipping a beat, I replied, "I would say, 'I want a ride on that helicopter to Pakistan.' " I pointed to the EAR/GSK file sitting in front of him and tapped the desk with my finger. "I want a ride on this helicopter." I got up and walked out of his office without another word. As I did so, Rod just grinned and rocked back and forth in his chair.

Later that afternoon, Rod asked me to walk over to DA Schubert's office. She was seated at her conference table with Rod and Steve Grippi. After taking a seat, Schubert cut to the chase. "Congratulations, we are assigning you to prosecute the Golden State Killer. You will be leading the case with Amy Holliday from our office."

"Thank you, Anne Marie," I somehow managed to utter. "And thank you, Rod and Steve. I won't let you down." My life had turned upside down in a matter of seconds.

I later found out that, soon after the arrest of DeAngelo, the upper echelon of the DA's Office had settled on me to prosecute the Golden State Killer. Considering the magnitude of the case, they wanted to assign a second attorney to help shoulder the load. Both Rod and Steve Grippi had suggested Andy Solomon, the longtime supervisor of the Major Crimes Unit and one of the most experienced trial lawyers in the office. Despite the recommendations of both her Homicide chief and her chief deputy, Schubert selected Holliday, who had only tried one homicide case and a handful of sex crimes.

But I didn't let that derail my excitement at my new assignment. I pumped my fist and promised, "We are going to get justice for the victims!" Little did I know just how challenging the assignment would be—for all of us.

3 American Riviera: New Beginnings

October 1979

Known as the American Riviera because of its mild Mediterranean-like weather, Santa Barbara County is located along Southern California's crystal blue coastline, about one hundred miles northwest of Los Angeles. Covered by mountain ranges that frame picturesque green valleys and coastal plains, much of Santa Barbara retains a rustic Spanish colonial feel. In the southern part of the county, nestled between the Santa Ynez Mountains and the Pacific Ocean, sits the small town of Goleta. Scenic views of the water and the soft sea breeze caressing groves of avocado trees soothe the souls of those who live here. In the late 1970s, a predator committed a series of violent and sadistic crimes that shattered Goleta's serene nights.

Catherine and Anthony* were a fit and active couple who had been dating for several years and lived in a ranch-style home on Queen Anne Lane. Their house sat at the end of a long driveway, and its backyard was dotted with arching palms trees and a small pond filled with green lily pads. The back of the property faced an open field that led to San Jose Creek. At the end of a long weekend, they went to bed Sunday evening and settled in for the night. In the early morning hours of October 1, 1979, Catherine and Anthony heard a stranger's voice in their bedroom. Feeling someone kicking the bed, Anthony opened his eyes but was blinded by the white light of a flashlight. "Wake up, wake up! Don't move, motherfucker, or I'll kill you."

It was the East Area Rapist, who had escaped the intense manhunt in the Bay Area by fleeing to Southern California.

The EAR ordered them to turn over onto their stomachs and made Catherine bind Anthony's wrists behind his back. When Catherine tied them too loosely, DeAngelo told her, "Make it tighter, or I'll fucking kill you!" He then secured Catherine's wrists and ankles, saying, "I gotta have money!" and asking them where their purse and wallet were located. As he pillaged the house, he kept yelling, "I'll kill you, you motherfuckers!"

I have often thought about what I would do in that situation. Would I resist, or run, or would I simply surrender? Would I scream or stay silent? Would I sacrifice myself so that my wife would live? Thankfully, few of us ever have to face these dark deliberations in our minds, but when we do, we realize there are no good answers. Catherine and Anthony could hear DeAngelo rummaging through their house, going through various rooms and opening drawers. Tied up and lying on their stomachs, they were at the mercy of the masked intruder.

When he returned to the bedroom, DeAngelo ordered Catherine to help him find her purse and money—a ruse he often used to separate one victim from the other. After untying her ankles, he led her into the living room while pressing a knife against her flesh. Forcing Catherine onto the floor, he retied her ankles and placed a pair of shorts over her face. Catherine, who slept in the nude, was completely naked. Even with her face covered, she could still see DeAngelo shining the flashlight up and down her body. She knew what would come next.

After walking around the house for several minutes, DeAngelo came back and whispered in her ear, "Now I'm going to kill you and cut your throat." He then went back into the kitchen and could be heard rummaging through the drawers and refrigerator, repeating over and over, "I'll kill them, I'll kill them!" He seemingly enjoyed inflicting psychological torture and relished every flinch and whimper. Like a cat toying with a helpless mouse, he took pleasure in the perverse power he held over their lives.

When Catherine heard him head down the hallway toward the bedroom, she quickly wiggled the bindings around her ankles, loosening them enough to slip them off her feet. This was her chance. She got up and ran to the front door. Barefoot and naked, her arms still tied behind her back, she stepped out onto the porch and felt the cold autumn air against her skin like the prick of a thousand needles. Just as she began to run down the long driveway, a hand grabbed her head, and putting a finger in her mouth like a fishhook, jerked her violently backward, causing her to fall on the ground. Growling, "I told you to be quiet," her assailant yanked Catherine to her feet and forced her back into the house, pressing his knife up against her neck. Back inside, he retied her ankle bindings.

Hearing Catherine scream from the front of the house, Anthony thought DeAngelo had killed her. He rolled off the bed onto the floor and managed to get on his feet. He hopped to the sliding glass door that led from the bedroom to the backyard and was able to unlock and slide it open although his hands were still cinched behind his back. Like Catherine, he was barefoot and naked, his heart beating so fast he could hear it echo in his head. He hopped behind some shrubs and lay down next to an orange tree, curling his body into a tight fetal position. The dirt, rocks, leaves, and prickly bush all seemed to dig into his flesh as he panted heavily in the dark. How long would he have to hide? What exactly was the monster doing to Catherine?

The EAR wasn't used to people fighting back, but this couple was different, and he was going to make them suffer. He headed to the bedroom only to realize that the sliding glass door was open and Anthony was gone. He ran into the backyard and started searching frantically for his victim, flashlight in hand. Anthony could see the bright spot of light flitter from place to place. Anthony held his breath and remained still. He heard footsteps and saw the light approach, then pass right by him. The EAR had not seen him lying there at his feet.

While DeAngelo was in the backyard looking for Anthony, Catherine heard a car speed away. Thinking her assailant had left the house, she loosened the ankle bindings once again and ran to the bedroom but couldn't find Anthony. Seeing the open glass door, she assumed her boyfriend had been kidnapped or murdered. She ran out the front door, screaming loudly for someone, anyone, to help her. Her cries woke next-door neighbor Stan Los, a special agent with the FBI. He ran out of his house to see the shocking sight of his neighbor naked, her hands tied behind her back. "Help! Anthony is dead. He killed Anthony!" At that very moment, Los saw a white male wearing a Pendleton patterned shirt hop on a bicycle and pedal westward on Queen Anne Lane.

Agent Los yelled out "Hey, stop!" but the EAR only pedaled harder. Los grabbed his keys and gave chase in his truck. Weaving through the streets of Goleta at 3:00 a.m., he chased the intruder while contacting dispatch on his CB radio. With every twist and turn, Los was getting closer and closer, but just west of San Patricio Drive, DeAngelo dumped the bicycle and leaped over several fences. Just like that, the East Area Rapist was gone in the night.

Next to the abandoned bicycle, Santa Barbara County Sheriff's deputies recovered the serrated steak knife DeAngelo had used to threaten Catherine. They also noticed star-shaped shoe impressions in the dirt along the path he used to escape on foot. Officers later found similar footwear patterns in Catherine and Anthony's yard. The bike turned out to have been stolen earlier in the evening from a nearby residence. The EAR often arrived at and escaped from his crime scenes on stolen bicycles. Agent Los grabbed the discarded bicycle to secure the evidence and drove back to his house, where he saw Catherine running down the street, still naked and bound, searching for Anthony and calling for help.

Deputies investigating the scene noticed that molding had been pulled from the siding near the kitchen door; they found pieces of the same molding near San Jose Creek, which ran next to the open field behind Catherine and Anthony's backyard. They also spotted bicycle tire tracks leading toward and away from the same creek bed, indicating that DeAngelo had emerged from a path along San Jose Creek on the stolen bike, ridden into the victims' backyard, and jumped over the fence before entering through the kitchen. Just as in Rancho Cordova, where the EAR had used the American River and concrete canals to move from one location to the next, DeAngelo was using San Jose Creek to discreetly stalk and find his prey.

Almost three months after Catherine and Anthony's terrifying ordeal, the EAR would return to Santa Barbara, and this time, there was no escaping his evil intent. Robert Offerman, a successful orthopedic surgeon, resided in a condominium complex on Avenida Pequena, which backed up to San Jose Creek. In his mid-forties and recently separated from his wife, Offerman lifted weights, played tennis, and lived life to its fullest. He was casually dating a petite brown-haired divorcée named Debra Manning, a psychologist who ran her own local practice.

Offerman's complex contained one- and two-story condos grouped together in multiple buildings, all painted brown to blend into the surrounding trees and gently sloping hillside. The upscale development featured a pool and several tennis courts, and a narrow concrete walkway connected the buildings and lawns of green grass. Just a few feet away from his home sat a grove of avocado trees. The grounds sloped downhill and spilled into a thick-brushed ravine, which dropped directly into San Jose Creek.

The days are sunny and the evenings mild in Goleta, even in winter. Over the weekend of December 29, 1979, Manning planned to stay over at Offerman's condo. The couple was scheduled to play tennis on Sunday morning with another pair, Joan* and William,* who were mutual friends. A little past 11:00 a.m., Joan and William knocked on the door of Offerman's home. No one answered despite repeated knocks and rings of the doorbell. Offerman was always punctual, and the condo seemed eerily silent. Sensing that something was amiss, William walked to the rear of the condo and found an open sliding glass door that led into the living room. A few feet from the door, William found a plastic bag with a cooked turkey carcass. The bag seemed out of place. The door jamb had been pulled away from the wall, and pry marks could be seen on the door.

William stepped inside the living room and yelled out for Offerman and Manning, but there was no response, just silence. Not sure what to do next, William walked towards the bedroom, calling out to his friends. When he passed the first bedroom, he saw that the mattress had been pushed off the bed. He walked to the next bedroom and slowly pushed the door open. He froze at the horrifying sight before him. Lying face down on the waterbed, Manning was completely nude, her arms and wrists tied behind her back with a white nylon cord. Dark red blood spatter and brain tissue were splattered on the headboard and bed around her body. Seeing a dead body on television or in a movie fails to prepare you for the real-life sight of a bloated purple body, stiff from rigor mortis, lying perfectly still on a bed awash in a gooey pond of vibrant red blood.

William turned to see Offerman lying face down and nude on the floor to the left of the door. His legs were splayed apart in an awkward position, and he clutched in his hands the same type of cord used to tie his girlfriend's wrists. Standing nearly six feet tall with a body builder's physique, Robert had been able to snap the nylon rope and free his hands. Described by his friends and coworkers as charismatic and aggressive, Robert had tried to fight back.

Offerman suffered three gunshot wounds, two to the neck and one to the buttocks. According to the pathologist's report, the bullets traveled in a downward trajectory, as if the victim were moving in an upward direction, perhaps to tackle his attacker. One bullet entered Offerman's lower neck and traveled through his upper right chest, exiting the body at his upper right back. As he fell to the ground, a second round penetrated his upper left chest, tearing through his aorta and lung; this was the fatal shot. A third hit him in the lower back, exiting through his left buttock. A fourth shot missed and lodged into the wooden dresser. After killing Offerman, DeAngelo, knowing he couldn't leave behind any witnesses, walked over to the bed and executed Manning. Detectives later found several rings lodged between the mattress and the wall. Before she was tied up, she may have believed they were only being robbed and removed her rings and stuffed them there for safekeeping. Unfortunately, she would never wear those rings again.

Offerman's condo was less than a mile away from Catherine and Anthony's house on Queen Anne Lane, and San Jose Creek intersected both locations. A predator could walk along the tree-covered creek bed unseen and undetected, emerging from the darkness to hunt his prey. Unable to torture Catherine and Anthony as he'd wanted, the EAR returned to Goleta to finish what he started. Far away from the dragnet closing in on him in Northern California, he found new victims farther down the coast.

Brenda* lived a few doors down from Robert Offerman. A little after 3:00 a.m., she heard one gunshot, then a pause, followed by three fired rapidly in succession, another hiatus, and then one final shot. The sounds of murder would no doubt be heard in a condominium complex in the middle of the night. DeAngelo had little time to flee the crime scene. He stole Brenda's son's Schwinn ten-speed bicycle, which had been left outside their home, and rode off into the night, eventually ditching it around the block from Queen Anne Lane. In the small rear lawn of Offerman's condo, county crime-scene investigators found star-patterned shoeprints matching those discovered in Catherine and Anthony's backyard.

As 1979 came to a close, Joseph DeAngelo left Santa Barbara, but he would return one more time.

— — —

A new decade, the 1980s, meant new beginnings, a new time. The preppy look of polo shirts, blazers, and chinos with boat shoes came into vogue, replacing the bell-bottoms and oversized collars of the 1970s. Big feathered hair, pastel colors, backcombed curls inspired by *Dallas*, and neon jumpsuits were the trend. Romantic ballads like "Lady" by Kenny Rogers topped the charts alongside rock bands like Foreigner and Styx. MTV debuted in 1981.

In January of that year, Ronald Reagan was sworn in as the fortieth president of the United States. America had chosen as its leader an actor turned politician with perfectly combed hair and a voice warm enough to melt snow. The country was emerging from a recession, crushing inflation, and a humiliating hostage crisis in Iran. Meanwhile, my family and I had settled into a regular routine in our tiny apartment off Hammer Lane. After cooking and eating dinner with our family, my mother would put on her uniform and drive to her graveyard shift at the local cannery. My father, who had graduated from college in Vietnam, had to start his education all over again in America. After driving a truck all day, he worked on an associate's degree at Delta Community College. After dinner, my father and I would stay at the dinner table and do our homework, learning how to read and write in English together.

In 1981, our family moved from Stockton to San Jose, roughly fifty miles south of San Francisco. Silicon Valley was still filled with orchards pushing up against the rolling hills that framed the city. The first and second wave of Vietnamese refugees settled on the East Side, creating the largest Vietnamese community outside of Vietnam. They formed the Little Saigon neighborhood, which filled with tiny shops selling pho and banh mi. In elementary school, I spent five years in English as a Second Language classes, but for the first time, I had Vietnamese classmates. And finally, we got to live in our own house. We moved into a small home on the East Side, just a block away from a restaurant where we could read the menu in Vietnamese. My little sister was born in 1981, and as the only girl in the family, she instantly wrapped my father around her finger with her precocious smile and round face. It was a time of new beginnings.

Three hundred miles to the south of San Jose, thirty-five-year-old Cheri Domingo was trying to get her new life started after a divorce. With curly brown hair and a bright smile, she lived in Goleta with her bright and independent fifteen-year-old daughter, Debbi. Their relationship was at times strained, and Debbi ran away from home to live with a friend. On July 26, Debbi called her mother from a pay phone; she wanted to stop by to grab a bathing suit. Their conversation quickly escalated into an argument, and Debbi screamed, "Why don't you just stay out of my life?" Those would be the last words she'd ever say to her mother.

That weekend, Domingo was doing a favor for her friend Robert,* a real-estate agent, who asked her to house-sit a home on Toltec Way in Goleta. A two-story residence with a red herringbone-patterned brick walkway leading up to the porch, it was known in the neighborhood as the "big red barn house" because a barn-shaped garage with red cedar shingle siding was attached to the left side of the residence. Above the garage, four large windows peered onto the street. The home was located approximately half a mile from Robert Offerman's condominium and nearly a mile from Catherine and Anthony's house. Down the street, a dirt trail led to San Jose Creek.

On the evening of July 26, Greg Sanchez, a friend whom Cheri had dated on and off for several years, drove to Toltec Way to spend the night with her. Tall and lanky with a mop of thick brown hair and a Tom Selleck mustache, twenty-seven-year-old Sanchez was kind and warmhearted.

Greg was supposed to spend that weekend with his fiancée, who was visiting from out of town, but for some reason chose to go see Cheri instead.

Robert, who worked for a real-estate agency in Santa Barbara, wanted to show the big red barn house to a client on the morning of July 27. When he called the house to inform Cheri about the showing, no one picked up. Robert met the prospective buyer at the home and rang the doorbell repeatedly, but no one answered the door. In the days before cell phones, if someone didn't pick up their house phone, you were out of luck. Robert used his key to unlock the front door, but the safety chain was still on. Concerned, he walked to the back of the house and realized that the sliding glass door was open. Seeing the lights were off, he called out for Cheri and headed for the master bedroom. The wood shutters were partially pulled down, and sunlight threw horizontal streaks of light onto the floor and walls. Walking toward the open closet, Robert came upon the body of a naked male crumpled on the floor, with piles of clothes haphazardly tossed over him. Robert ran out of the house and called 911.

Sixty-year-old Elizabeth* lived across the street from the big red barn. Around 3:30 a.m. on July 27, she was standing in her kitchen and looked out a window which faced the street. She spotted a white male wearing a T-shirt and dark pants standing near a hole in the fence that led into the backyard of the barn house. Terrified, she quickly turned off the kitchen light and watched the man squeeze through the hole in the fence. Elizabeth ran to her bedroom to wake up her husband, who was asleep in bed. About ten minutes later, they heard a single gunshot, followed by a loud woman's scream. The dogs in the neighborhood started barking and yelping. She suggested calling the police, but her husband told her it was probably just a firecracker. They went back to sleep.

When the Santa Barbara County Fire Department and paramedics arrived on scene, Captain Barzini* observed dried bloodstains on a white towel hanging off the stove. Robert led the way to the master bedroom but refused to enter. As Barzini walked into the room, he saw Sanchez lying face down with part of his body in the bedroom closet. Facing the bed, the captain noticed that all the covers on the left side of the bed were thrown back, but the covers on the right side had been pulled up toward the headboard, covering the pillow halfway.

Approaching the bed and seeing the pillow was covered in blood, he reached out to touch the bed and felt something hard. He jumped back before slowly lifting the covers to find Cheri's nude body. She lay face down with her hand crossed behind her back, as if she had been tied. However, the ligatures were missing; someone had removed and taken them. Cheri's head had been caved in with a blunt-force weapon. Sanchez had been rising out of bed when he was shot in the left cheek. He suffered a through-and-through gunshot, but that was not the fatal blow. He fought back valiantly and was viciously beaten, receiving twenty-four blows to his head; he died from hemorrhaging in the brain. Detectives did not find any evidence that he had been tied.

Unlike Robert Offerman, at whom DeAngelo shot four times, Greg was shot at only once, resulting in a debilitating wound to the face. The sound of a gunshot may be missed in the middle of the night, but four would definitely be noticed. DeAngelo needed time and secrecy to do what he wanted to do. He'd been reckless with Offerman, firing too many times and drawing attention to himself; he wouldn't make the same mistake again. A bludgeoning behind closed doors would allow him the time he needed to finish his predatory plan. No one came knocking at the door. No sirens approached.

After eliminating Greg as a threat, DeAngelo forced Cheri onto her stomach and tied her wrists to her ankles behind her back. He raped Cheri; then, with the same blunt weapon he had used on Greg, he bludgeoned Cheri's head ten times, causing a massive skull fracture and a gaping wound on the right side of her head. Not wanting to get blood spatter all over him, DeAngelo pulled the covers over Cheri's head before beating her to death.

DeAngelo had evolved as a predator, eliminating all witnesses. Detectives had examined the ligatures he'd used to tie his victims during his previous crimes, looking for patterns in his different knots. This time, crime-scene investigators could still see the ligature marks on his victim, but he cut and took all the bindings with him. He then slipped out of the big red barn and into the dark.

DeAngelo did, however, leave his semen behind. Investigators developed a DNA profile from a sample collected onsite and uploaded it into the Combined DNA Index System, or CODIS, a national database of DNA profiles managed by the FBI. It would take forty years before a match would be found. But no matter where he ran and hid, or how long he was gone, the truth would come for him.

— — — — —

April 2018

A year before DeAngelo was arrested in 2018, I prosecuted Shauna Burton for killing an elderly couple, Melvin and Jean Bain, in their mobile home. The defendant used a heavy metal flashlight to bludgeon the victims to death, leaving behind a gruesome murder scene. In closing arguments, addressing the jury, I talked about the importance of forensic evidence.

"The defense attorney told you in the opening statement, 'There's only one witness to this murder, Shauna Burton. She will take the witness stand and tell you what truly happened. She will be the only witness that knows the truth.' This is what the defense attorney told you, and he said it as if the defendant should get bonus points for killing the two other witnesses, leaving Shauna Burton's story supposedly unchallenged."

I went on to explain to the jurors that the defense was wrong. There were two more witnesses, who saw and heard everything: the Bains. And the physical evidence in this case would speak for them since they could not. Burton's DNA was found on the murder weapon. Paraphrasing the famous criminalist Paul L. Kirk, I told the jury that wherever the defendant stepped, whatever she touched, and whatever she left behind, consciously or not—her footprints and fingerprints and DNA served as a silent witness against her. Evidence does not forget. It is not confused by the excitement of the moment. It is not clouded by personal bias. It cannot perjure itself. Only human failure to find it, study it, and understand it can diminish its value.

Several of the jurors leaned forward and nodded their heads. I continued, my voice growing more urgent, "Mel and Jean were the silent witnesses in this case. In those last few minutes of their lives as they struggled with all their might to live, they struggled with all their might for one last breath, and in the process, they left behind clues as to who killed them. Each cut, each wound, each ounce of blood and even where their bodies were found represented clues they left for us. The clues they left point directly to this defendant, the woman who in cold blood took their last breath."

The closing argument is our last chance to convince the jury. We pour every last ounce of intellect, logic, and passion into our final entreaty. We spend the entire trial taking in all the evil and eating all the sins of the world, and in that final argument, we try to purge it all and make sense of it. After making my final argument, I sat down, feeling utterly spent. As with any trial, I had barely slept during the proceedings, often waking up in the middle of the night with my heart racing and my bedsheets soaked with sweat, my mind jumping from argument to argument. I dreamed about the case—I was Melvin Bain, or the authorities investigating the case; sometimes my subconscious pulled me under the current, and I was the killer. But when I am in the courtroom, I still maintain control of the trial, at least until after the closing argument. I felt completely helpless in that moment, no longer in control of any aspect of the trial. A day later, when the jury found Burton guilty of two counts of murder in the first degree, I felt a tremendous amount of relief. The forensic evidence had done its part to bring justice to the Bains.

— — —

As a young boy in the 1970s, I loved watching television, and one of my favorites was *Kung Fu*. The show covered the exploits of Kawi Chang Caine, who escaped China after the murder of his master and traveled across the Old Wild West, defending the defenseless and helping the downtrodden with his martial-arts expertise. Watching the show, I wanted to walk through the halls of the Shaolin temple, study kung fu, and pick up a burning cauldron with my forearms to sear the image of a dragon and tiger into my skin. However, even as a child, I noticed that David Carradine, who played the lead character, was the whitest monk I had ever seen. I would later discover that Bruce Lee, the legendary martial artist and actor, had created a similar concept for a show, but television executives felt that the American audience would not accept an Asian actor in a lead role. So instead, some white executives created *Kung Fu* and cast a white actor, David Carradine, who knew nothing about martial arts. It was far from the last time Hollywood would whitewash Asian American stories.

I also watched the television drama *Quincy, M.E.*, starring Jack Klugman, which depicted the investigative exploits of a Los Angeles County medical examiner who used forensic evidence to outsmart criminals, the police, and his boss to solve crimes. The producers based the character of Quincy on the career of Dr. Thomas Noguchi, Los Angeles County Medical Examiner from 1967 to 1982, who was known as the "coroner to the stars." Noguchi conducted the autopsies of Marilyn Monroe, Robert F. Kennedy, Natalie Wood, and hundreds of other notable figures, becoming a celebrity himself in the process. Once again, Hollywood wasn't ready for an Asian American male lead of a primetime television show, so they cast Jack Klugman. In a nod to Noguchi that can be described as problematic at best, they gave him a Japanese American assistant, Sam Fujiyama, played by Robert Ito.

As it happens, *Quincy, M.E.* influenced a major player in the GSK case: former Contra Costa County Investigator Paul Holes, who was renowned for pioneering the use of DNA evidence to solve cold cases. He and his fellow criminalists had used new DNA profiling and genealogy technology to identify Joseph DeAngelo as the Golden State Killer. Paul and I were attending a meeting regarding the GSK case in Santa Barbara, and we ran into each other at a restaurant and started talking over cocktails. His drink of choice was a bourbon neat, and I ordered an old-fashioned. Since the case broke, Paul had been interviewed on every news outlet on the planet. I wanted to know about his role in the investigation, but more than that, I always enjoyed learning about the human being and the arc of their life that brought them to that moment.

Growing up as a military brat in Northern California, Paul loved watching *Quincy* on television and rarely missed an episode. In fact, it was Klugman's character that inspired him to become a criminalist and cold-case investigator. Paul attended the University of California, Davis, with the goal of becoming a forensic pathologist. His grades dashed those dreams, but when one door closes, Paul told me, another opens. Attending a job fair, he met a veteran criminalist who described his job to him: investigating crime scenes, analyzing forensic evidence, and solving crimes through science. Paul changed his career path and trained to be a criminalist, graduating from UC Davis the year before I showed up on campus.

With his chiseled jaw and good looks, Paul Holes looks like a Hollywood actor straight from central casting. He started his career as a criminalist with the Contra Costa County Crime Lab, under the aegis of the Sheriff's Department. As one of the few departments that required their criminalist to be a sworn peace officer, Paul went through the police academy. Although he has never issued a citation or arrested anyone, he carried a firearm and badge. He began his career in the early 1990s working in the serology unit, earning the trust of his superiors and being promoted to the position of division commander over forensic science at the lab. He ended his stellar career as a cold case investigator at the Contra Costa County DA's Office. I had left that office by the time Paul joined, and we never crossed paths.

In 1994, as a young criminalist, Paul discovered an old, dusty file cabinet sitting in the basement of the Crime Lab. Out of curiosity, he started looking through it; the bottom drawer was stuffed with file folders labeled "EAR," containing police reports documenting the East Area Rapist's crimes. From the moment he read the very first words of the very first report, Paul became obsessed with the case. Many people had developed various theories over the years regarding the EAR's identity. Despite the massive police response, he had always evaded capture, prompting many to believe he wore a badge. Paul discounted this theory at first because he could not fathom how someone working full-time as a police officer could possibly have committed the sheer number of crimes over such a broad area.

Paul's work on the EAR cases began as a side project but soon became a personal passion as he learned more and more about the devastation the predator had wrought. He secretly worked on solving the EAR cases, even taking time away from his regular assignments on occasion. Once he started speaking to the survivors, it became an obsession, plunging Paul into the depths of despair but also lifting him to the highest peaks. The victims yearned for closure, and justice demanded accountability.

Over many years, he chased potential suspects down one rabbit hole after another, feeling the excitement of identifying a potential lead, the adrenaline of the pursuit, the moral certainty of building the case, and the heartbreak of a DNA test or other evidence excluding a prime suspect. Each time, his dedication to catching the EAR only grew. Paul was part of three generations of law-enforcement officers who felt the ups and the downs, the ebbs and flows, and the powerful currents of emotion that came with hunting the Golden State Killer. The rollercoaster of emotions took its toll on them all. In our conversations and in his bestselling book, *Unmasked: My Life Solving America's Cold Cases*, Paul talked about the sleepless nights, the drinking, the panic attacks, and the toll it took on his family life and his mental health. It was, and is, the price we pay.

Encountering failure after failure, Paul began analyzing where his investigations went wrong. He realized that he often identified a suspect and chose to focus on the details that made them a match to the EAR's profile, whether they were the right fit or not. The case was so complex that Paul could pick and choose details that conformed to his theory. He grew frustrated with the constant dead ends and felt he needed a fresh perspective. While serving on the same task force as Sacramento Sheriff Homicide Sergeant Jim Barnes in 2012, he heard about an investigative journalist and true-crime blogger, Michelle McNamara. She intended to write a story for *Los Angeles* magazine about the East Area Rapist/Original

Night Stalker. (Authorities in Southern California gave him the second nickname because his crimes predated those of Richard Ramirez, a.k.a. the Night Stalker, who killed at least fourteen people between April 1984 and August 1985.) She had reached out to a detective and asked to interview folks on the taskforce. Cops typically display a healthy, if not paranoid, aversion to speaking with the media, fearing their words could be taken out of context and portray their department in a negative light. The members debated whether it would be prudent to speak with McNamara. Forty years had passed, and the possibility of solving the cases seemed to dim with each passing year. They decided to talk to her, hoping that the publicity might draw renewed public interest in the case and bring forth new witnesses and evidence.

When Paul first talked to McNamara, he gave short, guarded answers. The journalist then asked additional questions that demonstrated she knew a lot more about the case than he realized. As they talked further and he began to trust that her heart was in the right place, Paul shared his list of potential suspects. In turn, she shared her own list, prompting him to do some research on their viability as perpetrators. They bonded over their hunt for the monster, talking on the phone several times a week. He gave McNamara a tour of the crime scenes in Contra Costa County, sharing details that few people knew outside of law enforcement. She became a full-fledged ally, a fresh set of eyes through which to view the quest.

After her *Los Angeles* magazine article—in which she coined the moniker "Golden State Killer"—appeared, McNamara signed a book deal to chronicle her obsessive search to identify him. By day, she took care of her family as a stay-at-home mom; at night, while her husband and daughter slept, she scoured the Internet as an amateur detective. Like Paul, she suffered from insomnia. I am certain she dreamed about the GSK because our demons always invade our sleep. Try as we might, we can never truly escape our monsters until and unless we confront them. Unfortunately, McNamara died in her sleep in April 2016. At the time of her death, she had completed about two-thirds of her book. Her husband, actor Patton Oswalt, hired investigative journalist Bill Jensen and true-crime writer Paul Hayes, and they finished her book based on her notes and drafts.

I'll Be Gone in the Dark became an instant bestseller, launching the Golden State Killer case into the stratosphere.

After I was assigned to prosecute DeAngelo, I read McNamara's book at night before bed, wanting to glean any insight I could from someone who had lived and breathed the case for several years. She had absorbed the GSK into her very skin, as if she were eating the sins of this monster. As a writer, she displayed an uncanny ability to convey her emotions, making her obsession relatable and accessible. But true-crime writing can sometimes focus too much on the criminal rather than the victim. The salacious nature of the crimes appeals to the prurient and voyeuristic side of human nature. It is much easier for us to delve into the fetishistic nature of a crime, glorifying the gore and imbuing the evildoer with a certain romantic invincibility, because focusing on the struggles and soul-crushing pain of the victims reminds us that at any moment, we could become one of them. Monsters are scariest in the dark because under the bright light of scrutiny, we see all the lines, cracks, and ugliness of who they truly are. Reading her book, I didn't learn any specific new facts; however, the popularity of her book made me realize that the Golden State Killer had become a worldwide phenomenon, and we needed to be prepared with how the media frenzy might impact the prosecution of the case.

When Paul learned of McNamara's death, he was devasted at losing a trusted confidant and ally. Undeterred, Paul forged forward, turning his focus to the DNA evidence. In the 1970s, when DeAngelo began his campaign of terror, the technology didn't exist to enable the use of DNA evidence. Forensic evidence often consisted of biological materials revolving around serology and ABO blood typing. Every human being has one of a few possible blood types: A, B, AB, or O. Using a genetic test, criminalists can identify blood type from bodily fluid, potentially linking crime-scene evidence to suspects. It is very limiting in that it cannot identify a specific person, only a group of people with the same blood type. Additional advancements were made in the use of enzymes and proteins from biological samples, which helped narrow the group of potential suspects.

New technology can revolutionize the field practically overnight. Although forensic DNA evidence is now universally accepted, it only recently took its place in the continuum of scientific discovery. On September 10, 1984, British geneticist Sir Alec Jeffreys experienced an epiphany while looking at photographic film of extracted DNA cells. Staring at the blurry, black-and-white pattern of barcodes, he noticed that the patterns were unique and inherited within each family. His new discovery was used to match a young boy's DNA to his biological parents, granting the child British citizenship.

In 1986, the police asked Jeffreys for his help in solving the rape and murder of two teenagers attacked while walking home from school. The crimes, committed two-and-a-half years apart just a few miles from Jeffreys's laboratory, were nearly identical in how they were executed. Police had arrested seventeen-year-old Richard Buckland as the killer behind both murders. But to the surprise of many, multiple tests by Jeffreys exonerated Buckland. Later, when another man, Colin Pitchfork, was arrested after police received a tip, DNA tests tied him to both murders.

Today, DNA evidence can be extracted from biological samples such blood, semen, saliva, and hair. Using this genetic material, a criminalist creates a DNA profile of specific loci, or locations, on the chromosome. That profile is then compared to that of a suspect; when law enforcement does not have a suspect to seek a match, they will upload the information into the Combined DNA Index System. The FBI established CODIS in 1998, and the national database now contains over fourteen million DNA records captured from individuals arrested or convicted of crimes. But back in the late 1990s and into the new millennium, the agency struggled to expand its database. Most law-enforcement agencies and crime labs worked in silos and rarely shared evidence, much less DNA samples.

In the late 1990s, the Orange County Crime Laboratory introduced a new, state-of-the-art DNA technology known as short tandem repeats, or STR, which examined areas that repeat on the human genome. Unlike older techniques, STR was much better at differentiating among human samples. Through the new testing, the lab connected four murders and rapes that occurred in the 1980s to the Original Night Stalker. Around the same time, Paul utilized an older technology to connect three rapes in Contra Costa County to the EAR, but it could not be compared to the STR profile developed by Orange County. By 2001, the Contra Costa Crime Lab adopted STR testing, and Paul used it to confirm that the EAR had committed all three Contra Costa rapes. On a hunch, he asked the assigned criminalist to contact Orange County to compare the Contra Costa STR profile with theirs. To Paul's absolute shock, it matched the sample from the four murders and rapes. The East Area Rapist was the Original Night Stalker. Upon hearing the news, Paul sat at his desk in utter silence. We had his DNA, but we didn't have his name—yet.

After Michelle McNamara's death, Paul felt lost and discouraged, fearing that he would never solve the case before his retirement. But when one door closes, another door opens. The world of cold-case investigation is a small one. In 2002, detectives found Eunsoon Jun's corpse, mummified and buried beneath bags of cat litter in the crawl space of a house in Contra Costa County. Her boyfriend, Terry Peder Rasmussen, was arrested for her murder and immediately pled guilty. In 1986, a five-year-old girl named Lisa Jensen was abandoned in an RV park in San Bernardino County by a man who she thought was her abusive father. With a fake name and no identification, this man left only two things behind when he left in the middle of the night: Lisa, and his fingerprints. After his arrest for murder, Rasmussen's fingerprints connected him to the abandoned Jensen girl. DNA eventually connected him to the Bear Brook murders in Allenstown, New Hampshire, where the bodies of Marlyse Honeychurch, her two daughters, and Rasmussen's own daughter were found stuffed into two barrels.

As investigators dug into Rasmussen's background, they began to question whether he was in fact Lisa's father. A DNA test revealed that he was not, and authorities concluded that he had kidnapped her when she was a baby. When he died in prison, Rasmussen took with him the secrets of Jensen's past. While watching television one night, Lisa came upon a show about how DNA testing and genealogy could give people insight into their family's history. She reached back out to San Bernardino Detective Peter Headley, who had previously tried to help determine her true identity. They discussed using genealogy to help solve this mystery. Headley reached out to DNAadoption.com, a nonprofit organization that helps adoptees find their biological parents.

Before the advent of DNA, we traced our personal history through civic records, faded memories, stories passed on at family gatherings, and scraps from photo albums. But many adoptees lack the information they need to research their family tree. But the proliferation of genealogy websites revolutionized the whole process. A group of dedicated and kindhearted volunteers, known as "search angels," stepped forward to help people find their birth parents using DNA. One such helper, Barbara Rae-Venter of New Zealand, took up genealogy as a hobby after retiring as a patent lawyer. Smart and compassionate, she was the perfect search angel. As a volunteer with DNAadoption.com, she agreed to help Jensen unearth her identity through information found on websites and open-source information.

Jensen didn't even know her true date of birth; all she had was her unique genetic material. She joined the major genealogical databases. Ancestry and 23andMe required her to provide a DNA sample, which they would convert into a special profile used by the sites. She also registered on GEDmatch and FamilyTreeDNA, which allowed users to search their databases by uploading their profiles from other sites. The degree of relatedness was measured in centimorgans (cM), a unit that measures the distance between genes on a chromosome. The higher the number, the more closely related you are. For example, the highest cMs occur between a parent and their child since we receive half of our DNA from each parent. Those trained in genealogy can use cM figures to estimate how closely two individuals are related.

The various site searches identified several cousins of Jensen's. Rae-Venter determined that many of her closest relatives lived in New Hampshire and noted that a woman named in two relatives' obituaries appeared to be the same likely age as her mother. Detectives located the woman's father, who told them that his daughter had left town with her boyfriend and her daughter in 1981 and was never seen again. The man agreed to take a DNA test; it confirmed he was Lisa's grandfather.

Detectives believe that Rasmussen was the boyfriend and that he killed Lisa's mother and kidnapped Lisa when she was an infant.

The detective who originally investigated Rasmussen for Eunson Jun's murder in Contra Costa County invited Paul to attend a conference call with Detective Peter Headley, one of the investigators of the Rasmussen case. Upon hearing about the breakthrough in identifying Jensen, Paul asked Headley how the case was solved. When Headley explained genetic genealogy, a lightbulb went off in Paul's head. He telephoned Barbara Rae-Venter immediately upon returning to his office and asked if the method could be used to identify an unknown suspect who left his DNA at a crime scene. She said it could.

The jurisdictions affected by the Golden State Killer combined to create a large task force comprised of local, state, and federal partners. Steve Cramer, general counsel for the FBI's Los Angeles office and fellow member of the group, approached Paul after a meeting in March 2017 to offer his help with genetic genealogy. Over the next several months, they went down the rabbit hole of the technology together, researching its viability to solve the case. But first, Paul had to locate crime scene DNA to test as well as navigate the complicated political landscape of a case that spanned eleven different jurisdictions.

— — —

From 1976 to 1979, the East Area Rapist committed upwards of fifty sexual assaults in Sacramento County alone. He left behind semen and biological evidence at the crime scene, but when the statute of limitations expired after three years, law enforcement in Sacramento discarded the biological evidence. After being assigned the case, I was shocked when I was told we no longer had any DNA left to test. Sacramento, Yolo, San Joaquin, Alameda, and Santa Clara Counties had all discarded their biological evidence when the statute of limitations expired. Although Contra Costa kept the DNA evidence from three of their rape cases, their crime lab used up the remaining evidence when it conducted STR testing. By 2017, there was none left for Paul to conduct his experiment with genetic genealogy testing. He learned, however, that Orange County still possessed a significant amount of pristine DNA from the rape and murder of Janelle Cruz in 1986. Needing only a tiny fraction of its sample, he reached out to the Orange County District Attorney's Office—the third largest in the state, employing nearly 400 prosecutors with an annual budget reaching almost $200 million. Elected in 2002, District Attorney Tony Rackauckas sat as the highest law-enforcement official in Orange County. Running a large DA's office carries a certain gravitas and influence in the law-enforcement and political world. As a four-term incumbent who sailed through multiple reelection campaigns, Rackauckas was a mainstay of the local Republican Party. His office strived to innovate, especially in forensic science. It started its own local database with DNA samples collected from those charged with crimes in the county. It also invested in state-of-the-art DNA equipment to conduct rapid testing of samples collected from crime scenes, which could be completed in just an hour.

Orange County has a reputation for being the antithesis of Los Angeles County. People speak of an imaginary "Orange Curtain" that protects its residents from the crime and chaos of its neighbor to the north. Some view its DA's office as siloed and willing to take a different path than other offices, refusing to "play well in the sandbox." The Golden State Killer committed three major crimes in the county, which poured considerable resources into solving the cases. To conduct genetic genealogy testing, Paul needed enough pristine DNA to create a SNP (single nucleotide polymorphism, pronounced "snip") profile. In simple terms, SNPs are genetic markers, and each human contains approximately five million of them. Spread throughout the entire human genome, SNPs allow genealogy databases to identify common blocks of DNA between people. The more two people share with each other, the more related they are. With a SNP profile in hand, the investigator could upload the SNP data to certain genealogy databases to find relatives of the offender.

During my cocktail session with Paul Holes in Santa Barbara, he described his efforts to secure additional DNA samples and expressed frustration that the Orange County DA's Office was playing politics and refusing to collaborate with him. Orange County had previously sent some of the crime-scene DNA to a company called Parabon to develop a new genetic profile, or "snapshot," of the killer. In the process, Parabon also created a SNP profile but would only provide it to Paul with the Orange County DA's permission. When Paul reached out, the office requested time to run the decision past Rackauckas. Weeks passed without a word from Orange County. Paul decided to speak with the Irvine Police Department since its investigators had worked on the original 1986 murder/rape and still possessed DNA evidence. The Irvine PD loved the idea and agreed to cooperate.

A few months later, the Orange County DA's Office finally met with Paul, who presented his novel idea to find the Golden State Killer using the technology that had been pivotal in finding Lisa Jensen's true identity. At the conclusion of the meeting, Rackauckas refused to share Parabon's SNP profile. Paul felt that the DA had already made up his mind before the meeting. According to Paul, one of the Orange County prosecutors approached him afterward, angrily accusing him of going behind their back by approaching the Irvine Police Department. Paul explained that he was merely exploring all options after hearing nothing from Orange County.

Rejected by Orange County, Paul devised a back-up plan. If he couldn't get the SNP profile from Parabon, Paul would just obtain a DNA sample from the Irvine Police Department and have a private lab develop the SNP profile. The Irvine PD agreed to do so. But the evidence never arrived because Rackauckas had told the Irvine police chief not to hand it over. In Paul's mind, this was about politics, not public safety. Prosecutors from Orange County would later vehemently dispute Paul's version of the events, claiming that they wanted to further vet the genealogy process. Regardless of which version represents the truth, that DNA sample never arrived from the Irvine Police Department.

The resentment and distrust lingered on. Prior to DeAngelo's arrest, Orange County officials were not informed of his identity as a suspect; they only found out after DeAngelo's arrest. When Detective Sergeant Kenny Clark first stepped into the interrogation room to interview DeAngelo, Orange County investigators had not yet left for Sacramento. They had to wait with detectives from other counties to interview DeAngelo the next morning.

When one door closes, another one opens. In March 1980, when Charlene and Lyman Smith were discovered dead in their home, Ventura County Assistant Medical Examiner Claus Peter Speth collected two semen samples from Charlene's body. He routinely collected two rape kits from crime scenes, one for the crime lab and the other for the Medical Examiner's Office. The crime lab's sample was used for testing over the years. But forty years later, while searching for evidence in an unrelated case, a Ventura County Sheriff's detective stumbled upon Charlene's second rape kit at the bottom of a freezer. When Paul Holes asked Ventura County officials for a sample, they immediately agreed. Paul kept his conversations with them a secret, worried that Rackauckas might try to intervene and stop the transfer. Once the DNA sample from Ventura arrived to his tremendous relief and excitement, Paul assembled a team that included Barbara Rae-Venter and Steve Cramer and Melissa Parisot from the FBI to collaborate on the genealogical testing. But he needed more resources and a bigger team.

— — —

Sacramento DA's Office Investigative Lieutenant Kirk Campbell and Investigative Assistant Monica Czajkowski are two very different personalities, but underneath the surface, both exemplify the same tenacious drive. Wiry thin, with close-cropped white hair and smiling eyes, Kirk moves about like a ball of pure energy, always ready to leap into action. In charge of all the investigators in the Homicide Unit, he displays discipline in all aspects of his work and life. Walking by his office, I would see him sitting at his desk counting out pistachios, making sure that he only ate the right amount of protein and carbohydrates for his daily snack. A former officer with the Sacramento Police Department, he flew an Air Support Unit helicopter and later supervised its Homicide Unit before retiring and joining our office in 2011 and worked his way up through the Investigative Bureau. Kirk can be gruff and to the point. You can tell when he disagrees with you because he will cock his head to the side, squint his eyes, give a long pause, and smile before launching into his argument. When it comes to investigating cold cases, Kirk displays a relentless desire to find the truth.

Monica started in our office as an intern, and in her words, "I never left." She has a friendly disposition and warm, kind eyes, and always greets everyone with a smile. She is a brilliant researcher, able to uncover every scrap of information and connect seemingly disparate sets of data, and she throws herself into the pursuit with passion. Humble to a fault, Kirk and Monica share an intense desire to fight for victims and disregard any attention or adulation for their success.

Having secured the DNA from Ventura County, Paul Holes needed a district attorney's office willing and able to provide the resources and commitment to carry his quest through to the end. He was a few months away from retiring and could not let this final opportunity go to waste. The Sacramento County DA's Office is one of a handful in the country with its own crime laboratory. Paul drove up to Sacramento from Contra Costa County in November 2017 to make his pitch for one last opportunity to solve the case. Paul met with then Sacramento District Attorney Anne Marie Schubert and Monica. Although both women were well versed in the use of DNA to solve cases, they struggled at first to absorb the novel use of genealogy Paul was proposing. But as Monica would later say, they had a good feeling that this was their best hope of solving the case. Kirk expressed even greater confidence that the case could be solved with genetic genealogy. Once Schubert approved the investigation and the team began to form, Paul sent the secondary sample from Charlene Smith's rape kit to a private laboratory to develop the SNP profile.

After the profile was obtained, the team uploaded the data to GEDmatch.com and FamilyTreeDNA in January 2018. The genealogy sites provided very distant relatives, making the process of building a family tree a laborious prospect. A few weeks later, Barbara Rae-Venter uploaded the SNP profile to MyHeritage, which yielded a closer relative to the suspect. The databases provided law enforcement only information that the account holders had agreed to make disclosable. Some privacy advocates have argued that the use of investigative genetic genealogy (IGG) violates people's constitutional rights. However, the US Supreme Court has repeatedly based the violation of search-and-seizure protections under the Fourth Amendment on a person's expectation of privacy. For example, people cannot credibly and reasonably expect privacy when they carry on a conversation at a café where other people might overhear the discussion. Additionally, inviting people to attend a speech you are giving does not afford you privacy protection if undercover officers sit in the audience and hear your speech.

Law enforcement utilizes tools open to the public, looking for information from those who provided public access. Prior to utilizing IGG, both the FBI and my office researched constitutional law, vetting the legality of the process before proceeding. In the years since IGG was used to find the Golden State Killer, this process has solved over a thousand cases worldwide and brought child molesters, rapists, and serial killers to justice, providing closure to countless families.

Under the guidance of Barbara Rae-Venter, Kirk, Monica, and the team undertook the tedious job of building family trees. The genealogy database supplies a list of persons related to the suspect, called a match list. Team members identify a cluster of relatives who share a common ancestor in their lineage. They then build each person's family tree, and working backward in time, pinpoint the common ancestor. Once multiple clusters have been delineated, the team again looks for a common ancestor that unites them. Depending on how closely related the suspect is to the original match from the genealogy database, the team may need to go back multiple generations to determine the common ancestor between the match list and the suspect. Once that ancestor is identified, the genealogy team works forward in time, building out the family tree of the common ancestor until reaching the generation of the suspect.

The team pored through census records, old newspaper articles, birth and marriage records, obituaries, other public databases, and social media to build the lineages. Additional research into probate documents, land records, and even religious records provided essential information on identifying relatives. Barbara Rae-Venter's upload of the SNP profile to MyHeritage provided Kirk and Monica with the right lead, narrowing down the cluster for them to follow. The team focused on this branch of relatives, building out a large family tree with hundreds of descendants. Along the way, the team sorted and filtered names of males who lived in the jurisdictions where the crime occurred and had the same general physical characteristics as the Golden State Killer—race, age, eye color. On March 14, 2018, Monica contacted Paul Holes and Kirk. "I think I found him."

For the first time since the Visalia Ransacker broke into his first home, since the EAR assaulted his first victim in Rancho Cordova, since the Original Night Stalker committed his brutal murders in Santa Barbara, Ventura, and Orange Counties, we finally had a name: Joseph James DeAngelo Jr.

As they dug deeper into DeAngelo's past, they found piece after piece of the puzzle: He served in the military; he attended the College of the Sequoias in Visalia, where Professor Snelling taught; he worked as a police officer in Exeter, near Visalia, then transferred to the Auburn Police Department, a thirty-minute drive from Sacramento; he grew up in Rancho Cordova. He had a relationship with a woman named Bonnie, who broke off their engagement; a victim of the EAR in Davis reported that her assailant had started crying and mumbling about a woman named Bonnie.

Disillusioned by two decades of hope turning into disappointment, Paul Holes was skeptical that DeAngelo was in fact the Golden State Killer. But all that changed when he reached out to DeAngelo's former chief at the Auburn Police Department, Nick Willick. After the chief fired DeAngelo for petty theft, he came to the chief's house one night. The next morning, Willick's four-year-old daughter told her father that a man with a flashlight had peered through her window. When the police searched DeAngelo's house, they found items from different stores. Upon hearing this story, Paul realized we had our man.

District Attorney Schubert was attending a dinner event when she received a call from Chief Deputy Steve Grippi. "Are you sitting down?" Grippi asked her before telling her that the results from a DNA sample taken from DeAngelo's garbage can was conclusive. Having tried multiple DNA cases, she grilled Grippi about the test results. He then interrupted her, saying, "All I can tell you is that it matches him, and the lab people are shaking." Schubert had grown up in Carmichael amid the East Area

Rapist's crime spree, and it had left a lasting impact on her and the community. Like so many people, she never gave up the pursuit, and she never hesitated to use the resources needed to find him.

After notifying the Sacramento County sheriff of the results, Schubert called Monica and Kirk. Monica later described her boss's call as a "surreal moment . . . Deep down inside, I knew DeAngelo was the guy, but there had been so many false alarms and false suspects over the years that I just conditioned myself for disappointment." As for Kirk, he described Schubert's call as one of those "moments in your life when you remember exactly where you were and what you were doing." He had been driving in his car and pulled off the road to take her call. As soon as they hung up, he called Paul Holes.

Paul had retired and moved to Colorado to look for a house. His wife and he had just been seated for dinner at a restaurant. Seeing the call coming through, he assumed it was just another update from the surveillance team following DeAngelo. But as soon as he answered, he could tell something was different. Kirk jumped right over the pleasantries and dived into the news. "You can't tell anybody about this. The crime lab found twenty-one [matching DNA] markers!" Without skipping a beat, Paul exclaimed, "That's him!" After hanging up the phone, Paul returned to his wife, but his heart wouldn't stop racing.

The road to find the Visalia Ransacker/East Area Rapist/Original Night Stalker/Golden State Killer had contained many twists and turns, stops and sprints, new trails and dead ends, peaks and valleys, and moments of pure excitement and crushing disappointment. Ultimately, it led to Joseph James DeAngelo. With his masked ripped off, the monster had a face and evil had a name. Though Paul's journey came to a close, our quest was far from over and the result far from certain as we steeled ourselves to prosecute the Golden State Killer. We were intimately aware of the potential headwinds of bringing a perpetrator to trial decades after they were committed and securing his conviction. What we didn't know, however, was that we would have to do it in a world that had changed forever.

4
Ventura: The Voices

March 1980

Bordered by Santa Barbara to the north and Los Angeles to the east, Ventura County boasts forty-three miles of majestic beaches. Thanks to swells rolling in from the Channel Islands off the Pacific coast, Ventura is renowned for its surfing spots, where herds of surfers in wetsuits catch and ride cresting waves. Rugged and unspoiled wilderness dominates the northern part of the county, encompassing the Los Padres National Forest and the ancestral home of the Chumash people. Most residents live in the southern portion of the county, where the coastal plains and valleys come together. Many divide the county between the east and west; the western part of Ventura straddles the ocean all the way down to the edge of the famous Malibu beaches, while the more densely populated eastern section pushes up against the San Fernando Valley—the Valley, as everyone in Southern California calls it.

Ventura has a vibrant music scene, having hosted John Lennon and Johnny Cash at the height of their careers. On any given summer day, street musicians busk as folks walk along the palm tree–lined boulevards against a backdrop of rolling green hills. In the 1980s, Ventura County saw a sudden boom in real estate as people fled Los Angeles for the coast. But Ventura refused to become just another L.A. suburb, maintaining its eclectic vibe with a burgeoning punk rock scene.

In 1980, after a successful career as a prosecutor at the Ventura County DA's Office, forty-three-year-old Lyman Smith waited patiently for his imminent appointment to judgeship. Sporting a glowing tan, brown hair, and long sideburns, he had left the DA's Office a couple years earlier and started several businesses, including a company that shipped cattle to the Middle East. Divorced and remarried to Charlene, Lyman still maintained a relationship with his three children. Ten years younger than Lyman, Charlene, who had long hazel-brown hair and a golden tan that matched her husband's, had gone to high school in Citrus Heights, the same suburb to which Joseph DeAngelo would retire. Lyman and Charlene lived in a ranch-style home on High Point Drive in the city of Ventura, a quiet and peaceful street nestled into the hillside overlooking the valley below. An empty dirt lot flanked the Smiths' residence to the right, and behind it was an open space dotted with trees and grass that backed up to a concrete drainage canal. The occasional streetlamp provided sparse lighting at night.

On the evening of March 13, as Charlene cooked dinner, she talked on the phone with her former mother-in-law, Isabelle, about an upcoming ski trip. According to Isabelle, Charlene never sounded happier than that night. A few hours later, everything would change. Less than two months before, DeAngelo had murdered Robert Offerman and Debra Manning in Goleta, forty-five miles to the north. Offerman fought back and forced DeAngelo to fire multiple gunshots, preventing him from being able to torture and rape his victims before fleeing the scene. With the Smiths, he would make sure that no one could hear or detect him while he committed his crimes, allowing him to escape in complete anonymity at a time of his choosing.

Lyman's twelve-year-old son, Gary, rode his bicycle to his father's home to mow the lawn on Sunday afternoon, March 16. Arriving just before 2:00 p.m., he knocked on the front door and rang the doorbell, but no one answered. He walked around to the back door, but it was locked. When he came back around and tried to open the front door, he realized it was unlocked. Once inside, Gary saw that the couch cushions had been pulled and tossed aside on the living room floor; cabinet doors and drawers sat open with their contents in disarray. The house was "made to look as though it had been ransacked," he recalled later. The sink was filled with dirty dishes, and an open box of crackers and a carton of milk were left out on the counter, as if someone never got a chance to put them away. Sensing something was horribly wrong—he knew Charlene took great pride in maintaining a well-kept home—Gary called out for his dad and stepmom, but the only sound he could hear was a beeping sound coming from the back. With a growing sense of dread, Gary followed the noise toward the master bedroom, where he saw his father and stepmother lying in bed with the blankets pulled over their heads. Thinking they were asleep, he moved to wake his father, but as he got closer, he saw blood on the blanket. The horror of a twelve-year-old child discovering his father's dead body can never be erased; the experience remains forever etched in his memory. Gary quickly backed out of the room and called the police.

Ventura Police Department detectives discovered Lyman face down, his wrists tied behind his back and his ankles also bound. He had sustained blunt-force trauma to the top of his head, resulting in massive skull fractures that caused his death. Charlene lay on her back, her ankles tied and her wrists tucked underneath her, bound with drapery cord. Wearing a white T-shirt and nude from the waist down, she had suffered blows to her head that shattered the base of her skull. Investigators found the murder weapon in the bed, a piece of firewood taken from a stack outside their bedroom door. Blood had spattered on the wall above the victims' heads and soaked into the blanket. The bindings on Charlene and Lyman were white cotton drapery cords with a copper-colored cloth center, tied in diamond and granny knots. After raping Charlene in her own bed next to her husband, the killer eliminated the witnesses to his depravity. To prevent getting blood on himself, he pulled the bedsheets over the victims' heads before beating them to death.

After detectives and crime-scene investigators examined the bodies, Ventura County Assistant Medical Examiner Dr. Claus Peter Speth arrived. A Dutch immigrant who had grown up in Amsterdam, Speth was meticulous and thorough in his work. He conducted rape examinations as soon as crime scenes were secured and before the bodies were removed so as to obtain samples in an undisturbed state. He then secured the evidence immediately in sterile tubes, placing it in dry ice before transporting it directly to the evidence freezer. He learned through experience that rape kits sent to the Crime Lab were exposed to repeated thawing and refreezing as tests were done, deteriorating the sample, so he routinely collected two sets of evidence, one for the lab and the other for the Medical

Examiner's Office. With Charlene, he collected two kits: The first went to the Crime Lab, where it underwent repeated testing and was completely consumed over the years. The second sat in pristine condition for nearly forty years at the bottom of a freezer at the Ventura Medical Examiner's Office. Speth's careful practice changed the course of our hunt for one of the most gruesome predators to ever walk among us.

— — — — —

April 2018

After more than four decades, the man behind the monikers—the Visalia Ransacker, the East Area Rapist, the East Bay Rapist, the Original Night Stalker, the Golden State Killer—finally had a name: Joseph James DeAngelo. At 10:30 a.m. on April 24, 2018, DA Homicide Chief Rod Norgaard filed a complaint accusing DeAngelo of committing two counts of murder in the death of Brian and Katie Maggiore. We further filed a special-circumstance allegation pursuant to Penal Code section 190.6 that he had committed multiple murders, thus making him eligible for the death penalty. The complaint and arrest warrant were all filed under seal with the court—and remain so to this day. The files are sealed to maintain the integrity of the case, ensuring that witnesses testify from their memory and not from a warrant or police report or other information accessed elsewhere. More charges would be filed by the other counties in which he committed his crimes.

The previous week, Sheriff's detectives had DeAngelo under surveillance, following him around to collect a DNA sample. They followed DeAngelo to a Hobby Lobby store, and while he was inside, they secretly swabbed his driver-side door handle, but it yielded insufficient biological material. Two days later, on garbage collection day, the Sheriff's Department commandeered a sanitation truck and lined the interior with plastic covering. Sergeant Darryl Meadows drove up to DeAngelo's house and picked up his trash. After driving around the corner, they sorted through it, collecting various items, including a tissue, to be analyzed. As Rod and Steve read aloud the Crime Lab's test results from the paper, I was eavesdropping on the other side of the wall.

As part of the surveillance, the Sheriff's Department flew a plane mounted with cameras over DeAngelo's house, videotaping his every movement. On one occasion, detectives observed him doing yard work in front of his house. He abruptly stopped and stood on the sidewalk, staring up at the plane for several minutes before going back inside the house. Did he know he was being watched? The next day, DeAngelo rode his motorcycle northbound on Highway I-5 toward Sacramento International Airport. Several unmarked Sheriff's vehicles followed him from a distance as a plane flew overhead. DeAngelo began driving erratically, slowing down and then suddenly speeding up and weaving in and out of traffic at almost 80 mph. He then took an exit that led to the airport terminals. After passing by the exit to the rental-car area, DeAngelo unexpectedly pulled to the side of the road and stopped underneath an overpass, forcing the unmarked vehicles following him to pass by. Either he knew he was being followed, or through force of habit, employed countersurveillance techniques.

By April 2018, the Golden State Killer was a seventy-two-year-old retired mechanic living in Citrus Heights, a quiet Sacramento suburb. He enjoyed riding his motorcycle and taking his aluminum-bottom boat for short fishing trips on local lakes and along the delta and wetlands in the southern part of the county. He spent hours mowing his lawn, trimming his bushes with precision, and organizing his garage in carefully labeled bins or buckets. He exuded an almost maniacal compulsion for order.

As we began to narrow our focus on DeAngelo, detectives started developing a strategy for a "takedown." As a former police officer, DeAngelo owned several legal firearms, including handguns, rifles, and shotguns. We were worried that, given a chance, DeAngelo might barricade himself inside his house and engage in a shootout—after forty years on the run, constantly looking over his shoulder, he wasn't likely to be taken into custody easily. Killing was something he was intimately familiar with, and he wouldn't hesitate to take a life in order to save his freedom.

After the arrest warrant was lodged with the court on April 24, the Sheriff's Fugitive Apprehension Team—which had an ominous nickname, the "Body Snatchers"—began preparations for the takedown. They typically hunt suspects at night and are not known for their subtlety or sophistication. While serving in Homicide, I had reviewed numerous search warrants from their leader, Sergeant Steve Girdlestone, while they were pursuing a suspect. Nobody called him Steve, or Sergeant, just Girdlestone. I would receive a call at 2 a.m., pick up the phone, and hear on the other line, "Hey, it's Girdlestone. We are looking for this guy and need you to review a search warrant so we can get in his phone." We had talked on the phone countless times but never met in person.

The first time Girdlestone and his team walked into my office, I thought they were a motorcycle gang led by a cowboy. After he introduced himself, I noticed that his footwear of choice was cowboy boots; he would wear a cowboy hat on duty if allowed. A ball of muscle and aggression, with dark sunglasses sitting on top of his shiny bald head, Girdlestone was the proverbial bull in a china shop. The rest of his crew had tattoos running up their arms and shoulders, bushy hair, scraggly beards, and a uniform consisting of T-shirts and dirty blue jeans. If you were going to snatch the Golden State Killer off the streets, the Body Snatchers were the perfect team to do it.

The plan called for detectives in a minivan a few doors down from DeAngelo's house to determine the right time to call in the Body Snatchers, who waited just around the corner for the signal to "release the Kracken." A gaggle of patrol vehicles, Crime Lab personnel, and an FBI forensic team gathered at a staging area in the parking lot of a nearby shopping center, likely provoking curiosity and concern from anyone shopping at the grocery store. Finally, the garage door opened, and DeAngelo walked outside and started working on his front yard. On the police radio, detectives debated as to how to approach DeAngelo. Some were worried that he might be armed, while others thought he might retreat inside or swallow a cyanide pill. Growing tired of all the chatter, Girdlestone took matters into his own hands, got out of his pickup truck, and started walking toward DeAngelo.

DeAngelo turned around to see who was approaching. Girdlestone nonchalantly pointed down the street and said, "Hey, do you know how I can get to . . ."

Before DeAngelo could register a thought or utter a word, the head Body Snatcher grabbed him by the collar and arm, swung him around, and pinned him to the ground in one continuous motion. Detectives rushed immediately to surround the suspect, and he was handcuffed, dragged to his feet, and thrown inside the back of a minivan. With his eyes glazed over in shock, DeAngelo cried in a high-pitched voice—just like the one he used the night he shot Officer McGowen in December 1975—"I have a roast in the oven!" The monsters of our imagination can look and feel very different in the bright light of reality. The bogeyman who had stalked the nightmares of so many was finally in custody.

— — —

A police interrogation room hears and sees everything. It never sleeps. Cold, bare, and bathed in fluorescent white light, it records the anger and the anguish, the fear and the frustration, the tragedies and the lies told within its walls. It never forgets.

Assigned by the Sheriff's Department as the lead detective on the Golden State Killer case, Detective Sergeant Kenny Clark possessed a near-photographic memory of the GSK's cases, not just the ones in Sacramento but throughout the eleven counties as well. He had an uncanny ability to recite the facts, at times veering too deeply into minutiae. His encyclopedic knowledge made him an invaluable resource whom I relied upon from time to time as the case proceeded forward.

A twenty-plus-year veteran of the force, Clark spoke with a calm, soothing radio voice. When he first arrived in the Homicide Bureau over a decade earlier, he, like all new detectives assigned to Homicide, was directed to the Cold Case room, a chamber filled with information and evidence related to a myriad of unsolved cases, sitting on dusty metal shelves, just waiting for someone to come along and solve them. In the left corner of the room, boxes pertaining to the Deputy Jeff Mitchell murder case sat next to the files for other notorious murders. But the case taking up the most boxes and shelf space belonged to the notorious East Area Rapist.

Clark's superiors ordered him to review the EAR case, and he attacked the assignment with relish. Over the next decade, he chased down numerous leads and developed multiple theories from the evidence at hand. He pored over all the police reports and developed new suspects. He once convinced my boss, Rod Norgaard, that a worker at a telephone company was the EAR because the suspect had stocky legs, could tap into people's phone lines, and lived in each of the areas affected by the Ransacker and the EAR at the exact time of those crimes. His theory was compelling enough that the Sheriff's Department followed this suspect as he drove his RV all the way to Oklahoma, where he discarded a McDonald's wrapper out of his window. They collected the wrapper and ran a DNA test, but the sample failed to match the EAR's DNA. At one point, Clark had the hunch that the Visalia Ransacker had evolved into the EAR, but none of his colleagues believed him. Now, they had found the real monster, and Clark was on the verge of interviewing the Visalia Ransacker/East Area Rapist/Original Night Stalker/Golden State Killer.

In 2005, the Federal Bureau of Investigation brought together experts from multiple fields to develop a uniform definition of a "serial killer." Ultimately, they defined a serial killer as someone who commits "the unlawful killing of two or more victims . . . in separate events." The FBI categorizes serial killers into three basic categories: organized, disorganized, and mixed (who demonstrate both tendencies).[1] Organized killers engage in extensive, methodical planning, selecting and observing their prey before formulating and executing their crimes. They are master manipulators who often lure or kidnap their victims. They control every aspect of the crime scene. They tie up or disable their victims so they can take their time torturing, sexually assaulting, and murdering them. Their crimes bear the hallmark of repeated patterns and recognized modi operandi. They follow their exploits in the media, reliving their crimes and relishing the

1 Federal Bureau of Investigation, *Crime Classification Manual*, 2nd edition, 2006.

attention they garner with their heinous actions. Disorganized serial killers, on the other hand, act impulsively, with little planning. They tend to commit crimes of opportunity that reflect a certain level of randomness and lack any coherent repeating patterns. Mixed serial killers demonstrate characteristics from both categories.

No matter how they are categorized, serial killers have been among us since the beginning of humanity. Liu Pengli was a Han Dynasty prince in the second century BCE who, according to historians, killed over a hundred people for sport.[2] The infamous Jack the Ripper killed and mutilated five women in London's East End from late summer to early fall 1888. He slashed the throats of his victims, mutilated their faces and genitals, and removed their internal organs. John Wayne Gacy, a professional clown, lured, raped, and murdered thirty-three boys and young men, prompting newspapers to call him the "Killer Clown."

But not all serial killers work as clowns or stand out with the wild-eyed look of a crazed and unhinged loner. Some are handsome and charismatic, like Ted Bundy, who raped and murdered over thirty women in the 1970s. Many, like Joseph DeAngelo, avoid capture for decades by blending in with the masses. They are our neighbors, coworkers, and friends. DeAngelo wasn't too tall or too short, too muscular or too obese. Nothing about him stood out. He had the appearance of an everyman.

Like a dance, an interrogation requires finesse, timing, and a precise, choreographed set of steps and moves. A skilled interrogator needs to have the right feel and intuition for the moment. It helps if you have a partner who is willing to talk. As a common law-enforcement tactic, perpetrators are placed in an interrogation room and made to sit and wait a long time before anyone speaks to them. This allows them to wallow in their predicament, their minds running wild with fear and anxiety. They may fidget, talk to themselves or to us, get up and pace about the room to break the monotony. Sometimes, suspects fall asleep at the table before being awakened by the loud clanging of the metal door opening and detectives walking in.

---

2 Qian Sima, Burton Watson, trans., *Records of the Grand Historian: Qin Dynasty*, 3rd ed. (New York: Columbia University Press, 1995).

DeAngelo was unusual, and so was his interrogation. At 5:20 p.m. on April 24, 2018, an hour after the Body Snatchers arrested DeAngelo, investigators placed him in a small interrogation room at the Sacramento County Sheriff's Department headquarters. DeAngelo, wearing a T-shirt, cargo shorts, and tube socks, sat down in a plastic chair at the table in the middle of the room. He was left to sit alone until 6:52 p.m. For an entire hour and a half, he sat motionless, his mouth agape, periodically taking in loud gulps of air but otherwise never moving an inch or even looking around.

After I was named the lead prosecutor of the case a week after DeAngelo's arrest, I watched the video of DeAngelo's interrogation. He reminded me of a sloppy grandpa or an alcoholic uncle whom you avoided at all costs during Thanksgiving dinner. He did not seem, at least to my eyes, particularly menacing. I noticed that he licked his lips constantly and made smacking sounds with his mouth. He was thirsty, I thought to myself. Upon reentering the interrogation room after the prolonged wait, Sergeant Clark asked DeAngelo, "Do you want some Dr Pepper?" (Officers had found Dr Pepper consumed by the EAR at several of the crime scenes. After DeAngelo's arrest, the Sheriff's Department and the FBI conducted a search of his home and found several cases of the soft drink.) No reply, no movement, no acknowledgment.

"Joe, do you want some Dr Pepper?" Clark asked again. Still nothing. No matter how many times he was offered Dr Pepper, water, or something to drink, DeAngelo never accepted. The beginning of an interrogation represents the most vulnerable and disorienting moment for a suspect. Questions run through their minds: How did I get here? What charges am I facing? What evidence do they have against me? Being offered Dr Pepper repeatedly fed into DeAngelo's paranoia that law enforcement wanted to collect his DNA from the can. What he didn't know was that we had already collected it from his trash can.

Clark began the interrogation by advising DeAngelo of his Miranda rights. "You have the right to remain silent. Anything you say can and will be used against you in a court of law. Do you understand?" The suspect remained motionless and mute. Clark repeated the warning. Still nothing. A few hours before, DeAngelo had been cooking a roast in the oven; now he found himself being interrogated. Knowing that curiosity is an itch suspects can't resist scratching, detectives will encourage suspects to start asking questions or talk. Sergeant Clark asked, "Would you like to know why you are here? I would be happy to share that with you. I'll give you a few minutes to think about it, and I will come back to see if you want to talk."

You don't want to press too hard at the beginning of an interview as the suspect might shut down the conversation. The worst-case scenario for any detective is when a suspect invokes his right to remain silent or asks for an attorney. But this situation represented a close second. DeAngelo didn't want to dance. Walking back to his office, where other detectives were watching a television monitor with a live feed, Sergeant Clark was unfazed. As the department's hostage negotiator, he was determined to use calibrated questions to entice the suspect to share information. He told his partners, "Inside, he's dying to find out what we know. Let's give him a few minutes to stew on it."

Every minute seemed like an eternity, the clock on the wall moving in slow motion. At 7:00 p.m., Clark walked back into the interrogation room and asked DeAngelo, "Would you like to know what's going on?"

"What have I done?" For the first time in almost two hours, DeAngelo spoke. Here perhaps was the opening, the crack everyone was waiting for.

"I will tell you, alright?" Clark replied. "I'm going to read you your rights. You have the right to remain silent. Anything you say may be used against you in court. You have the right to talk to an attorney and have one present with you before and while being questioned. If you cannot afford an attorney, one will be appointed for you, free of charge, before any questioning if you want. Understand those?" DeAngelo crawled back into his shell and stared at the wall.

Undeterred, Sergeant Clark began talking about the East Area Rapist nonstop for the next twenty-five minutes. Although DeAngelo sat there in silence, I could see the wheels turning in his head. Panic and despair must have been running through his mind. *They found me. They know. How do I get out of this?* He had been caught and cornered before, but this time, he was strapped to a chair, having lost all control.

Just a few hours before the interview, detectives observed DeAngelo doing vigorous yard work, jumping in and out of his truck, and lifting heavy objects. Now, sitting in the interview room, he feigned feeble incoherence. He had tried this parlor trick once before. When store security detained DeAngelo in 1979 for shoplifting dog repellent and a hammer, he pretended to suffer a heart attack and then fought with them to the point that they were forced to tie him to a chair. When police deputies arrived, he rolled around in his chair and screamed incoherently. Later that day, DeAngelo admitted to the deputies that he had acted crazily to avoid getting in trouble.

You can't dance if your partner doesn't want to. So Clark decided to leave the room and regroup, knowing that the silence of sitting alone might spur a suspect into filling that silence with words. A short while later, alone in the room, DeAngelo began talking to himself. "I've done nothing, I've done nothing. I've dreamed about him [unintelligible mumbling] . . . I was strong." Back in the monitoring room, Sergeant Clark wondered aloud, "Who the hell is 'him'?" He sensed something was about to happen. He went back into the interrogation room.

Seizing the moment, Clark pressed aggressively. Sitting down across from DeAngelo, he lobbed the first grenade: "Brian and Katie Maggiore, who were murdered in 1979 in Rancho Cordova. They were gunned down and executed. We have DNA evidence tying you to their murders."

DeAngelo snapped out of his silence. "I don't remember anything you've said. I don't remember any of that. . . . I've done nothing. Please let me go home. I don't remember any of that. I've done nothing." The panic in his voice was unmistakable.

Clark laid it on thick. "These are pictures of Brian and Katie. They were young. They had their whole lives ahead of them. They were walking their dog that night when you killed them."

Barely looking at the photos, DeAngelo said, "I don't remember any of those people. Or any of that. I want to talk to my wife."

"We might be able to make that happen. But not right now."

DeAngelo continued, "My wife's an attorney. I need to talk to her if I'm in trouble. I need to talk to my wife. I'm in trouble, yeah. Please." Sergeant

Clark's heart sank when he heard the dreaded A-word: "attorney." The request contained some ambiguity, however. Was he specifically invoking his right to an attorney? Or was he simply asking for his wife, who happened to be an attorney?

Knowing his window to obtain a statement was closing, Clark pressed on. "Well, let me go see if I can, if we even know where she's at. But I'll see if I can find somebody. See if your wife's available." He then left DeAngelo alone again.

Alone in the room, DeAngelo began murmuring to himself as detectives in the monitoring room leaned in and strained to hear every word. Through clenched teeth, he whispered, "I had no choice. I got stronger, stronger, stronger . . . He tried to [unintelligible]." His voice trailed off.

The detectives decided to change things up and offer DeAngelo another dance partner, Sergeant Michelle Hendricks. She was a twenty-year veteran of the Sheriff's Department, a no-nonsense cop who, like her legendary colleague Carol Daly, was known for her deep empathy for victims of sexual assault. Behind her soft voice and eyes, Hendricks worked relentlessly to obtain justice for her victims. I first met her when I prosecuted a serial rapist, Aaron Montgomery. He had lured and violently raped several victims; he pushed one woman into an abandoned house, where he assaulted her on the bedroom floor on top of stained bedsheets. Michelle interviewed the victim, who described a rainbow-colored stuffed teddy bear nailed to the wall, which helped deputies locate the house.

Before trial, Montgomery spat on and threatened to rape his own defense attorney. As we approached the hearing, Hendricks convinced each victim to come to court. One of them had moved to Mexico, but Hendricks talked her into boarding a plane and coming back to Sacramento to testify even though she was seven months pregnant. During the trial, the defense attorney referred to me as "DA Ho," and Montgomery kept calling me "Mr. Da Ho" the entire time. After the jury quickly returned a verdict of guilty, the judge sentenced the defendant to multiple life terms in prison. After the sentencing, Michelle stood next to me as the defendant kept screaming "Fuck you, Mr. Da Ho!" as the bailiff led him out of the courtroom. After a long career hunting rapists, Hendricks walked down the hall to question the most notorious and prolific rapist she had ever seen. She remembered hearing, as a young girl living in Sacramento, stories of the EAR attacks in the neighborhoods surrounding her home. She had spent nights hiding under her bedsheets, terrified that he might break into her home. Now she was about to come face-to-face with the bogeyman of her childhood.

As soon as she entered the interrogation room, Hendricks tried to gain DeAngelo's trust by appearing helpful. She told him she would try to get a hold of his wife and needed her number. DeAngelo stated that the number could be found in the phone the police had confiscated. When she asked for the passcode to get the number, DeAngelo, still playing games, claimed he didn't know the password to his own phone. DeAngelo then said, "All these things that they say I, I did a long, a long time ago. I, I need an attorney, right? An attorney?"

"Are you asking me a question? That's up to you, okay?" she responded.

"I need an attorney. I guess."

Shit, Sergeant Hendricks thought to herself. If DeAngelo explicitly asked for a lawyer, the interview would end, and she'd lose her chance to get anything useful out of him. She headed back to the monitoring room. We had one more tactic we wanted to try.

DeAngelo, his mouth agape and his eyes staring off into space, barely moved as Sergeant Clark and Investigator Steve Rhods walked into the interrogation room together. The night before DeAngelo was taken into police custody, we'd informed our colleagues at the Ventura County District Attorney's Office of the impending arrest. Ventura County was the only DA's office with which we shared the news because it had provided key DNA evidence to help us solve the case. They sent Investigator Steve Rhods to Sacramento the moment DeAngelo was in our hands. Rhods was thin as a nail, with silver hair and red, leathery skin. Loud and aggressive, he spoke with the subtlety of a long-haul truck driver—direct and to the point. We hoped he'd turn out to be the perfect foil in our "good cop, bad cop" routine.

Clark offered DeAngelo water, but he continued to stare blankly at the wall. Knowing we had to clarify the Miranda issue, the sergeant said, "I was told that you had mentioned a lawyer. That's a decision for you to make. It's not something that I can do for you. By the way, this is Investigator Steve Rhods, who drove up from Ventura to speak with you. Other detectives from throughout California are on their way and would like to speak to you. But the bottom line is, if you want to talk to them, that's something that we can make happen. If you'd like to talk to this detective, it's up to you what you want to do here. Any thoughts?"

Again, no response. Rhods, who had driven eight hours straight for a chance to interview DeAngelo, jumped right in. "Do you remember being in Ventura?" DeAngelo shook his head. In a voice that sounded like he smoked a pack of cigarettes a day, Rhods began to rattle off details of the murders of Charlene and Lyman Smith.

DeAngelo remained defiant. "I don't, I, I didn't do any of this stuff."

Without skipping a beat, Rhods leaned in close to the killer. "Well, the DNA says differently. Your DNA is inside of Charlene. Your semen is inside of her. You had sex with that woman."

"Where?" DeAngelo asked meekly, trying to regain his composure.

"In Ventura. March 13th, 1980." In a scolding tone, Rhods continued, "We spoke to your wife, Sharon. We told her that you wanted to see her, and she said she didn't want to see you. And I'm not lying about this." It was in fact a lie, all part of a psychological ploy to make DeAngelo feel isolated. After confronting DeAngelo for several minutes more, Investigator Rhods and Sergeant Clark left the room.

Within minutes, DeAngelo began talking to himself, and over the next three hours, he made puzzling statements about his struggle against an unidentified "him." He claimed he had taken charge and fought back. "I pushed him off. I got stronger, stronger. And now I am. And I pushed him off and that was the happiest day of my life. I see now, what he did to me. I took control of myself. I really controlled myself, and not him. He used to control me. I'm in control. My children all suffering so bad [unintelligible] so good [unintelligible]. They're all suffering, aren't they, but he's evil [unintelligible] self. It's so shameful [unintelligible]. I did all that. All these years, I was too weak. I was too weak to stand up to him. I don't remember any of it."

Startlingly, DeAngelo admitted aloud that he had committed the crimes. "I did all that . . . I didn't have the strength to push him out. He made me. He went with me. It was like, in my head, I mean, he's a part of me. I didn't want to do those things. I pushed Jerry out and had a happy life. I did all those things. I've destroyed all their lives . . . I raped. So now I gotta pay the price." DeAngelo was claiming that an alter ego named Jerry made him hurt, rape, and kill his victims. The detectives saw an opening. Since he was talking to himself, he might now talk to them as well. Steve Rhods returned to the room, sat across from DeAngelo, and leaned in. "A little while ago, you were sitting in here and you were speaking out loud and one of the things you said was, you didn't want to do those things. Who made you do those things?"

"I didn't, I don't understand what you're saying," DeAngelo responded feebly.

Using a classic interrogation technique, Rhods tried to find common ground with DeAngelo. "You know, Joe, you and I come from kind of similar worlds. I was in the navy during Vietnam, you were in Vietnam. You were a cop, I was a cop, okay? And we both learned how to take responsibility for our actions. Both in service of our country and of our communities, alright? So when I ask you a question, show me some respect, okay?"

When DeAngelo claimed he didn't know what he had done, Rhods pivoted into his bad cop persona. "You don't want to explain what you did? Because I can tell you what you did. You killed thirteen people. You raped over fifty young women. You terrorized little children. That's what you did. Could I be any clearer than that?"

"I don't remember," DeAngelo answered.

Rhods had had enough. He walked up right next to DeAngelo and placed his hand on his shoulder. "Had a happy life, didn't ya? Learned how to control it, remember? Do you remember that? How did you push that impulse down? That sexual urge. Tell me. C'mon, Joe. C'mon. You hurt those people. And you remember. C'mon, show me some respect. Either answer my question or tell me you don't want to. . . . Joe, you're not crazy."

Like a bad actor, DeAngelo began to whimper and cry. As the interview ended, we were left with the question: Was he crazy, or was he just pretending to be, as he had done during his 1979 arrest?

— — —

As deputies escorted DeAngelo from the interrogation room to the county jail for booking, four women who had never met or spoken with each other were getting ready for bed. One thing connected them all together: Joseph James DeAngelo. In a small house in Rancho Cordova with bars on the windows and doors, Phyllis prepared for a long night. Her sleep was never restful. She lived in a fortress; her house was her prison. When her husband traveled for work, Phyllis lived in fear until he returned. In her youth, she had exhibited a warm and outgoing personality, but now she was withdrawn and quiet. For over forty years, she wondered how she had been targeted, and why. She wondered how different her life would have been but for that night. Most of all, she wondered who the man was that tormented her every waking moment and slipped among the dark recesses of her nightmares.

A couple of miles away, Trish had worked long and hard to repair the broken pieces of her soul and create a new life. It had taken her many years to tell her children what had happened. Out of shame, mostly, and fear, she had kept a secret that forced her to the brink of despair and hopelessness. Many times, whether in quiet rooms or halls bustling with people, in moments of peace or times of chaos, the horrifying memories would return, stirring up a tempest of crippling emotions within her.

Twenty miles from the Sacramento County Jail, fifty-seven-year-old Kris got ready for bed. Forty-two years earlier, her life had taken a tragic turn, and she had never been the same. In defiance, she often left her doors and windows unlocked, challenging her nightmares to return. She wanted to take back control of her life; she refused to live in fear. But buried within her, all those thoughts and emotions would come roaring out of the depths of her psyche to consume her once more.

Three thousand miles away, in South Carolina, seventy-two-year-old Jane Carson was a retired United States Air Force major. Her first marriage had not survived the trauma of her assault. After getting remarried, she relocated from Sacramento to South Carolina. Years later, she wrote a book entitled *Frozen in Fear* that recounted her journey to recovery and resiliency.

For each of the four women, one night, one event had brought anguish and doubt into their lives. But this would be the last night they had to live with all those questions and all that torment. Tomorrow morning, when the sun came out, everything would change for Phyllis, Trish, Kris, and Jane.

— — —

In California, a defendant's first appearance in court is called an arraignment, during which a judge informs them of the charges they face and of their constitutional rights and assigns them an attorney. DeAngelo's arraignment was scheduled for April 27, 2018, in Department 61of the Sacramento Superior Court. Every local and national media outlet would be there. For the first time in forty years, the monster behind the mask would be revealed to the world.

For many of us in the DA's Office, the capture of the Golden State Killer seemed to come out of nowhere. Like a flash of lighting in the night sky, it sent a palpable excitement and nervous anticipation surging through the office. "Can you believe he's still alive?" "Can you believe we actually caught him?" "Who's going get the case, who's going to prosecute him?" I really wanted to see him up close and personal, but the tiny courtroom would be packed with media, victims, and law enforcement, and it was not yet my time. I walked to my office and clicked on the livestream link of the proceedings.

Kris Pedretti and her husband, Steve, arrived at 901 G Street in downtown Sacramento and walked into the lobby of the Sacramento County D.A.'s Office. She was shaking from head to toe with anxiousness, and Steve held her hand to help calm her nerves.

Friday, April 27, was a beautiful spring day with a slight breeze, and blooming flowers basked in the warm sun. The Honorable Michael Sweet presided over Department 61. With a ruddy face and a full head of silver hair, Judge Sweet had been a prosecutor and then served as the Executive Director of the California District Attorneys Association before being appointed to the bench. He always spoke with precision, as if reading from a script. Many years ago, I had appeared in front of Judge Sweet to prosecute a child molester who had sexually assaulted a young boy and his little sister. The trial occurred the week before Christmas, and he treated the children with such kindness, even allowing the little girl to hold a teddy bear on the witness stand to calm her anxiety. The jury convicted the defendant in less than two hours, and the judge sentenced him to multiple life terms in prison.

Although he exhibited a calm countenance from the bench, Judge Sweet occasionally flashed a piercing look or sharp word to keep the attorneys in line. The elected district attorneys for Sacramento, Santa Barbara, Ventura, Orange, and Alameda Counties sat in the front row, right behind a phalanx of cameras crammed in a five-by-ten-foot area behind the attorneys' desk. Spilling over and struggling for position, the cameramen tried to get the best angle of the steel cage in which defendants were typically held during their arraignment. With his hands clasped behind his back, Steve Grippi paced back and forth in the courtroom like a prizefighter waiting for the bell to be rung. Kris sat in the front row on the other side of the courtroom, right in front of the cage.

At the Homicide Unit four blocks away, I watched the screen intently as the courtroom came into view. Before every court appearance and trial, my heart begins to race, my palms sweat, and I feel butterflies in my stomach. Even though I was only sitting in my office, I felt as if I was standing there ready to address the judge. The wait was unbearable.

"All rise, Department 61 is in session," the bailiff announced authoritatively. As everyone stood up, the door to the judge's chamber opened, and Judge Sweet walked in and took his seat on the bench. Five minutes later, at 1:35 p.m., a deputy sheriff pushed Joseph DeAngelo, who was in a wheelchair, wearing an orange jumpsuit over a white T-shirt, into the courtroom. The defendant wore a dumb, confused look on his face. The deputy wheeled DeAngelo around to face Judge Sweet. I could hear the continual click of cameras in the courtroom. Everybody wanted a look, a picture, a memory of the moment.

The court clerk declared, "Your Honor, on the 1:30 calendar, page two. In custody, DeAngelo."

"Is Joseph James DeAngelo Jr. your true and correct legal name?" the judge asked the defendant. Staring ahead for a moment, just breathing through his mouth, DeAngelo hesitated before quietly answering yes. Judge Sweet continued, "You are before the Sacramento Superior Court for two reasons. One, there is a warrant, a hold for you out of Ventura County for two counts of murder, 187(a) of the Penal Code. There is no bail from Ventura County. In Sacramento County Superior Court, you are charged by way of a felony complaint, 18FE008017, filed on April 25, 2018, alleging two counts of murder and a special circumstance. Count 1 alleges that on or about February 2, 1978, in the county of Sacramento, you did willfully, unlawfully, and with malice aforethought, murder Katie Maggiore, a human being, in violation of Penal Code section 187 subdivision (a). It is a felony. It is further alleged that in the commission of that murder, that you personally used a firearm of unknown caliber, in violation of Penal Code statute 12022.5(a). This makes it a violent and serious felony. Count 2, for a further and separate cause of action with the charges set forth in Count 1, it is further alleged that on or about February 2, 1978, in the county of Sacramento, you did unlawfully, willfully, and with malice aforethought, murder Brian Maggiore, a human being. It is again further alleged during the commission of that murder that you used a firearm of unknown caliber. There is a special circumstance alleged against you, and that reads as follows: It is further alleged that the offenses charged in Counts 1 and 2 are a special circumstance in that the defendant committed multiple murders within the meaning of the Penal Code statute 190.2(c)(5)." The special circumstance allegation of committing multiple murders made DeAngelo eligible for the death penalty.

Judge Sweet then appointed Deputy Public Defender Diane Howard to represent DeAngelo. Howard, a public defender for nearly thirty years, was known as a straight shooter who was easy to talk to and had a dry sense of humor. She liked to put a hand on the defendant's shoulder to humanize her client. Accepting representation, she used the same playbook and placed her right hand on DeAngelo's shoulder. The judge announced the case would be continued for a couple of weeks. This gave the prosecution the time we needed to turn over the initial packet of police reports, assemble the litigation team, and simply get our bearings before plotting out the next steps in this unprecedented proceeding.

Sitting in the front row, Kris intently stared at DeAngelo's face from the moment he was rolled into the courtroom. Terrified that she had somehow known him all along, she was relieved to see that he was a stranger. Her anxiety and the sharp pangs in her stomach began to subside. Meanwhile, the case of the People of California vs. the Golden State Killer had only just begun.

5
The “OC”

Summer 1980

With over three million residents, Orange County, or the OC, as most people now call it, sits just south of Los Angeles. OC residents typically divide the county into three different areas—the coast and the northern and southern parts—and each has its own distinct geographical, demographic, economic, and cultural identity. The cities and towns in the northern part of the county tend to be flat and more densely populated; the towns to the south spread out in gated and master-planned communities that hug the beaches or nestle into the hillsides perched above the ocean.

The OC symbolizes eternal sunshine and evokes the chill SoCal vibe. It boasts forty-three miles of beaches that have long hosted a world-class surfing scene, and international competitions are regularly held next to the pier in Huntington Beach, known as "Surf City USA." Just south of Huntington Beach, along the Balboa Peninsula in Newport Beach, the waves reach upwards of thirty feet at the Wedge. Formed by the natural intersection of the land and a manmade jetty at the entry of the harbor, the Wedge provides opportunities to catch an epic wave on a surfboard or to go body surfing. When I lived in Newport Beach, I rode waves at the Wedge before changing into a suit for court.

Most of the Asian American and Latine communities live in the more densely populated and older cities of northern Orange County. In fact, the area is home to the largest Vietnamese population outside of Vietnam.

As a child, I remember jumping into my parents' station wagon and driving down from San Jose to the OC's Little Saigon, where I marveled at the restaurants and stores with Vietnamese names that filled every street. We would stop by Lee's Sandwiches to pick up a banh mi filled with Vietnamese ham, pâté, and pickled vegetables for less than a dollar before heading off to Disneyland. Little Saigon felt like a second home.

In the 1950s, the aerospace industry replaced the orange groves and farms that had given the county its name, and an influx of businesses took over the region. Large master-planned communities such as Irvine spread through the southern part of the OC, and young affluents and suburbanites rushed in to fill them, especially along the coastal areas of Laguna Beach and Dana Point. By 1980, Orange County began to see an increasing flow of immigrants from Vietnam and Mexico. At the same time, a vicious serial killer continued what he had started in Visalia, Sacramento, Contra Costa County, and along the coastal towns in Santa Barbara and Ventura. His new hunting ground brought him to Orange County.

That summer, my father took me for the first and only time to the movie theater. For months, I desperately wanted to see *The Empire Strikes Back* and pestered him about Darth Vader, Luke Skywalker, Han Solo, and a big-eared green creature named Yoda. I used thin tree branches as a light saber and dreamed of being a Jedi Knight. Given my dad's busy work schedule and our having barely enough money to get by, going to the movies was a true luxury. Glued to my seat, I didn't take my eyes off the screen for even a moment, wanting to absorb every last word and image.

I gasped and nearly fell out of my chair when Darth Vader, the personification of evil, shrouded in a black cape and mask, said, "Luke, I am your father." How could Luke Skywalker, our righteous hero, be his son? Many considered *The Empire Strikes Back*, the second installment of the original trilogy, the best movie in the entire franchise. It evoked an ominous tone in the eternal battle between the forces of good and evil—and darkness won, at least momentarily. This endless struggle is woven into the very fabric of our DNA and transcends all cultures and belief systems. Whether we live in poverty or in a palace, whether we work with a hammer or a scalpel, whether we run from our past or run a company, the never-ending fight against evil touches all our lives, sooner or later. Evil is patient and cruel. It always covets and consumes; it is never satiated or satisfied. It never sleeps.

That same summer, Keith and Patrice "Patty" Harrington, a young couple still basking in the blissful glow of their wedding, were enjoying their new and busy life as newlyweds. But evil would soon pay them a visit. With curly brown hair, a faint mustache, and a chiseled jaw, Keith was a twenty-four-year-old medical student about to embark on a successful career as an emergency-room doctor. Patty, a registered pediatric nurse a few years older than her husband, had shoulder-length brown hair parted in the middle and a beaming smile. They met while working at the same hospital. In addition to her day job, Patty worked as a nurse tending to newborn twins for a member of the Irvine family, which founded the OC city of Irvine.

Keith and Patty lived together in a one-story house on Cockleshell Drive, in what is now Dana Point, behind the Niguel Shores planned community. A short stroll from their home led to a beautiful golf course, and their backyard enjoyed a view of the Pacific Ocean and soft sea breezes. Far from the bustling freeway and adjacent to gates monitored by security guards, this location represented a distinct departure from DeAngelo's other crime scenes. On the surface, it appeared to carry an exponentially higher risk of being seen or captured. However, people living in such a place can be lulled into a false sense of security, letting down their guard with the belief that a tranquil place like this was safe. Outside the gates, narrow dirt paths wove through thick and heavy bushes, providing easy cover for a perpetrator on foot to climb up the hill, jump over the fence, and prowl through the neighborhood at night.

Keith's father, Roger Harrington, who owned the house the young couple lived in, spent most of August 19 installing a new sprinkler system in the front yard. Patty came home around 8:30 a.m. after working the graveyard shift and went immediately to bed. Keith headed off to work at the University of California, Irvine Medical Center. When he returned home at 5:00 p.m., his father was still working in the yard. After checking on his wife, Keith rolled up his sleeves and helped his dad finish up the yardwork. They enjoyed their one-on-one time together, and then Roger said goodbye to Keith before driving back to his home an hour away. Little did he know it was for the last time. Later that night, Patty's sister called around 11:00. Nothing seemed amiss, but Patty sounded tired, and the two sisters only spoke for a few minutes. That would be the last time their loved ones would hear from the couple.

The young newlyweds, who loved to entertain at their new home, had made plans to have their friends Jason and Liz* to dinner on the evening of August 20. As the sun began to set, the guard verified their names on the guest list and waved the couple through the gate. They knocked on the door and were greeted by silence. Liz looked in the window and peered toward the kitchen. The kitchen sat dark and empty—with no sign of cooking or preparation for a dinner party. She saw only a doctor's bag sitting on the desk. Had their friends forgotten about dinner? After fifteen minutes, Jason and Liz left a note on the door: "Patty & Keith—We came by at 7 and no one was home. Call us if plans have changed? Liz and Jason." The call never came.

Roger loved all four of his sons, but Keith, the youngest, held a special place in his father's heart. Throughout the day on August 21, he repeatedly called his son but got no reply. He drove to the house and knocked on the front door as the sun dipped toward the horizon. He looked in the window and saw the house was still and the lights were turned off. Roger unlocked the garage and found both cars parked inside. Walking into the home, Roger called out for Keith and Patty, but no one responded. He made himself a drink, took a sip and began walking toward the master bedroom.

At the doorway, Roger saw two lumps in the bed. When he pulled back the comforter, Roger saw pools of blood all over the bed and under Keith's head. He quickly left the bedroom and called 911. When the Orange County Sheriff's Department arrived on the scene, they found Roger sitting on the curb, sobbing uncontrollably. Deputies found Keith lying face down and nude on the bed, with pools of coagulated blood on the pillow and bedding. While the comforter covered Keith's entire body, the underlying bedsheet only came up to his armpits, with his arms lying on top of the sheets. Crime-scene investigators discovered ligature marks on his wrists; he had been bound during the crime, but the ligatures themselves were gone. Investigators located pieces of brown macramé rope near his feet. Since this type of rope sheds easily, detectives also discovered a few macramé fibers on his wrists.

Patty also lay face down on the bed, with puddles of blood surrounding her head. She wore a white terry-cloth robe that was untied in the front. Officers also found rope marks on her wrists and ankles but not the ligatures themselves; tape lifts taken by investigators detected fibers that matched the brown macramé rope found on the bed. Keith's autopsy revealed that he had suffered massive skull fractures and lacerations caused by blunt-force trauma. Patty suffered severe skull fractures and brain contusions. Although investigators did not locate a murder weapon at the scene, the coroner found a small piece of brass in Patty's head wound. Detectives noted that a brass sprinkler head was missing from the front yard and believed that was the murder weapon. The coroner estimated, based upon the condition of the liver, the extent of rigor mortis, and skin slippage, that they had died between the late evening hours of August 19 and the early morning hours of August 20.

Investigators searching the area found a single glove on the golf course a short distance away. At that time, forensic science had not yet advanced to the point where authorities could have collected sufficient contact DNA to develop a full profile of a suspect. However, using fluorescent light, they discovered semen on the back of Patty's thigh, who had been sexually assaulted. The vaginal swabs collected by the pathologist also found semen. The Orange County Crime Lab developed a DNA profile from this sample, connecting the Harringtons' killer to the same perpetrator of two other crimes in the City of Irvine and, ultimately, to the Golden State Killer.

— — —

Born in Germany, Manuela Rohrbeck immigrated to the United States with her parents, Horst and Ruth. They eventually settled in Orange County, where Rohrbeck worked as a loan officer for a local bank in Irvine. Many Germans view language through the prisms of functionality and purpose. They value direct communication and dismiss small talk as useless and a waste of time. Manuela, who spoke with a German accent, embodied this characteristic, and some of her coworkers and customers found she could be abrupt. Her wavy blond hair and piercing blue eyes caught the attention of David Witthuhn, who worked as a salesman at a Mercedes-Benz car dealership, the House of Imports. About the same age as Rohrbeck, Witthuhn, who sported a thick brown mustache on his round, ruddy face, also came from a German family. As a salesman, he could talk easily with anyone. The two quickly became enamored of each other. By 1981, the Witthuhns had been married for five years. They lived in a one-story house in a new development in Irvine. An atrium at the center of the house was flanked by two sliding glass doors, one that led to the kitchen and the other to the bedroom. The front door looked out onto a strip of green grass dotted with giant eucalyptus trees, while the right side of the backyard butted up against Pepperwood Park.

Just two years earlier, Joseph DeAngelo had crept like a demon in the middle of the night along San Jose Creek and among the avocado groves of Goleta. Catherine and Anthony had escaped his clutches, and he'd had to escape on a bicycle while being chased by an FBI agent. He returned two months later, slithering along the creek bed before sneaking into Robert Offerman's condominium, where he shot Offerman and Debra Manning. Having tasted blood and feeling the power of death, he could not resist the pull to Ventura, where he bludgeoned Charlene and Lyman Smith with a piece of firewood after torturing them. DeAngelo then hopscotched down the coast to Dana Point, where he took his time in a house perched above the ocean to brutalize Patty and Keith Harrington. None survived his rampage of rape and murder. Now, six months later, he arrived in the middle-class suburbs of Irvine.

Suffering a viral infection and a fever, David Witthuhn couldn't stop vomiting. On February 1, 1981, Manuela Witthuhn drove her husband to the local hospital, where doctors admitted him for treatment. His condition deteriorated, and he spent several days in the hospital. Manuela did not like sleeping alone, feeling unsafe even in suburbia. Careful to lock all the doors and windows to her home, she also often wrapped herself in a sleeping bag like a protective cocoon in bed. Her father offered her a German shepherd for protection, but she declined.

Four days later, on the evening of February 5, Witthuhn was still in the hospital, and Manuela stopped by her parents' place for dinner before heading to see him. Her parents described their daughter as happy and hopeful that the doctors would soon send her husband home. She left the hospital around 9:00 p.m. and headed home. A call log showed that Witthuhn's last call to his wife occurred at approximately 9:30 p.m. The next morning, Witthuhn called his wife several times, but no one answered the phone. In fact, the answering machine never came on, which he thought was suspicious. When he called the bank where she worked, they told him she had not yet come in.

Growing more concerned, Witthuhn asked his father-in-law, Horst, to check on Manuela. Before the advent of cell phones and location tracking, the only way to find someone was to physically track down the person. Horst asked his wife, Ruth, to drive over to their daughter's home to check on her. Just before noon, Ruth arrived and knocked on the front door, but no one answered. Using her key, she unlocked the front door and went inside to find an eerily quiet house. As Ruth went into the bedroom, she saw Manuela lying face down on the bed with massive amounts of blood around her head. Reeling in total shock, Ruth reached for her daughter's arm, but it felt ice cold to the touch.

Responding officers found Manuela wrapped in the sleeping bag she slept in and wearing a velvet robe that was open in the front. Again, they discovered ligature marks on her wrists and ankles, but the bindings had been removed. Based on the tear marks on the sleeping bag and a lack of blood spatter above the victim's head, they believed the killer had pulled the bag over her head before bashing her skull in with a heavy object. A bedside lamp the size of a cannonball with a square chrome base had been removed from the house. Investigators theorized that the killer had used it as the murder weapon.

The police canvassed the neighborhood, looking for witnesses. Detectives interviewed a woman who had driven by Witthuhn's house on the night of the murder and seen a man sitting at the kitchen table with his back toward the front window. Unfortunately, she could not provide any additional description or information. Crime-scene personnel scoured the house and found a screwdriver lying on the backyard patio. The killer had used it to break the locking mechanism and pry open the rear sliding glass door. Although multiple pieces of jewelry had been stolen, Manuela's wedding ring was not. On a raised cement slab in the backyard, officers found a small television set that the killer had removed from the house and put up against the fence as a stepping stool to jump over the fence. As he left the house, the killer had also taken the cassette tape in the answering machine. Prior to his illness, David had placed an ad in the newspaper to sell his Mercedes, and the killer might have called the house as part of his plan of attack.

Even though Witthuhn lay several miles away in a hospital bed, the police quickly focused their suspicion on him. He possessed a solid alibi, but law enforcement knows that sometimes those closest to the victim have the most to gain by their death. When Witthuhn moved in with a new girlfriend only a few months after his wife's death, the police intensified their attention on him. Even his former in-laws began to suspect him. They moved back to Germany, forever haunted by their beloved daughter's absence, their missed dinners and conversations, and the grandchildren that never came. Although he wasn't home, David was also a victim. He was always looking over his shoulder, fearful that the killer would come for him as well one day. Although he passed a lie-detector test, Witthuhn remained the prime suspect. He returned to work, but people looked at him differently. He could see the judgment in their eyes. He could never escape the dark cloud of doubt that cast a shadow over his life. He used alcohol to dull the pain. Over the years, the stares and whispers and rumors crushed David's soul until he died in 2008, a broken man who never got to learn the name of his wife's murderer.

Manuela's body gave us clues, however, as to his identity. Her autopsy revealed multiple depressed skull fractures and lacerations on the left side of her head, resulting in hemorrhaging and death. The coroner saw a significant bruise to her left buttocks from being hit by a large object. Vaginal swabs and smears confirmed that Manuela had been brutally raped before being killed. However hard he may have tried to wash away the stain of his presence at that crime scene, the killer failed to do so. Patterns were emerging.

— — —

For years, Janelle Cruz struggled to find stability in her life, especially through her tumultuous teenage years growing up the 1980s. She spent time in a psychiatric hospital—the same facility where Patty Harrington had worked. But each time she fell down, Cruz got back up again. After spending nearly a year in an all-girls program in Utah, she returned home feeling a renewed sense of determination to get her life back on track. In March 1986, she enrolled at Orange Coast College—the same school Patty Harrington attended. Resilient and full of grit, the eighteen-year-old stood out in a crowd with an energy that pulled people towards her.

Cruz was particularly close to her little sister and best friend, Michelle. They had remained close through the ups and downs of their young lives. They lived with their mother in a one-story track home at the end of a cul-de-sac, which backed up to a greenbelt. A few steps outside the house, a hedge-flanked pedestrian walkway led to a nearby park. Less than three miles away from Witthuhn's home, this slice of suburbia looked like every other street in Irvine. Standing at the access point to the walkway, a person could blend into the background while watching the front of Cruz's house before moving through the park and out onto the surrounding streets that intersected with the freeway. Just like the crime scenes in Rancho Cordova or the sleepy towns sitting parallel to the interstate freeways in Contra Costa County, a patient and thoughtful predator could slip quickly in and out of Irvine.

Cruz disliked being at home alone, so on May 4, 1986, she invited a male coworker to the house after work. Dylan* met Janelle when she started working at the pizza parlor and they quickly struck up a friendship. As they sat on her bed, Cruz and Dylan heard rustling noises outside of the house. Startled, they looked out the window but saw only darkness. They went back to their conversation, but a few minutes later, they heard a door or a gate close in the garage area. They went to look around, but nothing seemed out of place. Dylan needed to get home as it was almost 11 p.m. Once Dylan left, Cruz went to bed.

Cruz's home was up for sale, and since it was a newer home adjacent to a greenbelt, the house garnered significant interest. A real-estate agent stopped by the house the next day around 5 p.m. to show the house to a potential homebuyer. When she walked into the bedroom, she found Cruz lying naked on the bed. The agent called her boss, who arrived at the house to find the victim bloodied and dead. As they came into the house, Irvine Police Department officers discovered blood by the front entryway and in the kitchen. In the bedroom, they found Cruz's body in a different position than other victims of the Golden State Killer. Her feet were resting at the head of the bed, while her face was pointed toward the foot of the bed. Her killer had likely placed Cruz so he could see himself raping her in the mirror on the closet door. She had been bound and gagged, as evidenced by the ligature marks on her body, but as with other GSK victims, the killer had taken the bindings with him. Crime-scene investigators discovered small blue fibers on the bed and on Cruz's body from pieces of fabric that the killer had ripped and used to bind her. In several of the East Area Rapist cases, including the rape of Jane Carson, the EAR had torn small pieces from a towel to gag and tie his victims.

A blanket covered Cruz's face. When investigators pulled the blanket back, they found her skull caved in and caked with dried and smeared blood. Again, the cowardly killer had covered his victim's face with the blanket. He wanted to minimize the spatter, but he also didn't want to see their fear and pain as he brutally pulverized their faces. In those last few seconds, he couldn't look them in their eyes because he would see the reflection of a monster. After raping and murdering Cruz, he slithered out the sliding glass door, put a chair next to the wall in the backyard, and escaped in the night. In years past, witnesses had described how he leaped easily and adeptly over fences. But time catches up to all of us.

The autopsy revealed that Cruz had died from blunt-force trauma with multiple skull fractures. Investigators believed the murder weapon was a pipe wrench, which the family reported missing after the murder. Vaginal swabs and smears found semen, and the DNA profile developed from the sample connected her murderer to the Harringtons and Manuela Witthuhn—and, ultimately, to Joseph DeAngelo.

The rape and murder of Janelle Cruz on May 5, 1986, marked the last known crime attributed to the Golden State Killer. In the three decades that followed, the investigations became less and less urgent, making way for more recent cases; the cold-case files were gathered and tucked away in banker boxes and metal drawers. Residents living in the shadow of the East Area Rapist passed on stories of a bogeyman who had invaded their dreams and pushed entire communities into a frenzied panic. He gained mythical status as an urban legend, leaving behind dead bodies and broken lives. He gained notoriety with names like the Visalia Ransacker, the EAR, the Original Night Stalker, and finally, the Golden State Killer. But the victims and those who had lost loved ones never forgot, nor did three tenacious generations of officers who pursued him through thousands of dead ends and false leads. Robert Louis Stevenson, author of *The Strange Case of Dr. Jekyll and Mr. Hyde*, wrote, "Everybody, soon or late, sits down at a banquet of consequences." Although it would take thirty-two years after Janelle Cruz's rape and murder, Joseph DeAngelo would finally be forced to sit down at the banquet of his consequences.

— — — — —

May 2018

I arrived early to the airport to board a 9:00 a.m. flight to Los Angeles, where Chief Deputy Steve Grippi, fellow prosecutor Amy Holliday, and I were to meet some of the other GSK prosecutors from Southern California. L.A. was a neutral and central location to convene the various teams: Santa Barbara, Ventura, and Orange Counties. As we began our descent, I looked out the window to contemplate the City of Angels below me, sprawled out in the blistering heat of early summer. Home to ten million souls, L.A. County and the city proper were always a source of fascination in my heart. Larger than life, full of glitz and grime, it's a place where dreams come true or get extinguished. It's also the site of some of America's most notorious criminal cases—Sirhan Sirhan, the Manson Family, the Menendez Brothers, the LAPD officers who assaulted Rodney King, O. J. Simpson, and the Grim Sleeper Killer were tried here.

My mind inventoried the myriad sex crimes and homicide cases I had tried over the years. The accumulation of those experiences had brought me to this point. After countless hours reading and prepping cases, I could close my eyes and see the police report for each witness and piece of evidence, facts and pages and line numbers etched into my memory. But prosecuting a case involves more than regurgitating facts. We need to listen, absorb, and retell the story of those who were wronged, some of whom may not be able to tell it themselves. It's the space in between the walls that make up a room, and if you truly listen, the space will speak the truth. You cannot tell the story unless you understand what is left unsaid above and beyond the facts. When I dedicate nearly every waking hour and even my dreams to a case, the story begins to weave itself into the strands of my own DNA. But the Golden State Killer represented a challenge unlike any other case I'd ever handled.

Sitting on the plane, I felt an overwhelming sense of panic wash over me at the sheer magnitude of the case, an anxiety that would return time and time again. There was so much to take in: thirteen known murders, upwards of fifty sexual assaults, and over one hundred twenty burglaries in eleven different jurisdictions spanning the breadth and length of the state. Millions of pages of police reports. Tens of thousands of witnesses, victims, and law-enforcement officers. Four decades. Not to mention the innumerable books, documentaries, newspapers, and blogs obsessed with every case and fact. Where should I begin? Whom should I talk to? What should I read or listen to? I leaned back and closed my eyes, repeating the words that had calmed me down over the years when I felt control slipping through my fingers and my throat tighten. *Take a deep breath, Thien*, I told myself, inhaling deeply and exhaling slowly. *Take care of the things you can control, and the things you cannot control will take care of themselves*. I slowly repeated my mantra. I could feel my heart rate drop. As I opened my eyes and my vision came into focus, I reminded myself of an old saying that would guide my approach: How do you eat an elephant? One bite at a time. I would devour the Golden State Killer case, one bite at a time. One step at a time, I would move the case closer to justice for all the victims. But first, Los Angeles lay before us.

After Judge Sweet arraigned DeAngelo in court, the main prosecuting counties feverishly assembled their prosecution teams. After landing at LAX, we headed to the Los Angeles County District Attorney's Office's Airport Branch location, where the Los Angeles DA graciously provided us a place to assemble and discuss the next steps. No elected officials would attend this meeting, only executive leadership and grunts like myself, who would ultimately be tasked with doing the dirty work of litigation.

The receptionist led us to a windowless conference room with a large square table, fluorescent light, and air conditioning on blast. As we took our seats and made small talk with the other prosecutors, I could sense the nervous tension undulating like a wave around the room. My office had discussed internally the possibility of trying the case in Ventura County. After all, they had provided the crucial DNA sample, and our offices worked well together. But with limited resources and a small courthouse, Ventura colleagues privately expressed to us their deep reservation about hosting the trial. For similar reasons, Santa Barbara District Attorney Joyce Dudley didn't want the Golden State Killer case tried in her county either. Moreover, she opposed the death penalty, an option the other DAs wanted to preserve as a possibility. Orange County, the third largest office in the state, possessed the resources and facilities to host the trial. But could its team, which carried a reputation for "not playing well in the sandbox," work collaboratively with the other counties? According to Paul Holes, OC officials had obstructed his efforts to obtain extra DNA from the Janelle Cruz case. Despite these concerns, my office was ready to transfer Joseph DeAngelo to Orange County and try the case there. I embraced the idea of returning to the OC, living in a small beach house on the Balboa Peninsula and surfing at the Wedge before heading to prosecute the Golden State Killer.

We went around the table with introductions. People asked how DeAngelo was adjusting to life in custody at the Sacramento County Jail. I responded that he was being held in one of the few cells with a camera affixed inside it. Deputies monitored him twenty-four hours a day to make sure he did not harm himself. He loved candy and junk food, constantly eating them in his cell. As we talked about the next steps in prosecuting DeAngelo, the chief prosecutor from Orange County Homicide, Ebrahim Baytieh, quickly jumped in to speak. Not very tall or physically imposing, he nevertheless caught your attention when he spoke. His gesticulating hands cut through the air with a magnetic energy, his words spilled out in spurts, and he would occasionally enunciate certain syllables for emphasis. "We have a lot of experience trying *big* cases in Orange County," Baytieh started, "and as the head of the Homicide Team in OC, *I have* tried a lot of them." I heard Grippi, sitting to my immediate right, let out a long sigh and adjust himself in his chair.

"We spearheaded the use of Rapid DNA testing and started our own local DNA database," he continued. "Our DNA prosecutors are *the best* and can lead the forensic part of any trial." Grippi mumbled to himself about how we'd had to request Ventura's DNA sample to solve this case. The conversation took a turn for the worse as Baytieh began to draw comparisons in his off-putting pitch. "Some of the smaller DA offices don't have the resources that *we* do," he said as Santa Barbara Chief Deputy DA Kelly Duncan, sitting to my left, shifted in her seat. She knew their resources could not match up, but that didn't need to be thrown in her face in front of everyone. One of the other prosecutors tried to pay him a compliment and pivot the conversation, but Baytieh spoke over him and pushed his agenda further. "Yes, *I* did win the Prosecutor of the Year award, and *I* would be honored to lead the prosecution of this case. We have the most homicide victims in this case, more than any other county. We have a lot of great attorneys in my office who could help *you* try your case."

An awkward silence filled the room. I could see the embarrassment flash across the other Orange County prosecutors' faces at their boss's cringeworthy closing argument. We prosecutors spend our lives in the courtroom, measuring the years not in birthdays, but in the trials that dominate our lives. We are a proud group. Instead of being gracious, Baytieh's braggadocio alienated the other prosecutors in the room. In his mind, he was simply extolling the virtues of his office, but the "Orange County is bigger and better than you" message reaffirmed the perception that Orange County lived in a bubble and would not collaborate well with the other prosecution teams. Baytieh snatched defeat from the jaws of victory.

Ventura County Chief Assistant DA Chuck Hughes was the first to break the uncomfortable silence. Sporting thick glasses and a spiky goatee, he spent many years as a prosecutor in neighboring Riverside County before joining the Ventura office and quickly moved up the ranks. Cutting straight to the point, he asked, "Let's say we try it in Orange County. Tony Rackauckas is the midst of a tough reelection fight against his challenger, Todd Spitzer. What if your DA loses that campaign? What's going to happen to our case? Don't we need stability in leadership in whatever county we try the most prolific serial killer of our lifetime?"

"Tony is not going to lose his race," Baytieh uttered sheepishly.

Chuck added quickly, "But you can't guarantee that, can you?"

"No, I cannot."

As we left the building to catch our flight home, Steve Grippi went full Grip. "Ebrahim Baytieh believes that only OC can try a fucking case? Who the fuck do they think they are to shit on everyone else!" The veins around his temple began to pop as he defended our honor. "In any given year, we try more cases than they do. They didn't solve this case, and they want to just take over the whole thing." An accomplished prosecutor in his own right, Grippi rightfully demanded and expected respect. As we weaved through L.A. traffic, I brought up the fact that we didn't have DNA in any of our cases and thus had the most challenging cases to prove. "If we try this case in the OC, Baytieh will sever our cases out of the trial or at the very least treat our victims as second-class citizens."

— — —

A week after our return from Los Angeles, Homicide Detective Sergent Kenny Clark stopped by my office. “Have you seen this?” he asked, handing me a piece of paper. My eyes widened and my blood began to boil as I read it. An Orange County Superior Court judge had signed an order directing the Sacramento County Sheriff to hand DeAngelo over to the Orange County Sheriff’s Office for transport to Southern California, where he would be tried for the murder of the Harringtons, Manuela Witthuhn, and Janelle Cruz.

“They’re trying to take him and it ain’t gonna fucking happen! Where did you get this?” I yelled out loud to Kenny, who shook his head. “The Orange County Sheriff’s Department sent this to our jail, who gave it to me, and I immediately came over because the sheriff is asking how he should respond.”

I had spent my entire career in the courtroom, assiduously avoiding the political machinations of those sitting in the executive suites. Figuring out how to admit a crucial piece of evidence was more enjoyable for me than navigating political waters, shaking hands, and chewing on dry chicken breast at stuffy functions. When it came to stratagems of power, I felt like a club-level chess player going against grandmasters. But now, I could no longer bury my head in my files as the Orange County DA’s Office made its Machiavellian moves. The court order reinforced our worst fears about Orange County. Unable to convince us of their superiority, they wanted to take DeAngelo by force.

Sergeant Clark and I walked into Rod’s office and handed him the court order. Reading the document, Rod chuckled and leaned back in the red leather chair, rocking back and forth and rubbing his goatee. He thought back to the day four years earlier when the Body Snatchers had walked into the hospital room in Auburn and grabbed Luis Bracamontes. On October 24, 2014, Bracamontes, with his wife by his side, had cut a bloody path of death and terror through the Sacramento region. In a Motel 6 parking lot, he shot at Sacramento County Sheriff’s Deputies Danny Oliver and Scott Brown, killing Oliver. He then carjacked a vehicle, shooting a civilian in the face. As the entire Capital Region went on high alert, he stole a red pickup truck from a landscaper and headed eastbound on Interstate 80 into a rural area of neighboring Placer County. When county deputies followed civilian tips to a quiet street in South Auburn, Bracamontes shot at them and stole a patrol car. In the ensuing chase, Detective Michael Davis was shot and killed by Bracamontes, who then grabbed a shotgun from the patrol car and retreated into a nearby house. After a standoff that culminated in the SWAT team firing tear gas rounds into the house, he gave himself up.

Placer County Deputies transported Bracamontes to a small local hospital to treat a hand wound. Thinking ahead, Rod knew we would seek the death penalty against Bracamontes, and his mind started running through the possible issues. A case with this degree of notoriety and media coverage would certainly force a judge to weigh whether the defendant could obtain a fair trial in a jurisdiction. One of the main factors involves the size and demographics of the jurisdiction, and Placer had a far smaller and less diverse population than Sacramento. A judge was liable to change the venue since a smaller jury pool would be more vulnerable to the influence of media coverage.

In law school, we learned that "possession is nine-tenths of the law," meaning that a person in physical possession of a disputed object has a strong legal argument that they should keep it, even if they are not the rightful owner. Turning to Sergeant Steve Girdlestone, Rod asked where Bracamontes was.

"He's sitting in a little hospital up in Placer County getting treatment on his hand," Girdlestone responded.

"We need to try this case in Sacramento, and he should be sitting in our jail," Norgaard said in his gravelly voice. Sergeant Girdlestone replied, "Copy."

The same group of detectives that would grab Joseph DeAngelo off the streets of Citrus Heights four years later headed off to Placer County. Six members of the Body Snatchers entered the hospital and "checked" Bracamontes out of his room. The lone Placer County deputy guarding the prisoner could only sit there as they wheeled the cop killer out of the building and took him to the Sacramento County Jail. Placer County District Attorney Scott Owens, enraged that we had taken Bracamontes, met with then Sacramento District Attorney Jan Scully. In her twentieth year in office, Scully carried a certain gravitas as one of the longest tenured elected prosecutors in the entire state. And as the elected DA of California's capital, she moved in the orbit of state power. Wanting to talk at a neutral location, Owens set up a meeting at a Claim Jumper restaurant in downtown Sacramento. Rod joined Scully, and they listened to Owens rant about how we had "kidnapped" the cop killer from his county. With a steady gaze, Scully calmly told Owens, "Bracamontes is in our possession, in our jail, and you are not getting him. Rod is going to try Bracamontes in Sacramento, and you are more than welcome to have your prosecutor partner with Rod and try the Placer County charges in Sacramento." Four years later, in a Sacramento courtroom, Rod Norgaard and Placer County prosecutor Dave Tellman would convict Luis Bracamontes of two counts of first-degree murder in the deaths of Deputy Danny Oliver and Detective Michael Davis. A Sacramento jury issued a verdict of death.

— — —

A Superior Court judge in Sacramento possesses the same and equal authority as a Superior Court judge in Orange County. Sitting at the same judicial level, they cannot override each other; that authority belongs to the appellate court or the State Supreme Court. After staring at the ceiling, Rod looked at Sergeant Kenny Clark and me and said, "Type up a court order for one of our judges to sign directing the Sacramento County Sheriff to hold DeAngelo in our jail, pending trial here. The sheriff is expressly ordered not to release the defendant to anyone without prior written authorization from our judge." This directive would give the Sacramento Sheriff cover to ignore the Orange County judge's instruction.

After typing up the order, we needed the right judge to sign it—someone who would understand the dynamics driving it. The Honorable Steve White had signed the arrest warrant for DeAngelo. In his early sixties, with a square jaw and steady blue eyes, Judge White still possessed the energy of an attorney half his age. I had tried several sex-crime and homicide trials before him and knew his piercing questions demanded the utmost level of preparation and advocacy in his courtroom. White's portrait hung on the wall back at the office as he had been the thirtieth

Sacramento County DA. Appointed to the position, he lost his reelection bid to Jan Scully, who as a supervisor in the office challenged her boss for the position. Steve White understood politics. He was the perfect judge to sign the order.

I handed the document to Sergeant Kenny Clark. "Kenny, let's have Judge White sign this."

"Copy, heading over there now."

Walking into the packed courtroom, Kenny quickly caught Judge White's eye. Moving his way through the crowd of defendants, he went up to the side of the bench and whispered, "It's about the GSK case." With barely a glance or pause, Judge White pivoted out of his chair and glided down from the bench. With his characteristic swagger, he walked into his chambers with Kenny. His office resembled a museum—his chair crafted of Indonesian teak wood, portraits of presidents and Supreme Court justices on the walls, a large magnifying glass with an ivory tusk handle, a collection of glass weights spread across his ornate desk.

"What's going on?" Judge White asked. Without taking a seat or saying a word, Sergeant Clark handed over the order. As his eyes scanned the page, the corners of the judge's mouth turned slightly upward, and he began to nod his head. Without hesitation, he signed it with an emphatic tap of the pen to dot the "i" in his signature. "So, what triggered this?" the judge inquired with amused curiosity. Kenny handed him the order from the Orange County judge. He read it, looked up at Kenny, and smiled. "The case will be tried in Sacramento." In that moment, Judge White could not foresee the important role that his signed order would ultimately play in making sure the voices of all the victims would be heard.

6
The California Penal Code

May 1977

In the early days of the series of attacks attributed to the East Area Rapist, he sexually assaulted the women, including Phyllis, Jane, Trish, and Kris, while they were home alone. Once the spokesperson for the Sheriff's Department pointed out this common theme at a community town-hall meeting, the predator, taking this as a challenge, began targeting couples—a pattern he would repeat over and over in various locations up and down the state. This unique aspect not only allowed us to connect the Sacramento incidents to those in other jurisdictions, but it also gave us a way to charge him with more crimes beyond the murders.

By early 1977, Sacramentans froze in panic and fear as the EAR seemed to strike with utter impunity. Women gathered downtown in front of the courthouse to give speeches through bullhorns demanding safety and accountability and to march in the streets holding signs. In town-hall meetings organized by community associations, the public demanded the police catch the EAR. Groups of men banded together to patrol their neighborhoods at night. Each time another victim was reported, the media covered the assault for days.

Recently married, Linda and David O'Dell moved to California in early 1977 to start a new life and enjoy the California sun. Having grown up in Ohio, Linda embodied the sensibilities and traditions of a large Midwest Catholic family. Twenty-two years old, with blond hair parted down the middle and bright blue eyes that stared right through you, she worked as a server at a local restaurant, serving lunch a couple of days a week. Eight years older than his wife, David worked at a Mexican restaurant close to home. They moved into a small single-story house in a residential neighborhood in Citrus Heights. The house, which sat at the end of a cul-de-sac, had a wide concrete driveway and a small porch with a decorative arch. White exterior siding gave their home a rustic ranch-style look. Linda kept a clean and orderly house, and its shaggy brown carpet, plaid-colored couches, and simple décor made it feel warm and welcoming. The couple had just gotten a tiny German shepherd puppy that constantly snuggled against Linda. The triangle-shaped backyard pushed up against a large apartment complex with a parking lot that led directly out to one of the main thoroughfares in town.

On May 13, 1977, after a long day at work, the O'Dells were enjoying a quiet night together at home. After watching television, they went to bed. As they settled in, Linda heard the sound of something scratching against metal. Believing that the noise came from her cat, she gave it no further thought. At 2:00 a.m., they felt someone kicking their bed and opened their eyes to a blinding beam of light shined right in their faces. A masked man stood at the foot of their bed, pointing a flashlight at them. "Don't look up, or I'll blow your heads off," the intruder threatened them. "You make a sound, and I'll kill you. I have a .45, and I'll kill you if you move. I'm going to take your money, and I want some food. Then I'll leave in my van."

Holding a gun to David's head, he threw over some shoelaces he'd brought with him and ordered Linda to bind David's hands behind his back. After she did so, the masked man told her to retie the knot. He then tied Linda's hands and both their ankles with granny knots, all the while repeating, "Shut up." Panic paralyzed the couple as they lay helplessly in bed, shrouded in darkness.

"Where's the money?" the intruder demanded. He found a jar of pennies, broke the top of it with his gun, and poured the coins onto the ground, then picked out some Canadian coins and quarters and put them in a mug. After rummaging through the house, he came back into the bedroom and asked where Linda's purse was. When she told him to look on the couch, he left only to return empty-handed and pretending to be frustrated, a ruse to separate Linda from her husband. First, he stacked dishes on David's back and leaned forward to growl menacingly, "If I hear this move, I'll slit her throat and cut off her ear and bring it back to you!"

The EAR untied Linda's ankles and took her to the family room. Walking down the dark hall, Linda realized she was about to be raped. She could barely breathe as he pressed the tip of the knife against her throat. The fear washed over her like a wave of jagged glass cutting and ripping her skin. Once in the family room, he laid Linda on her stomach and told her to cross her legs. After he retied her wrists and ankles, he went off to rummage through the kitchen, taking time to drink their beer and eat their food. Returning to Linda, he warned her, "You'd better cooperate with me, or I'll kill you."

He ripped a towel and draped it over the television, securing it in place with a candle before turning the TV on. He muted the sound, but the light from the TV screen cast a glow over the family room, creating an ambience for his sexual sadism. Forty-one years later, when they arrested DeAngelo, investigators found a towel draped over his computer monitor; while in custody, he hung a towel over the fluorescent light in his jail cell. Some people never change.

As Linda lay face down in her family room, bound and helpless, the EAR stacked dishes on her back. He repeated to her, "I'll kill you if you make any noises." He took great pleasure each time Linda flinched in fear. Each grimace, each whimper, each tremble seemed to ratchet up his excitement. The intruder returned to the bedroom to torture David further, reveling in the power he held over another person's life. Pressing the gun to David's head and running the knife blade against his neck, he threatened to kill him if he made any sound whatsoever.

The masked man moved back and forth several times between husband and wife, taking his time with each of them. Returning to Linda, he blindfolded her with a torn piece of towel. When she heard a zipper being unfastened, Linda begged for mercy, but he gave her none. "Be quiet, or I'll kill you. I'll slit your throat." After sexually assaulting Linda, he told her, "You are so beautiful. I am going to take you in the van with me. How would you like to be down by the river?" The rapist rolled Linda back onto her stomach and retied her ligatures and stacked the dishes again on her back.

He returned to the bedroom to dump the coins into a bag and to threaten David. The theft of the coins and the references to a "van down by the river" were part of the EAR's elaborate effort to hide his true identity and lead investigators astray. The masked monster utilized variations of this strategy in many of his crimes. To compensate for the impotent sense of smallness and weakness he felt about himself, the EAR craved power over his victims. It wasn't enough for him to invade the sanctity of their homes, eat their food and drink their beer. Tying their limbs like cattle ready to be culled and using sexual violence to violate their bodies wasn't enough for him—not for the deep hole he needed to fill.

In nearly all the East Area Rapist's crimes involving couples, he took their wedding bands, including the O'Dells' rings. A wedding band represents the bond between a husband and wife, its circular shape symbolizing an eternal and unbroken commitment. Only a few of the couples attacked by the EAR managed to stay together. David and Linda would later divorce, unable to heal the trauma and guilt they felt over the attack.

— — —

In her early thirties, Mia* enjoyed being a doting mom to her two young daughters. She raised the girls in a small but comfortable home with her husband, George,* in the Contra Costa County suburb of Danville. The single-story home with big windows faced a quiet street and sat against a backdrop of rolling hills and oak trees. Neatly trimmed green grass and round rocks framed the front yard, where a small white Buddha statue watched over the house. By early summer, the grass on the hills began to turn a golden brown. The inside of the house featured a shaggy red carpet, white tiles, and flowery wallpaper. Clothes, toys, and furniture were scattered throughout the home.

After a slow weekend with the girls, the couple settled in on Sunday night. At around 4:00 a.m. on June 11, 1979, Mia woke up to a masked man dressed in black hovering at the foot of her bed. He shined a flashlight in her face and ordered her to wake up her husband. After the suspect forced George onto his stomach, he threw pretied shoelaces to Mia and ordered her to bind her husband's wrists behind his back. The suspect walked over to George and growled into his ear, "You motherfucker, you motherfucker, I'll blow your head off." While Mia tied her husband's hands, the suspect shoved a large caliber revolver into the base of George's skull and cocked the hammer. Thinking he was going to die, George thought of his family. Once she finished tying George's hands, Mia was ordered to flip onto her stomach, and the EAR fastened her wrists and ankles.

As with the other rapes by the EAR in Sacramento, the intruder kept saying, "I just want your money. Where's your money?" After searching the house, he came back with a hand towel, which he used to blindfold Mia. After removing the bindings from her ankles, the suspect forced her to the family room and made her lie on her stomach. After retying Mia, he returned to the bedroom and gagged George with a torn strip of towel, threw a blanket over his head, and placed several bottles of cologne taken from the dresser onto his back. Before leaving the bedroom, he warned George that he would kill everyone in the house if he heard any glass fall to the ground. Throughout the night, the assailant returned repeatedly to the husband, making threats while cocking the hammer on his gun. On the last occasion, he taunted George. "You don't like it, do you? There's nothing you can do about it."

The EAR sexually assaulted Mia in the family room as her husband lay immobilized in their bed. Mia prayed that her daughters would be left unharmed and sleep through this nightmare. After the last assault, the intruder caressed Mia from her neck area down to her thighs and took her wedding band. He told her he needed to take some things out to his van and warned her, "Don't move, or I'll blow your head off. I'll be back." But he never returned.

Just before dawn, a neighbor saw a man ride away from the area near Mia and George's home on a ten-speed bicycle. The Sheriff's Department recovered the stolen bike and brought it back to the owner, who lived about a mile away from the victims. Next to where the bicycle had been parked the night before it was stolen, deputies found a set of pretied shoelaces identical to the ones used to tie the couple up. In 2001, the DNA profile from the semen discovered in Mia's vaginal swab matched the profile generated from semen found at the March 1980 double homicide of Charlene and Lyman Smith in Ventura—and the DNA profile of Joseph DeAngelo.

— — — — —

June 2018

I loved the first season of the television show *True Detective*, starring Matthew McConaughey and Woody Harrelson as detectives who pursue a sadistic serial killer. The opening scene of the first episode reveals the pale white body of a young woman found dead in a burning field of crops in a Louisiana bayou. Her killer has mounted a crown of deer antlers on her head and painted ritualistic symbols on her back. I found the series most fascinating when it delved into the souls of monsters and of the men who chase them. It stripped away the veneer to reveal the frailty of human beings. We see McConaughey's character, now retired, being interviewed by two new detectives assigned to reopen the case that he solved many years earlier. Gaunt and hollowed out like a skeleton draped with oily skin and long stringy hair, he speaks in the interrogation room in slurring diatribes while drinking beer and smoking cigarettes. Meanwhile, his seemingly straightlaced partner, also long since retired, sits alone in front of a television eating leftovers reheated in the microwave. These detectives took in all the sins of the world, and the years were not kind to them.

My wife, Jenny, loves to watch true-crime shows such as *Law & Order* and *NCIS*. The glossy gore, the splashy blood, the detectives chasing their main suspects before a last-minute twist reveals the true killer—such formulaic plotlines always keep her glued to the screen. She also enjoys the courtroom scenes, where the prosecutor catches the defendant lying on the witness stand during cross-examination. Truth be told, I find it difficult to watch these types of programs because I inevitably end up yelling at the TV, "A defendant would never be able to give a long speech in the middle of the DA's questioning! You can't do that during cross-examination!" Having endured enough nonsense, I get up from the couch and storm out of the room, but not before Jenny throws a pillow at me for interrupting her show. I already live in the world of true crime; I don't need to see Hollywood's version of it.

Onscreen, we see lawyers flipping through old law books and poring over dusty files, hoping to find a loophole in the statutes or an overlooked piece of evidence to break a case. Rarely does real life mirror fiction, but sometimes it does—and sometimes we need it to.

"What the fuck, Rod!" I yelled, not at my supervisor but at the predicament we were in. Being tactical and constantly playing chess in the courtroom, I am my father's son. Fueled by passion and running hot because I care deeply about justice, I am my mother's son. "Why the fuck did we throw away all the DNA evidence? Are you telling me that we don't have any semen or blood left from any of the rapes in Sacramento?"

"No. In the early eighties, it was all tossed after the statute of limitations ran out and we couldn't charge those crimes anymore," Rod responded quietly, rocking back and forth in his red chair with his eyes closed.

I lowered my head and started rubbing my temple, my mind racing. "Wait, wait . . . we still have the pretied shoelaces found next to Brian Maggiore, right? With the advancements in DNA technology, we can do more testing?"

Rod opened his eyes. "I'm not sure. I think we may have lost it after we sent it to Orange County for more testing back in the early 2000s." The pretied shoelaces found next to Maggiore's body, in a neighborhood where the EAR frequently prowled and attacked, was a key piece of circumstantial evidence tying him to the Maggiore murders. And now, we couldn't find the shoelaces. Overwhelmed with disbelief and anger, I couldn't stop cursing like a sailor.

Rod tried to place their actions into context. "In their defense, law enforcement back then couldn't have foreseen the advancements that brought us genetic genealogy."

"Contra Costa didn't throw away their DNA!" I responded, my blood still boiling.

I returned to my office and closed the door. I began pacing back and forth, frustrated by the constraints caused by the lost and discarded evidence. An old Zen koan came to mind: A master asked his student if the stick he held in his hand was real. No matter how he answered, the young pupil kept getting hit with the stick. With no good options, he grabbed the stick and broke it. The lesson to be learned is, if you find yourself in an untenable and unsustainable situation, you break the situation. Like the student, I needed to break free and find a solution outside of that paradigm.

We desperately needed to connect the probable EAR rapes in Sacramento to the cases in Contra Costa County where DNA confirmed DeAngelo's identity. In both places, he had the same modus operandi: He confronted the victims as they slept; he made the woman bind her partner up with shoelaces that he pretied and brought to the crime scene; he tied up the woman before ransacking their home, eating their food, and drinking their beer; he separated the woman from the man and brought her to another part of the house; he stacked objects on the man's back, threatening to kill him should any items fall to the ground; he returned to the woman and sexually assaulted her before leaving. The extensive similarities among these cases meant we could reasonably link our cases to ones that left no question as to the EAR's identity. But even if we could match up those crimes, we had another hurdle to overcome.

The criminal-justice system viewed rape through a different lens in the 1970s. Sexual assaults often went unreported, and even when they were filed, many in our society deflected the blame onto the victims, who had few rights and protections. And while the law categorized it as a felony, the statute of limitations for rape was only three years. This meant that from the time the crime was reported, the District Attorney's Office had to file charges within three years, or it would be barred from doing so.

On the other hand, there was no time limit to charge a defendant with certain serious crimes. A "life crime" granted prosecutors an unlimited length of time to file charges, as was the case with "special circumstance" murder charges, which made the defendant eligible for the death penalty or life in prison. In such instances, charges could be brought against a suspect even after decades had passed. Thus, we could still charge DeAngelo with the murder of Brian and Katie Maggiore. The fact that he committed more than one murder constituted the "special circumstance." However, the assault victims who had waited four decades to learn the identity of their rapist were now unable to obtain the justice they had sought. I needed to find a loophole to charge those cases.

When trying to solve a problem, we lawyers are taught to start with the law. Much of our jurisprudence, or system of law, is predicated on writings contained in dusty books written long ago. I pored through the laws concerning rape and sexual assault, looking for a crime that carried a life sentence. By 2018, actual law books had become a relic of the past; we did our research online, scanning through digitized volumes containing cases spanning the entire history of the American legal system.

Since these crimes were committed in the 1970s, the actual laws of that time governed the case. But there was a problem: The old statutes covering murder and rape from the 1970s were missing from the online database we used. We had physical copies of the penal codes stretching back decades in our office, but the earliest book dated only to 1981. I headed to the Sacramento County Law Library, hoping to find the penal codes from that era.

Although rape was not a "life crime" in the 1970s, I suspected that kidnapping might be. As I walked out of my office to head over to the library, my phone rang. Contra Costa Deputy DA Paul Graves was on the line. I had met Graves many years ago when I was hired as a snot-nosed kid straight out of law school, becoming a rookie prosecutor in "CoCo" County. The year was 1998. Sporting tiny round glasses and thick black hair held in place with tons of hairspray, I was a baby-faced assassin in the courtroom. A rising star in the office, Graves worked in the main office, located in downtown Martinez. The oil refineries a few miles away spewed out white smoke, and loud sirens occasionally blared in town when a fire broke out at the factory, causing everyone to close their office windows. As a senior attorney in the office, Graves tried felony cases in the downtown courthouse. As a rookie prosecutor, I was relegated to handling low-level misdemeanors in the outlying courts.

My supervisors instructed me to drive out to the Delta Courthouse in Pittsburg, located in the eastern part of the county. The Delta branch of the Contra Costa DA's Office consisted of one twelve-by-twelve-foot room inside the courthouse. As I walked in, a few Pittsburg cops spilled out into the hallway. I could see and smell smoke billowing out of the tiny office. You couldn't smoke in the building, but whoever was in that room obviously didn't care about the rules. The room was awash in fluorescent light, and a single cobalt gray desk with rusty brown trim sat by a tiny window whose bent aluminum blinds didn't open. On the desk was a beige rotary phone, a penal code book from 1985, and a stack of files. Sitting at the desk was Prosecutor Bob Law, an old-school, straight-shooting attorney with a full head of white hair, a brown short-sleeve dress shirt, and a wide, short striped tie. From his lips dangled a cigarillo that had been smoked all the way to the end, the ashes still hanging on for dear life. As I approached the desk, Bob looked me up and down, then blurted out, "Ho?"

"Yes sir, that's me," I responded quickly.

He threw me a file and said, "The jury's waiting down the hall for you. Good luck. You're gonna need it." A slight smile accompanied those brief words of encouragement. Despite appearances, I could feel that he cared about the young lawyers under his direction. I started walking down the hall, feeling a mix of excitement and anxiety coursing through my veins. It was only my second jury trial, and the first time I had ever seen this file. This is known among attorneys as a "handoff"—I didn't know what the charges were, nor had I read a single line of the report or spoken to any of the witnesses. I slowed my pace dramatically to give myself more time to read its contents. It was a "242," an assault-and-battery charge, section 242 of the Penal Code. Two soccer moms had gotten into an argument, and one pulled chunks of the victim's hair out and hit her in the face.

The courtroom was presided over by the Honorable Samuel Mesnick, who was as old as dirt and as pleasant as whiskey poured on an open wound. I walked past the rows of prospective jurors sitting in the audience.

The judge looked me up and down just like Bob had done a few minutes earlier. "Ho?"

"Yes, your Honor?"

"You ready to pick a jury?" he barked down at me, sitting high up above everyone.

"Yes, sir, I'm ready." I tried to sound confident, but on the inside I was trembling in fear.

That same day, I picked a jury, gave an opening statement, called my victim to the witness stand along with the police officer who found the clumps of her hair on the ground, cross-examined the defendant, and gave a closing argument. After an hour, the jury returned a verdict of guilty.

Contra Costa County felt like the Wild West of prosecution, where we flew by the seat of our pants and forged our litigation skills in the crucible of the courtroom. We worked hard and played hard, arriving early in the morning and staying till late, and finishing our night with cocktails and beer at Crogan's in nearby Walnut Creek. A few miles away from my office, in Martinez, a veteran criminalist named Paul Holes obsessed over a serial rapist. I left Contra Costa in 2000; our paths would not cross until much, much later.

When Paul Graves called, we briefly reminisced about the old days in CoCo County. He had stayed in the office and was currently supervising the Sexual Assault Unit. He then turned to the business at hand. "I heard you're prosecuting the East Area Rapist. Congrats, that's as big as it gets. The statute of limitations ran out on all the rape cases, including the ones in CoCo and Sacramento. Have you thought about other possible charges with a life sentence?"

"I'm looking at kidnapping charges but need to get a hold of some old penal code books to confirm my theory," I answered.

"Check out kidnapping for robbery, or aggravated kidnapping," Graves offered. I was glad to hear that another experienced prosecutor was thinking along the same lines as I was. But I needed to find those old law books.

I headed over to the Sacramento County Law Library in order to track down the penal code books from 1976 to 1979, the time frames the EAR committed his sexual assaults in Northern California. I rushed up and down the aisles with anticipation. 2018, 2000, 1999, 1998, 1986, 1981, 1980 . . . 1975. Where were the books from 1976 to 1979? I began to panic, and my heart pounded louder and louder. Did someone purposely take the books for these years? I saw the books for 1970 through 1975. What were the odds that only the books for the years I was looking for would be missing? Did DeAngelo take them somehow? Crazy thoughts ran through my mind as I scanned up and down the rows. Beads of sweat rolled down my forehead, my chest tightened, and my breath became shallow. First the discarded DNA and the missing shoelaces, and now this. I double-checked the same aisle of books no fewer than three times, to no avail. But then, behind me and to the left, I saw the four missing penal code books wedged in between random books about California criminal procedure. I brought my hand to my chest and started to breathe normally again. To this day, I cannot explain how the penal codes for those exact years ended up stuck between unrelated books. Feeling utter relief, I grabbed the first book.

The yellowed pages of the 1976 California Penal Code were stuck together and made a crumpling noise as I pulled them apart. The crime of kidnapping for robbery, or aggravated kidnapping, was set forth in Penal Code Section 209. However, I went straight to Section 799, which covered the statute of limitations for life crimes. In a quiet whisper, I read aloud:

> "There is no limitation of time within which a prosecution for murder, the embezzlement of public moneys and a violation of Section 209 . . . must be commenced. . . . Prosecution for . . . a violation for section 209 may be commenced at any time after the discovery of the crime."

"Yes!" I yelled loud enough for everyone in the library to hear and pumped my fist in the air. The librarian sitting at her desk gave me a dirty look. I then went through each of the penal code books for 1977, 1978, and 1979 to confirm the same language in Section 799. We had a loophole to solve the statute of limitations issues; now we needed to pore through the dusty old reports looking for the right facts to support the charge of aggravated kidnapping.

Our system of jurisprudence is predicated on *stare decisis*, meaning "to stand by things decided" in Latin. Lawyers and judges are bound to follow the legal decisions made in the past by the appellate courts and the Supreme Court. We are chained to history. A key element of aggravated kidnapping is asportation, or the forced movement of the victim. The prosecution must satisfy a two-pronged test to have a crime qualify as aggravated kidnapping for robbery: First, the movement of the victim must be more than incidental, in the sense that it is unrelated and unnecessary, to accomplish the robbery; and second, the movement has to increase substantially the risk of harm to the victim. The courts have repeatedly emphasized that the analysis must be done on a case-by-case basis.

In 2011, the California Supreme Court decided *People vs. Vines*. During a robbery of a McDonald's restaurant in South Sacramento, the defendant ordered the manager at gunpoint to move past the front counter back through the kitchen until they reached the safe. From there, the defendant walked the manger into the back of the restaurant, encountered three other employees, and ordered the whole group downstairs into a locked freezer where the temperature was 20°F. In upholding the defendant's conviction for aggravated kidnapping, the court decided that, although the movement was confined to the interior of the restaurant, the scope and nature of this movement were more than incidental to the robbery. Additionally, the movement substantially increased the risk of harm to the victims due to the low temperature inside the freezer, the decreased likelihood of their being detected, and the inherent danger of any attempt to escape the locked compartment.

In DeAngelo's case, we needed to focus on the crimes in Sacramento and Contra Costa where he moved the victims and substantially increased the risk of their being harmed. For example, when he punched Trish in the mouth and dragged her limp body from the driveway along the side of the house and through a gate, she could no longer be seen or heard from the street and thus put in greater peril.

For Linda, Mia, and the other victims who were moved, I analyzed every aspect of their cases. To meet the first criterion, the movement of the victim had to be "more than merely incidental" to the robbery. At first glance, this may seem contradictory. At the time a victim is moved, the defendant must possess the intent to commit robbery; but the movement must be more than what is simply necessary to facilitate it. Examining the reasoning behind this rule places the contradiction into its proper context. Without this rule, all kidnap robberies where the victim is moved even slightly would qualify as aggravated kidnapping, which carries a life sentence.

In every case where the defendant took property from the victim, from the moment he entered the residence to the second he left, DeAngelo possessed at least two criminal intents—to rape and to rob. The whole time he was in their homes, he maintained the intent to take the victims' property, looking for trophies, taking their photographs or their jewelry, particularly items of great emotional value, such as a wedding band or a class ring. DeAngelo's purpose for moving the victim was not just to find her purse or take her ring or eat her food, but also to separate her from someone who could protect her or prevent the sexual assault. In doing so, the movement was beyond what was necessary to accomplish the robbery itself. Therefore, that act was "more than merely incidental" to the robbery.

DeAngelo's intent to rape and rob was a means to an end. Sexually violating someone and taking their property were the tools he chose to achieve his real goal: to utterly dominate and control both the female and male victims. Sexual gratification was a byproduct of his rapes. Taking whatever he wanted, whenever and however he wanted it, was his way of exerting and demonstrating control. Even the act of lingering in their homes for hours, rummaging through their refrigerators, and eating their food as they lay helpless was meant to violate the sanctity of their bodies, their homes, and their relationships. He always intended to commit robbery, and he always planned to perpetrate sexual assault. DeAngelo moved his victims to exert dominance and control of them. Crucially, it also had the effect of substantially increasing the risk of harm to the victims.

Moving her away from the only male adult in the house facilitated her sexual assault. DeAngelo knew that raping the female victim in front of her spouse, fiancé, or boyfriend could lead to resistance and possibly a violent confrontation. A basic military strategy is to divide and conquer, and that was exactly what he did. Moreover, being moved under these circumstances exacted a tremendous psychological and emotional toll on the victims, increasing their risk of harm.

Ten sexual assaults that occurred in Sacramento and two in Contra Costa County matched these specific criteria. I also found six such incidents in the surrounding counties. However, Sacramento DA Schubert felt that adding them would "muddy up the waters" since they lacked DNA evidence and would not provide any tactical advantages. Whether they did or not, each one of these victims deserved the justice they had long sought. Her decision did not sit well with me. Better than many, I understood the cold logic that represents a foundational pillar of our justice system. However, justice without humanity is a marriage without love—a cold, transactional relationship. Reducing justice to nothing more than calculated decisions denies our empathy and compassion. But ultimately, I was not the elected district attorney, and the call was not mine to make. Determined to find a way to give these six victims their day in court, I recommended that we call them as witnesses during trial to establish a pattern of conduct for DeAngelo.

As for the new sexual assault incidents that we would now charge, the prosecution path went as follows: DNA connected DeAngelo to the rapes and murders in Southern California; the same DNA connected him to several rapes in Contra Costa County; and the modus operandi/pattern of the rapes in Contra Costa matched the rapes in Sacramento. Just like on television, we found the loopholes and scoured the files for overlooked evidence. We would finally deliver justice to these victims, and in the process, unequivocally identify Joseph DeAngelo as the East Area Rapist and the Original Night Stalker. We felt confident about the path we had chosen, but the legal battles were only just beginning.

7
The Team

August 2017

The People's Team

Eight months before the Body Snatchers grabbed DeAngelo off the streets, I grabbed three chocolate ice cream bars shaped like Mickey Mouse's head and hurried back to my family. Drenched in sweat, I weaved among the crowds of people moving slowly through Disneyland. Trying to enjoy one last vacation before the kids went back to school, we decided to spend an ungodly amount of money and time at the "Happiest Place on Earth." Suddenly my cell phone began to buzz. I handed the treats off to the kids and reached into my pocket. I could feel the scathing look my wife sent in my direction.

Detective Rob Peters's name popped onto my screen. Over the years, I'd worked with countless detectives, and without question, Peters ranked in the top three investigators I'd ever dealt with. A former Marine who wore Clark Kent glasses and a bowtie, he also had tattoos covering both his forearms. I recall Peters briefing our office about an execution-style murder that he had spent months investigating. Homicide Chief Norgaard had gone on vacation and asked that I attend the presentation. After laying out the particulars of the case, Peters recommended that we file murder charges against a suspect who had been at the scene. I felt more evidence was needed to connect the accused to the crime. Peters eventually found a witness who identified her drug dealer, not the person he'd wanted to charge, as the murderer.

He called me to get a warrant to track the new suspect's cell phone. Before approving the search warrant, I couldn't help but give Peters a hard time. "What happened to the guy you originally wanted me to charge?" I asked with a chuckle.

"Ah . . ." Peters admitted, laughing at himself, "I was wrong about that first guy. We have the true killer now." It takes a smart and humble person to admit they made a mistake and correct course to find the right answers, and he did not hesitate to do so. When the Sheriff's Department assigned Detective Peters to assist Sergeant Clark on the GSK case, I knew we had an all-star law-enforcement team.

Some DA offices assign multiple prosecutors to handle big cases, but Sacramento rarely did. For most of my career prosecuting child molesters, serial rapists, gang crimes, and homicides, I tried those cases alone in the courtroom. Sacramento consistently litigates the third-most jury trials in California, behind only Los Angeles and Riverside Counties. Those jurisdictions have either ten times or double the population, respectively, of Sacramento. Considering our high volume, we simply don't have a sufficient number of lawyers to assign more than one prosecutor to each case on a consistent basis. Plus, we typically employ the "Lone Ranger" ethos of trial work. In the nearly one hundred trials I'd conducted, I alone carried the burden of delivering justice.

But the Golden State Killer case was unprecedented. For Sacramento's EAR cases alone, we had nearly fifty sexual assaults and a death penalty–eligible double homicide to litigate. DA Schubert decided to assign Sacramento prosecutor Amy Holliday, a relatively inexperienced trial lawyer, to assist me. Some in the office whispered about her lack of experience in the courtroom; she had only a handful of serious cases under her belt. She heard the criticisms, and it stung. Although we had never worked together, I considered Amy a friend and knew she cared deeply for victims of violence. I pushed back against the whispers, defending her as best I could against the negative comments.

The various district attorneys across California designated prosecutors from each of their respective offices to serve on the GSK Prosecution Team. The Golden State Killer had cut a particularly violent path through Santa Barbara County, including the attempted assault of Catherine and Anthony in Goleta; and the violent murders and rapes of Robert Offerman and Debra Manning and Cheri Domingo and Greg Sanchez. With limited resources, Santa Barbara DA Joyce Dudley asked Sacramento to prosecute the crimes from their jurisdiction. Their top trial lawyer, Chief Deputy Kelly Duncan, was already prosecuting ten members of the infamous MS-13 gang—Mara Salvatrucha, a particularly violent criminal gang with ties to El Salvador—for committing nine murders. The gang's subset in Santa Barbara trafficked drugs, guns, and humans for sex work, and it used murder to rule the streets. With Kelly as our liaison, we would handle the actual litigation of Santa Barbara County's cases.

Standing nearly six feet tall, with closely cropped light brown hair, Kelly Duncan was sharp and direct, adept at assessing any situation quickly, and stood out in a crowd. She was sitting next to me when Ebrahim Baytieh and the Orange County DA's Office tried to take over the case, and she immediately recognized their power play. Upon her return from that meeting, Kelly recommended against the case being tried in Orange County. Before joining the DA's Office, she represented the Santa Barbara County Sheriff's Department. During her time there, she got a front row seat to the investigation of pop star Michael Jackson for child molestation. Jackson owned Neverland Ranch, located in a rural part of the county. Multiple young boys accused the pop singer of sexually assaulting them. Many of the victims had accepted cash settlements or had sued Jackson. Although the evidence against Jackson seemed convincing, the lawsuits for money weighed upon the jurors in the criminal trial, who eventually found Michael Jackson not guilty. As Kelly knew firsthand, high-profile cases created their own gravitational pull and could easily spin out of control, and her steadiness was a credit to her office and a valuable asset to the investigation of the cases in her jurisdiction.

Our colleagues in Ventura County had already been collaborating with us on the EAR investigation before we identified DeAngelo. Crucially, they provided the DNA sample from Charlene Smith's rape kit which allowed Paul Holes and others to conduct their investigative genetic genealogy work. District Attorney Greg Totten led the Ventura County office with a steady hand for almost two decades. His second-in-command, Chief Deputy Cheryl Temple, ran the day-to-day operations with precision and smarts. She was thoughtful and rarely wasted any words when articulating her position. Cheryl had tried multiple death-penalty cases and commanded instant credibility thanks to her tremendous courtroom experience. For instance, she handled the gut-wrenching 1999 case of forty-four-year-old Socorro Caro, who shot and killed her three young sons with a revolver because she believed her husband was divorcing her. During the trial, Cheryl used an innovative computer animation to recreate the crime and played the wrenching 911 call from Caro's husband when he arrived home and found their children dead. After a grueling four-month trial, she was able to convince the jury of Caro's guilt and obtained a sentence of death for the murderer.

Contra Costa County had multiple rape cases, including several with DNA evidence matching DeAngelo. In 2017, DA Mark Peterson resigned in disgrace after illegally using over $60,000 in campaign funds for personal items such as groceries, jewelry, and movie tickets. Appointed to replace Peterson, Judge Diana Becton was in the midst of an election battle to remain the DA. As such, she asked Sacramento County to litigate Contra Costa's cases, and we dutifully obliged.

Orange County contributed a team of prosecutors and investigators led by Senior Prosecutors Deborah Lloyd, Scott Scoville, and Jim Mulgrew. Debbie had retired from the DA's Office but returned to prosecute the Golden State Killer. Earlier in her career, she had convicted Eric Bechler for bludgeoning his wife, Pegye, with a dumbbell and dumping her body in the Pacific Ocean during a wedding anniversary boat trip. The Coast Guard never recovered her body despite an extensive search. During the trial, Debbie, who was then a deputy DA, argued that the defendant, who had been penniless before meeting his wealthy wife, had killed her in order to collect her $2 million life-insurance policy and "maintain the lifestyle he had become accustomed to." The jury convicted Bechler of first-degree murder. Debbie received the California District Attorneys Association's Prosecutor of the Year Award and earned national recognition for her expertise on "no body" homicide cases. For the DNA portion of the GSK case, Orange County also assigned Deputy DA Scott Scoville, who helped form the OC's cutting-edge DNA Unit. With the mind of a scientist, he could counter any attempts by the defense to undermine the forensic evidence.

The other main Orange County prosecutor, Jim Mulgrew, spoke with a voice that reminded me of the legendary sportscaster Howard Cosell. As the supervisor of the Law and Motion Unit of the Homicide Team, Jim possessed a wealth of experience arguing complex legal issues. Among his most important prosecutions was Rodney Alcala, a.k.a. the "Dating Game Killer," who committed five murders between 1977 and 1979 and appeared as a contestant on the popular *Dating Game* TV program in the midst of his crime spree. One of his victims was a twelve-year-old girl in Orange County, whose body he dumped in the Los Angeles foothills. Orange County prosecutors obtained a conviction for murder and a death sentence against him, but the case was overturned on appeal. After prosecutors tried him a second time, the California Supreme Court upheld the conviction, but a federal judge reversed it and ordered a retrial. While preparing to try Alcala for a third time, investigators discovered that his DNA matched semen found in three rape-murders in Los Angeles. Prosecutors from both jurisdictions decided to combine the murder charges into one case and try him in Orange County. After the jury convicted him of murder and the judge sentenced him to death, the California Supreme Court heard the appeal. One of the challenges filed by the defense focused on combining the multiple murders in different counties and trying them all in Orange County. Jim argued the case before the California Supreme Court on behalf of the prosecution—some described his legal arguments as "savant-like"—and got the conviction and sentence upheld. The landmark proceeding was one that Jim and I returned to repeatedly as the GSK case

Professor Claude Snelling.

Courtesy the Snelling Family

Golden State Killer crime map.

Courtesy the Federal Bureau of Investigation and the Sacramento County DA's Office

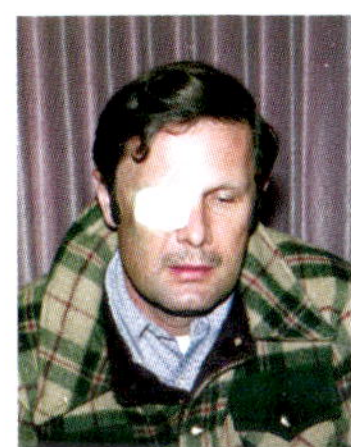

Visalia, CA, police officer Bill McGowen.

Courtesy Visalia Police Department

Pretied shoelaces found at Maggiore crime scene.

Courtesy Sacramento County Sheriff's Office

Katie and Brian Maggiore, July 1976.

Courtesy the Maggiore Family

Aerial photo of the Maggiore crime scene, February 1978.

Courtesy Sacramento County DA's Office

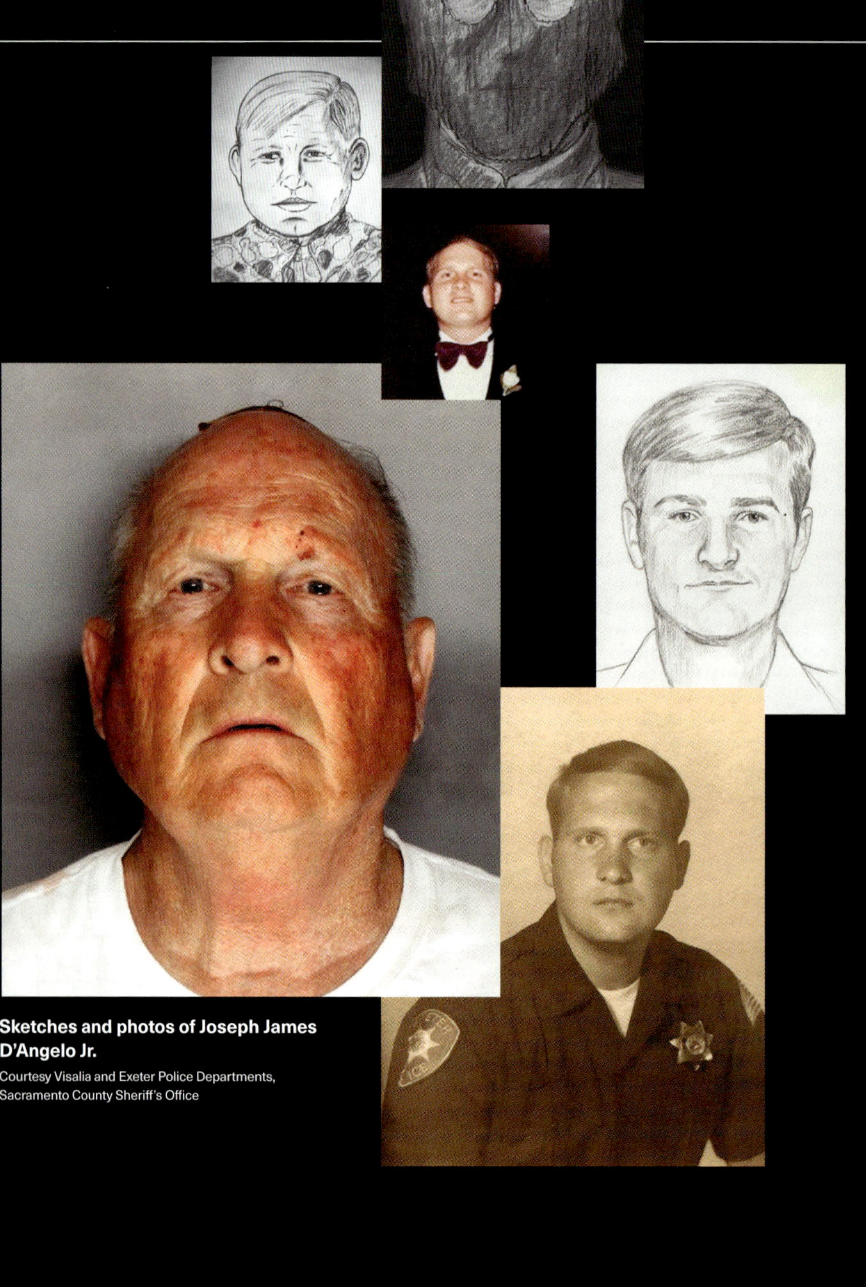

Sketches and photos of Joseph James D'Angelo Jr.

Courtesy Visalia and Exeter Police Departments, Sacramento County Sheriff's Office

Linda O'Dell with Porsche.

Courtesy the O'Dell Family

Phyllis Zitka.

Courtesy the Zitka-Henneman Family

Jane Carson.

Courtesy the Sandler Family

Gay and Bob Hardwick.

Courtesy the Hardwick Family

Kris Pedretti.

Courtesy the Pedretti Family

Detective Carol Daly.

Courtesy the Daly Family

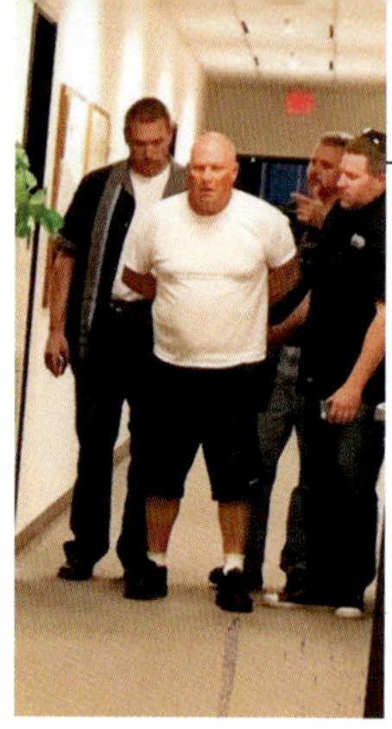

DeAngelo escorted into interrogation room hours after his arrest, April 24, 2018; in the interrogation room; moving around in his cell.

Courtesy Sacramento County Sheriff's Office

Search of DeAngelo's backyard for trophies using ground-penetrating technology.

Courtesy the author

The Golden State Killer investigative genetic genealogy team. From left: Sacramento DA Investigator Lt. Kirk Campbell, Contra Costa County District Attorney Investigator Paul Holes (ret.), FBI Los Angeles Associate Division Counsel Steve Kramer, FBI Los Angeles Analyst Melissa Parisot, Sacramento District Attorney's Office Analyst Monica Czajkowski. Not pictured: genealogist Barbara Rae-Venter

Books found in DeAngelo's home.

Courtesy the author

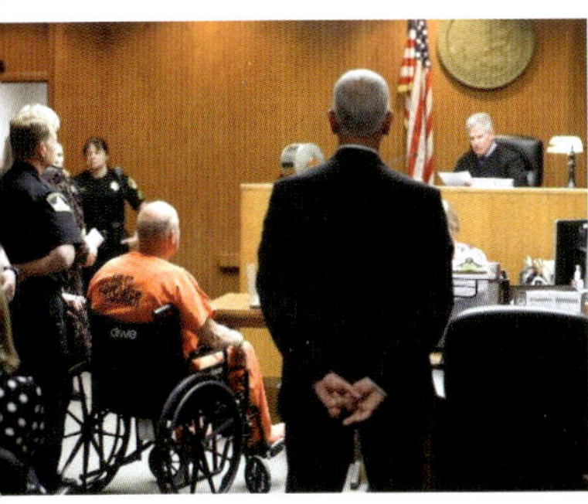

DeAngelo arraignment, April 27, 2018. Sacramento DA Chief Deputy Steve Grippi (center), Judge Michael Sweet (right).
Photo: Fred Greaves/Reuters

Sacramento County Assistant Chief Deputy District Attorney Thien Ho, lead prosecutor of the Golden State Killer case, arguing for setting of preliminary hearing.
Photo: Paul Kitagaki Jr./*Sacramento Bee*

DeAngelo with Public Defender Diane Howard.
Photo: *Sacramento Bee*

The Golden State Killer prosecution team. Alameda County DA Nancy O'Malley (ret.), Santa Barbara County DA Joyce Dudley (ret.), Santa Barbara County Assistant Chief Kelly Duncan, Orange County Senior DA Debbie Lloyd, Tulare County Chief Deputy David Alavezos, Contra Costa County Deputy DA Venus Johnson, Contra Costa County DA Diana Becton, Orange County Senior DA Pat Dixon, Ventura County DA Chief Deputy Cheryl Temple, Ventura County DA Greg Totten (ret.), Tulare County DA Tim Ward, Orange County DA Todd Spitzer, former Sacramento County DA Anne Marie Schubert (ret.), Los Angeles County Supervising DA Marguerite Rizzo, Sacramento County Chief Deputy Steve Grippi (ret.), Sacramento County Homicide DA Chief Rod Norgaard (ret.), Sacramento County Assistant Chief DA Amy Holliday, Sacramento DA Thien Ho, Sacramento County Assistant DA Mike Blazina. Not pictured: Orange County Deputy DAs Jim Mulgrew and Scott Scoville

DeAngelo's plea hearing, Sacramento State ballroom, June 2020.

Photo: Jay Czajkowski

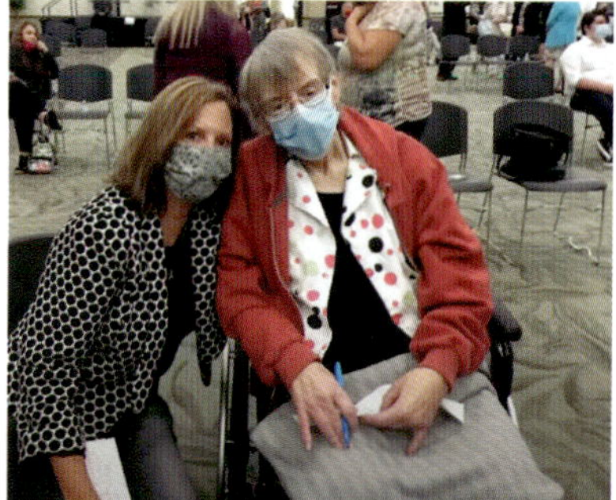

Kris Pedretti and Phyllis Zitka at DeAngelo's sentencing hearing, August 2020.

Courtesy the Pedretti Family

Kris Pedretti and Carol Daly.

Courtesy the Pedretti Family

Jane Carson at DeAngelo's plea hearing, June 2020.

Photo: Rich Pedroncelli/AP

Thien Ho and his father, 1976.
Courtesy the Ho Family

Thien Ho and his mother, 1973.
Courtesy the Ho Family

Standing with his wife, Jenny, Thien Ho is sworn in as the thirty-third Sacramento County District Attorney by Judge Carlton Davis, January 3, 2023.
Photo: Hector Amezcua/*Sacramento Bee*

Wall featuring the portraits of Sacramento DAs.
Photo: Kim Hudson

progressed. Like the Alcala trial, we had multiple murder charges from disparate counties combined in one case.

None of DeAngelo's known crimes occurred in Los Angeles County, but the biggest district attorney's office in the country possessed unrivaled resources. As the deputy-in-charge of the Forensic Science section of the L.A. County DA's Office, Marguerite Rizzo gained national recognition for her work on the Grim Sleeper serial killer, who raped and murdered multiple women in South Los Angeles in the mid-1980s. After four years, the crimes suddenly stopped, and the killer took a fourteen-year break before resuming his murderous ways, committing ten murders in all before law enforcement used familial DNA to identify him as the killer. This method compares DNA profiles developed from crime-scene evidence with those already in a criminal DNA database. It differs from investigative genetic genealogy, which searches databases maintained by private third parties, which are significantly larger because they are not limited to criminals. Investigators found a relationship between the killer and a man named Christopher Franklin, who had been convicted of gun possession in 2008. He was too young to have committed the murders in the 1980s; but his father, Lonnie David Franklin Jr., a retired sanitation worker, fit the profile.

Officers followed Franklin to a restaurant. Dressed as a waiter, an undercover officer collected Franklin's dishes, glasses, and pizza crust. DNA on the pizza crust matched saliva found on one of the murder victims. During the trial, then Deputy DA Marguerite Rizzo handled the presentation of the forensic evidence, explaining the science in clear and simple ways for the jury to understand. After his conviction for all the murders, the judge sentenced Franklin to death. For the GSK case, Marguerite and Scott Scoville from Orange County would provide us with an invaluable source of expertise on the forensic aspects, and they fit right in with the other phenomenal battle-tested prosecutors from across the state.

— — —

The Public Defenders

For nearly three decades, Supervising Public Defender Diane Howard roamed the halls of the Sacramento Superior Court. She wore colorful suit jackets and carried an elegant purse, and gaggles of young defense lawyers followed her around in the hopes that her magic would rub off on them. A fierce advocate for her clients, Howard's word was above reproach. A straight shooter, she would tell me, "Your offer was too high," making me reconsider my position, or "You gave me a fair offer, but the client is too stubborn to take it. Let me work on it." Although we never tried a case against each other because we were often able to negotiate a settlement or resolution beforehand, I respected her. Howard was cut from the old cloth of lawyers. She fought hard in the courtroom, leaving everything in there but never taking it with her. This meant that opposing lawyers would fight her tooth and nail at trial and then go out for a cocktail or coffee afterward.

When DeAngelo made his first court appearance before Judge Sweet, Howard handled the arraignment on behalf of the Public Defender's Office and accepted appointment of the case. The defense needed a lawyer with her experience, credibility, and gravitas to gain DeAngelo's trust, especially as she stood before the throng of media capturing DeAngelo's and her every move. But there was a problem.

After my assignment to the case, I ran into Howard outside the main courthouse, and we stopped to chat. "Diane, I saw that you're defending the GSK. I thought you were retiring?"

"I was, or actually I am, retiring sometime in the next year or so. We're going to assign a few other lawyers to the case to prepare for that," she responded. The identity of the opposing counsel is always one of the first details a prosecutor wants to know. Do they lie and cheat, or are they honest? Are they difficult to deal with, or do they pick and choose their battles? Are they bombastic or easygoing? Are they going to "age the case" by continuing over and over again as the case grows old, or will they actually try it?

My interest was piqued as to who would supplement and eventually replace her. A short time later, Deputy Public Defenders Joe Cress and Alice Michel, both of whom had over two decades of experience litigating major cases, were assigned to DeAngelo. Built like a triathlete with tossed brown hair and a goatee, Joe was easy to talk to and well respected by everyone. In fact, the union that represented both the public defenders and the prosecutors voted him president. Familiar with defending murderers and sex offenders, Alice could walk into any courtroom and handle any client. Between them, when it came to discussing a sensitive issue, Alice was more apt to say no right away, whereas Cress tended to take his time responding and seemed immensely practical. Knowing this, I picked and chose which battles to fight, and with whom.

— — —

After he was interrogated but before he was booked into the jail, DeAngelo lowered his head and ran into a wall in a half-hearted attempt to hurt himself. When officers took his booking photos, the blood on the top of his head had not fully dried. I was standing next to Rod when we received the media request for a picture of DeAngelo taken by jail officials.

"Please pull up the booking photos, Noems," Rod requested.

As we scanned through the photographs, Rod looked at me and asked, "How about this one?"

"Nah, this one is better. His eyes seem more dead, and he looks creepier," I suggested, pointing to another photo.

"All right, Noems, send that one to the media," Rod instructed.

Since that day, the picture I picked comes up whenever DeAngelo's name or the Golden State Killer moniker is searched on the Internet. It lacks the terror evoked by the 1970s sketches of a masked man or the duplicity of his photo as an Exeter police officer, taken at the height of his reign as the Visalia Ransacker. However, it shows the wrinkled face of a decaying monster whose dead and hollowed-out eyes caught my attention that day in court.

Concerned that DeAngelo would hurt himself further, deputies placed him in one of three cells equipped with a hidden camera—one was used to house the infamous Unabomber; the second was reserved for Omar Ameen, an ISIS terrorist who was also a member of al-Qaida in Iraq; and the third was specifically used to monitor the GSK—behind a light fixture above the sink. His every act would be recorded twenty-four hours a day, seven days a week. The guards were instructed to always keep an eye on him, making sure he did not self-harm.

The jail housed DeAngelo right next to Salvador Vasquez-Oliva, who was accused of a quadruple murder. In March 2017, he stabbed his niece and wife to death and killed his teenage daughter and son with a claw hammer before wrapping their heads and hands in plastic on the cement floor of their garage. Norgaard assigned the case to me, and we sought the death penalty. I will never forget the boy's chubby, innocent face with the side of his head caved in by his own father's violent hands. As a father with a young son, I shook in anger looking at those photographs. When I received the Golden State Killer case, the office reassigned all my other trials, including Vasquez-Oliva's, so that I could focus solely on GSK. The sergeant overseeing the floor where they housed these two criminals told me that they talked regularly, sharing snacks and suggestions of different books to read. I was not surprised that these heinous murderers would commiserate and find companionship with each other.

After DeAngelo's arraignment on April 27, 2018, the judge chose May 2 for further proceedings. I pored over all the videos of his first court appearance, when deputies pushed a seemingly incoherent and open-mouthed DeAngelo into a packed courtroom. The arraignment was but a continuation of his "feeble old man" routine from the interrogation room. It was yet another mask he wore to hide his true self and to manipulate us. I regularly watched videos of DeAngelo in his cell on one side of my computer screen as I studied reports and photos of his crimes during the 1970s and 1980s. Watching DeAngelo live the life of a caged animal in a jail cell, I felt the juxtaposition was fitting. What I saw was an animal, no longer in the wild hunting his prey, but a creature in captivity, pacing back and forth, unable to sit or rest for long, trapped, and on the lookout for an opportunity to pounce, kill, and escape.

In an iconic scene in the film *The Usual Suspects*, a detective interviews a small-time con man, Roger "Verbal" Kint, one of two survivors of a shooting at the Port of Los Angeles. Desperate to identify the mysterious crime lord Keyser Söze, the cop presses the petty criminal for more information, but Kint, who has a disabled hand and a pronounced limp, appears naive and powerless. Kint finally posts bail and hobbles out of the police station. As he gets farther and farther away, he begins to lose his limp and flexes his allegedly disabled hand to show a perfectly working limb.

Like Kint, DeAngelo's condition seemed to deteriorate with every court appearance. He seemed to be losing weight and acted more and more incoherent. He seemed barely able to hold himself up, much less walk. In the jail videos, DeAngelo shuffled slowly toward his cell, cane in hand. Once the door closed, however, he leaned the stick against the wall and began pacing around the cell in a triangle formation, without a single limp or pause. In fact, his speed increased as he walked, and he also climbed up and down on his bunk bed easily to retrieve items. Just like Kint became Keyser Söze, Joseph DeAngelo suddenly transformed into the Golden State Killer. The master manipulator could not hide from the camera's eye.

DeAngelo had just been arraigned a few days earlier. I barricaded myself in my office and tried to absorb his case with every pore of my body. I came up with an idea how to organize the discovery, the evidence we needed to turn over to the defense. This included all the police reports, video and audio recordings, and crime-scene photos, all of which needed to be labeled and tracked with unique identifiers. As thoughts randomly sprung up in my mind, I heard a knock.

"Come in!" I yelled out. As the door opened, I saw both Sergeant Kenny Clark and Homicide Detective Rob Peters standing there. "Gentlemen, to what do I owe the pleasure?" I asked with a big smile as I stood up to shake their hands. As they both looked sheepishly at the floor, my smile disappeared. "All right, what happened, guys? Don't tell me DeAngelo hurt himself again." I wanted them to cut to the chase and tell me the bad news.

"Oh, no, no, he's fine," Rob reassured me. My heart rate returned to normal.

"We might have a little problem," said Kenny.

Detective Peters chuckled and said, "Eh, funny you should say little . . ." His voice trailed off, and a devilish grin flashed across his face.

"Before we arrested DeAngelo, we got a search warrant signed by

Judge White to take pictures of his penis, collect his DNA and fingerprints," Kenny continued. "We were going to do all these things after his interrogation, but in the frenzy of the moment, we forgot to do so."

Rob offered, "We can still do it now if you want, but we wanted to check with you first considering he has a lawyer now."

With no DNA evidence connecting DeAngelo to the East Area Rapist crimes, we needed every piece of corroborating evidence. Many of the rape victims, including Jane Carson, described their attacker as possessing an unusually small penis. Some in law enforcement labeled it a "micropenis," and this was well known among investigators and profilers. If DeAngelo possessed a small penis, we needed confirmation.

"Since you have the search warrant already signed, you can just go take the pictures and collect his DNA and prints," I started thinking out loud. "But we'd better play it safe. The judge appointed Diane Howard as his lawyer." We had the authority to take DeAngelo out of his cell, strip him, and take pictures of his penis. But what if he started talking with investigators about the cases? It could go sideways really quickly since he had a lawyer and couldn't be questioned.

"What do you want us to do?" Sergeant Clark asked. Some cops were reckless cowboys who shoot first and ask questions later, living by the ethos that it's better to ask for forgiveness than permission. I appreciated that Kenny and Rob were thoughtful and careful enough to discuss sensitive matters with me before acting.

"I'll talk to Diane Howard," I replied. "I will let her know that we obtained a search warrant for his pictures, case prints, and DNA before his arrest, and we intend to collect it now. This will give her a chance to object, and we can fight it out in court. Hang tight, I'll let you know the next steps." Even before calling Howard, I knew what her answer would be. When I called and told her what we wanted to do, she immediately objected and claimed it violated her client's rights since he was now represented by counsel. We set the hearing date for May 3, 2018.

Our victims' advocates, who have a master's degree in social work, handle the day-to-day interactions with the victims. They ensure that the survivors receive updated information regarding court appearances and events and assist them with obtaining counseling and other services. For the EAR's victims in Sacramento, we assigned two of our best victim advocates, Ann Tran and Mailyn Chuong, empathetic and relentless in their advocacy for victims. I had worked with them on multiple sex and homicide trials over the years. Court appearances can turn into a media circus, with cameras stacked on top of each other and reporters shoving microphones in people's faces. To ensure that the victims and survivors received a seat in the courtroom for every hearing, the advocates escorted them into an adjoining room and then brought them into court before the doors opened to the public and media. Both Ann and Mailyn were experts at choreographing the whole process.

Early on May 3, Amy Holliday and I made our way from my office to Department 61, located on the first floor of the county jail. On that cool and lovely Sacramento spring morning, I tried to enjoy the walk but could feel the butterflies in my stomach. We speculated as to what might happen later that day: Would DeAngelo come to court in a wheelchair, acting feebly? How many times would Diane Howard place her hand on DeAngelo's shoulder to help humanize him? How was she going to get around the fact that we had a search warrant signed by a judge? How many victims would attend, and how many media outlets would cover the hearing? What questions would the reporters ask us?

As prosecutors, we cannot publicly comment on an active case because it could potentially prejudice the jury pool and thus affect the defendant's constitutional right to a fair trial. We walked through our possible responses to the media should we be asked questions. We practiced the art of giving an answer that isn't really an answer and saying "No comment" without actually saying "No comment." Walking down the long hallway that led to the courtroom, we saw a dozen cameras and throngs of media standing about with notepads. Clumped together in groups, they fanned out in the hallway whispering to each other as attorneys milled about. You could feel the excitement and anticipation in the air. We quietly ducked into another courtroom to access a private corridor reserved for court staff, law enforcement, and attorneys.

The courtrooms in the jail are designed for quick appearances related mostly to defendants in custody. The audience section was lined with about sixty padded folding chairs. A large cage with metal bars sat on the left side of the courtroom. A door at the back of the cage led to an access cell, from which the deputies brought inmates in for their court appearances. We were to sit at a curved black desk to the right of the courtroom just below the judge's bench. The media would be crammed up against the wall in the tight space behind the lawyers. Per my usual habit, we got to the courtroom before the defense attorneys. I had spent the previous day going over my arguments and counterarguments about the legality of taking pictures of DeAngelo's penis and collecting his fingerprints and DNA after appointment of counsel. I had studied all the cases and was ready to make the right arguments. But first, we needed to meet the victims. Having just been assigned the case, I had not yet met them all.

Ann Tran peeked into the courtroom and asked if we were ready to greet the victims. After I gave her a thumbs up, she disappeared for a few minutes. When the door opened, about a dozen women in their late fifties to seventies walked into the room. They smiled, laughed, and chatted among themselves, exuding a nervous excitement. But underneath their cheerful veneer, I could still sense a distinct undercurrent of apprehension. How could they not be filled with a mix of anxiety and anticipation? They were about to encounter their rapist for the first time in over forty years. Some had attended the arraignment the previous week, but for many, this was their first time in court.

As they prepared to sit in the front two rows with a prime spot to see DeAngelo, we walked over to them to introduce ourselves. A small woman in her mid-sixties with short gray hair parted to the side walked up and reached out to shake my hand. "Hi, I am Victim Number One, and my name is Phyllis Zitka." I immediately shook her hand and introduced myself with a warm smile. Peering through her thick round glasses, I saw the gentleness, but also the pain in her eyes. Reading the account of Phyllis's rape in a police report did not prepare me for the surge of emotion I felt as I held her hand and heard her voice. It was as if I had reached across time and space. She had aged, but I saw the young woman from 1976 in front of me.

As a prosecutor, I never promise a victim the outcome of a verdict. The one thing I always tell them is, "I promise you that nobody will work harder for you." But something about Phyllis caused me to break my own rule. Perhaps it was the pain in her eyes, or the fact that she had waited so long for this day. The words just came out of me. "I don't how and I don't know when, but I promise you, we will get you the justice you so deserve." Her eyes began to well up.

Only fifteen years old when DeAngelo raped her a few days before Christmas 1976 and now in her late fifties, Kris Pedretti walked over to me. "Hi, my name is Kris, and I am Victim Number Ten." I recalled the details of the crimes committed against her and the pictures of the house where they occurred. I could only imagine the pain she had endured. Her father told her never to discuss the rape again, making her feel ashamed. She had to sit at Christmas dinner only a few feet away from where she had been brutalized a week before. As a father with a daughter the same age as Kris when the EAR attacked her, my heart broke for her. The smiles and the words can tell a different story since they can hide the pain and deny the darkness, but the eyes never lie. Just like Phyllis, the hurt was still visible in her eyes. I made her the same promise I made Phyllis.

Linda O'Dell, who had moved from the Midwest to Sacramento with her spouse, was attacked by the EAR while her husband was forced to lie in bed covered in a bedsheet with plates and glasses stacked on his back. She was barely five feet tall, but her fierce blue eyes could burn a hole through a wall. Her marriage didn't survive the weight of the attack, but she endured and raised her sons with pride. "Hi, my name is Linda, and I was a victim of the EAR. Thank you for everything. You're my hero," she told me as we shook hands, although I hadn't yet done a single thing. I felt guilty accepting her appreciation; I hadn't yet earned it. The three generations of law enforcement that had pursued the GSK over the decades deserved the gratitude, not I. Looking over, I saw that Amy was meeting all the victims, shaking their hands, and listening to their stories intently. I could tell she was touched by this opportunity to come face to face with the people whom she had thus far seen only in the police reports. No one takes a job as a prosecutor to get rich. We do it for a cause. We toil away in courtrooms across every town and city in America because we are driven to help victims.

Mailyn Chuong tapped me on the shoulder and brought me over to Jane Carson. I had seen pictures of her in a nurse's uniform a few months after DeAngelo had raped her while her three-year-old son was nearby. I read how he had taunted her. After his arrest, I saw Jane was interviewed on *NBC Today with Megyn Kelly,* her unwavering resilience on display. At the age of seventy-two, she had never forgotten the pain the EAR had inflicted upon her. Although she retired from the air force as a colonel and had a successful career as a nurse, the trauma left deep scars. After the attack, she heard helicopters flying overhead looking for her assailant. To this day, loud noises and the sound of helicopters frighten her.

Living on the East Coast, Jane missed the other court appearances but would not miss this one. She wanted to sit in the front row and see him clearly—and she wanted him to see her. I walked over and introduced myself and thanked her for attending the hearing. Before I could explain what to expect, she said, "I saw him on TV pretending to be an invalid. I don't buy it one bit." Her eyes narrowed. "He's a manipulator and a coward!" Jane pulled no punches, and I admired her greatly for it.

— — —

Diane Howard, wearing a flamboyant jacket and toting a Louis Vuitton bag, walked into court trailed by a gaggle of young attorneys. When I walked over to her table, she flashed a confident smile. "Are you ready to lose today?" she asked.

I retorted, chuckling, "You got any advice, Diane? You're used to it." We both laughed. The joking tone of our banter notwithstanding, we deeply respected each other as ferocious advocates for our respective sides. It was still early in the case, and the other public defenders had not yet been assigned. While she did write the motion to stop us from taking the pictures and the DNA samples, she assigned Deputy Public Defender David Lynch to argue the motion in court. Sporting an English accent that became more pronounced when he argued before a jury, Lynch worked for over two decades at the Public Defender's Office, earning a reputation as a pugnacious attorney who fought you over every issue. Smart and relentless, he specialized in attacking DNA evidence. He would ensure that even someone like DeAngelo got the full rights guaranteed him under the US Constitution.

We had recovered DeAngelo's DNA from a discarded tissue in his trash can, but we ideally needed a clean sample using a buccal swab on the inside of his cheek. Equally important, without any DNA evidence from our rape cases, I needed circumstantial evidence corroborating his identity as the EAR. I needed to confirm the extreme smallness of his penis. I needed pictures. Law enforcement conducts searches all the time, mostly after establishing probable cause that incriminating evidence exists. Once they have a compelling reason, the officers can conduct the search immediately depending on the circumstance—to prevent evidence from being destroyed or compromised, for instance—or they can get a judge to sign a search warrant authorizing the search and seizure of the evidence.

To do so, an officer would write an affidavit listing their title, experience, and expertise, followed by a narrative noting the felony crimes involved and why there exists probable cause to believe that incriminating evidence would be found at a particular place or on a particular person. Courts apply greater scrutiny to evidence seized without a search warrant because it was acquired without a judge's authorization. The circumstances of the situation, the type of evidence sought, and the nature of the charges dictate whether a warrant is obtained. Given that we were investigating one of the most prolific serial killers and rapists in California history, we damn well were going to make sure every base was covered before collecting his DNA or taking pictures of his genitalia.

The bailiff called the court to order and instructed everyone to rise as Judge Sweet entered and took his seat. I had tried a case that went before him many years ago, and he was well prepared and fair. The back hallway door opened, and the deputies rolled DeAngelo into the chamber in a wheelchair. Audible gasps and whispers spread through the audience. Everyone strained their necks to get a glimpse of the Golden State Killer. Although the judge had excluded cameras from the courtroom, journalists and media filled every available seat to memorialize the moment. Longtime *Sacramento Bee* reporter Sam Stanton, who covered the crime beat and had seen all sorts of killers and rapists over the years, stood directly behind me. He had just finished covering the Bracamontes death-penalty trial and was jumping headfirst into the GSK case.

I looked to my left and saw Jane lean forward in her chair, glaring at her rapist. Her eyes narrowed and her breath seemed to quicken. She had waited so long for this moment. Phyllis and Linda, seated in the front row, also watched DeAngelo's every move. Kris leaned in toward her husband, Steve, for support. The Golden State Killer's face, shrouded these past four decades in darkness and anonymity, was exposed again to the entire world.

DeAngelo maintained the same vacant expression on his face, head cocked back and mouth hanging half open, as he had at his arraignment. He was still trying to manipulate us. But we'd seen the videos of his movements in his jail cell, when he thought he was not under surveillance. We knew the truth—and he didn't know that we knew.

I always stand when I address the court, even just to say "Good morning." It is a sign of respect. I stood at counsel's table while Howard stood next to DeAngelo with her hand gently resting on his shoulder. She filed a Motion to Enjoin, trying to prohibit us by judicial order from taking pictures of DeAngelo and collecting his DNA. Lynch stepped forward, stood next to Howard, and nodded to Judge Sweet, who asked him to proceed. Lynch launched into his argument:

"What the District Attorney seeks to do is seek evidence from a client without input from defense counsel," he began. "Once judicial proceedings have begun, the government's right to investigate and perfect the charged offense is limited by the adversarial process." His position centered on the notion that once DeAngelo was charged, the original search warrant, which Judge White had signed before the defendant was booked, no longer applied. He pushed for our having to rejustify and relitigate the need for the search. He further argued that forcing DeAngelo to provide incriminating evidence against himself by exposing his genitalia for photographs or giving his DNA amounted to forced "testimonial" evidence. Since he was represented by an attorney, he could not be forced to testify or give incriminating evidence since it would violate his right to due process.

To challenge the sufficiency of a search warrant, however, a defense attorney is required by law to go before the judge who signed it. Instead of going before Judge White, who had reviewed and signed the order, the defense went to Judge Sweet, who had just arraigned DeAngelo. I began my argument by highlighting their improper use of the law. "A valid search warrant has been issued by a neutral magistrate, authorizing law enforcement to obtain fingerprints and DNA samples as well as take photographs of his person," I reasoned. "The law is clear: The only way to challenge a signed warrant is through a Motion to Suppress. But instead, they filed a Motion to Enjoin. They used the wrong vehicle to drive to the wrong destination."

Further emphasizing my argument, I said, "They can dress it up any way they'd like. At the end of the day, they are challenging a lawful search warrant signed by a neutral magistrate." I then turned my attack to their claim that taking pictures of DeAngelo's penis or collecting his DNA amounted to the defendant being forced to provide "testimonial," or incriminating, evidence against himself. "Obtaining the defendant's major case prints and his DNA sample does not require him to speak or say even a single word. Taking photographs of his person does not require the defendant to share his thoughts and beliefs with law enforcement," I went on. "His right to remain silent, his right to his own feelings, and his right to a lawyer would remain untouched and untainted."

After listening to our arguments, Judge Sweet read a summary of all the legal precedents that supported my position that the defense's motion was baseless since the search did not involve testimonial evidence. He rejected each of the defense's claims, denying their motion in its entirety and clearing the way for the execution of the search warrant.

As the deputies began to roll DeAngelo back to his jail cell, I saw Jane lean even farther forward in her chair, her hand gripping the railing in front of her as she glared at the GSK, her defiance palpable to all. Before all the victims and survivors filed out of the courtroom, I walked over to Phyllis. She grabbed my arm and whispered, "Thank you." From that moment on, every time I went to court, I always looked for her in the front row. Before walking out of court, I texted Sergeant Clark and Detective Peters, "Good to go. Call me after you take the pics." They reached out to Howard and arranged to execute the search warrant the following day.

Early the next morning, Kenny and Rob woke DeAngelo up and brought him to the lineup room at the jail. Tucked away on the second floor, it is set up with a slightly elevated platform for suspects to stand on. Kenny and Rob were in the adjoining room, where witnesses and authorities can look at the suspects and observe the proceedings through a one-way glass window. Diane Howard joined them to ensure DeAngelo's rights were not being violated and to speak up on his behalf if she objected to any of the procedures. Sheriff's Homicide Bureau Detective Ralph Garcia, an identification technician, and a photographer conducted the testing. They started by collecting the DNA sample through a buccal swab; next, they took DeAngelo's master case prints, rolling each of his fingers and palms in black ink before imprinting them on a print card. Garcia then ordered DeAngelo to turn around and remove his shirt, and the photographer documented his face, neck, chest, arms, and hands.

Rob got on the intercom and said, "All right, Garcia, it's time to take pictures of his penis." Howard left the room, assigning her investigator to monitor the rest of the search. Under the bright fluorescent light, the monster that had terrorized California stood there, impotent and overweight. Nothing can ever fully erase the atrocities he committed against Jane, Kris, Phyllis, Trish, and others, but for a moment, the myth of the Golden State Killer was no more. The fear he had instilled, the force he had wielded, and the mystery and power he had lorded over victims, law enforcement, and journalists alike—it was all gone.

The photographer was instructed to take pictures of DeAngelo's genitalia from multiple angles. He kneeled down to do so, but he grew frustrated after several failed attempts. Detective Garcia threw up his hands in the air in exasperation and barked over the intercom, "There's nothing there."

"Tell DeAngelo to spread his legs and pull back the foreskin," Kenny directed.

I was sitting on the couch outside of Norgaard's office eating lunch when Detective Peters's name scrolled across my screen, just like it had eight months earlier in Disneyland. "It's smaller than the circumference of a dime and its length is equal to the tip of your pinky." We had the circumstantial evidence we needed in order to corroborate the testimonies of DeAngelo's victims.

8
The Monster Behind the Mask

August 2018

On August 21, 2018, the Sacramento County District Attorney's Office formally charged Joseph DeAngelo with twelve counts of murder with special-circumstance allegations, making him eligible for the death penalty.

As part of the analysis of whether or not to formally seek death, we had to look into the GSK's background. Investigators delved into the dark recesses of his life, leaving no stone unturned. We interviewed his ex-wife and ex-girlfriends, his family and friends, and his former coworkers, and we scoured his employment, financial, and military records. I read every report and interview transcript. I pored over every photograph and video, recording and reel.

Several months before DeAngelo's arrest, I walked through the aisles at a local bookstore and came across *Mindhunter: Inside the FBI's Elite Serial Crime Unit* by the legendary federal agent John E. Douglas, who profiled Ted Bundy, Charles Manson, and Jeffrey Dahmer. I brought it home, and it sat on my nightstand, untouched and gathering dust. A week before the GSK's capture, the book caught my eye for some reason, and I opened it to a random page:

> "Serial murder may, in fact, be a much older phenomenon than we realize. The stories and legends that have filtered down about witches and werewolves and vampires may have been a way of

explaining outrages so hideous that no one in the small and close-knit towns of Europe and early America could comprehend the perversities we now take for granted. Monsters had to be supernatural creatures. They couldn't be just like us."

What makes someone a monster? How are they different than us? Are they born evil, or do life's cruel circumstances turn them into monsters? The debate regarding the causes of criminal behavior—nature versus nurture—has raged for centuries. Advances in the field of genetics has focused on the MAO-A gene, nicknamed the "warrior gene," which helps to regulate neurotransmitters like dopamine, serotonin, and norepinephrine. Dopamine affects functions involving reward, motivation, and pleasure, while serotonin regulates mood, sleep, and social behavior. Norepinephrine affects focus, alertness, attention, and our response to threats. Han Brunner, a Dutch geneticist, published a study in the October 1993 issue of *Science* showing a correlation between a mutation in the gene to increased aggressive response to provocation. Additional technological improvements and use of brain imaging scans found a correlation between abnormal brain function in the amygdala and prefrontal cortex with aggressive behavior. These areas of the brain help regulate violent impulses, control emotions, and make moral decisions. However, correlation is different than causation.

Geneticist James Fallon subscribed to the belief that a person's genes created their physical and psychological profile, determining their actions. He examined countless PET scans of human brains for his research project, looking for physiological patterns that might correlate with criminogenic behavior. Some of the scans came from the brains of convicted murderers, others from people diagnosed with schizophrenia, depression, and other psychological disorders. He also reviewed scans from the brains of normal individuals. To maintain the integrity of the research, he conducted a blind trial, meaning he did not know the identity of the person from whom the slide came. Without fail, he correctly identified each of the brain scans belonging to murderers. He noted that they all demonstrated diminished function in the orbital cortex, which is responsible for regulating morality and ethics. It functions as a brake, stopping and regulating the amygdala, which is associated with aggression and appetite. Fallon reasoned that, without a conscience, an individual will lack the ability to control their behavior or conform to the rules of society.

In conjunction with his research on serial killers, Fallon examined PET scans from his own extended family as part of a project looking into Alzheimer's disease. One slide matched the brain scans of the murderers; in fact, it looked exactly like the brain of the worst serial killer. For him, it suggested that the poor individual was a psychopath, or they shared an uncomfortable number of traits with one. To his shock, the slide was his.[1]

Further genetic testing showed that Fallon possessed the mutated MAO-A gene linked to violence, aggression, and a lack of empathy. He was also distantly related to Lizzie Borden, who was acquitted of killing her father and stepmother with an axe in 1892. In addition to "Cousin Lizzy," Fallon investigated his father's lineage to discover seven other alleged killers. His great-grandfather was hanged for murdering his own mother. Against the backdrop of his family's own violent history, Fallon, by all accounts, lived the quiet life of a married man and scientist. He had never committed a crime, much less murder. So despite hitting the genetic lottery for serial killers, he somehow escaped his destiny of destruction and death. For a geneticist, that created a conundrum, and his views began to evolve. He came to believe that our genes could point us in one direction or the other, but our environment helped shape the person we became. Abuse and trauma in childhood could tip the scale in favor of violence.

Defense lawyers utilize these studies in "neural law" to help their clients escape responsibility or mitigate the consequences of their crimes. However, they often minimize the role of free will. In life, some are dealt losing cards, but it's how one chooses to play the cards that matters. As Stephen Hawking once said, "I have noticed even people who proclaim everything is predestined, and that we can do nothing to change it, look before they cross the road." On the scales of justice, how do we balance a defendant's horrific childhood with the

1 Fallon, James, *The Psychopath Inside: A Neuroscientist's Personal Journey into the Dark Side of the Brain* (New York: Current, 2013).

devasting pain and horror they inflict on innocent people? Does a serial killer's genes and upbringing absolve them of the vicious bludgeoning, the sadistic sexual assaults, and the lives ruined or cut short?

— — —

Joseph James DeAngelo Jr. was born on November 8, 1945, in Bath, New York. His father, also named Joseph, served in the military in World War II. Born three years after his older sister, Rebecca, DeAngelo also had a younger sister, Connie, and brother, John. Like many military families, they moved from assignment to assignment. According to military records, from 1951 to 1957, they lived in Ohio, Germany, and New York before settling in California. Around 1954, in Germany, nine-year-old DeAngelo and seven-year-old Connie were exploring the military base on which they lived and found themselves in an abandoned warehouse. Two military personnel found the children playing and trapped the kids in the building, refusing to let them go. Several months before her death in 2017, Connie told her son Jesse that the two men took turns raping her in the warehouse while the other held DeAngelo down. After their release, DeAngelo and his sister ran back home to tell their parents what had happened. The parents never reported the horrific assault and told the children to never speak of it again.

Particularly close to his mom, Jesse learned from her that his grandfather had physically abused his grandmother, especially when he was drunk. Joseph Sr. stopped beating her only after military police warned him of potential imprisonment and discharge. Having suffered at the violent hands of her husband, Kay DeAngelo also drank heavily and routinely struck the children. To protect herself from the beatings, Connie would wear multiple pairs of pants.

The family returned to the United States in January 1957 when Joseph Sr. was stationed in Southern California. DeAngelo attended Terra Bella Elementary School, located about a half hour from Visalia. In the summer of 1959, they moved to Rancho Cordova, and DeAngelo attended Mills Junior High. At the age of fourteen, DeAngelo worked at Mather Air Force

Base, where his father was stationed, cleaning the Bachelor Officer's Quarters. From 1961 to 1964, he attended Folsom High School.

During DeAngelo's senior year of high school, the air force reassigned his father to Orlando Air Force Base in Florida, and his parents divorced in 1964. Joseph Sr. eventually moved to Korea, where he married a woman and started a second family. In a creepy effort to recreate his life in America, Joseph Sr. gave the children from his second marriage the same names as the ones he left behind, Rebecca, Joseph, and Connie.

A key characteristic of the East Area Rapist involved his collecting trophies or souvenirs from his many crimes. He often stole a wedding band, an earring, or a photograph, wanting to retain an intimate item from the victim. According to a friend who first met DeAngelo in junior high and remained a good friend through high school, DeAngelo had a habit of collecting a peculiar souvenir. Around the time both boys were juniors or seniors in high school, they were cruising on Chase Drive, not far from the locations of the first rapes in the East Area Rapist series. Suddenly, DeAngelo reached into the glove compartment and pulled out a Gerber baby food jar and handed it to Gary*.

"What the heck is this, Joe?" asked Gary as he held the bottle in his hand and looked at its strange contents.

DeAngelo responded, "That's pubic hair." As Gary looked on in disgust, DeAngelo continued, "Whenever I have sex with a girl, I always get a pubic hair and put it in the jar." Gary didn't want to hear anything more about it.

DeAngelo spent his youth riding his bicycle everywhere, swimming in the river, and running in the concrete canals he would later use to escape from his crime scenes. On foot and on wheels, DeAngelo came to be intimately aware of every street and neighborhood in the Cho. But more important for his future as a criminal, he knew all the secret paths and shortcuts, the hideouts and blind spots. As a teenager, he also developed a penchant for deviant behavior. In summer 1962, Fred Kane, who lived in Rancho Cordova and was about to begin Folsom High School, was swimming in the American River when he heard gunshots and then felt the water around him splashing. Looking up, he saw a teenager on the shore, shooting at him; no fewer than six bullets whizzed past.

Kane quickly swam ashore and ran up the embankment to confront the shooter, who was walking away with two other boys. His fists clenched and ready to rush the shooter, Kane yelled out to the group, who turned around. The shooter still had the .22 caliber rifle in his hand and warned that he would shoot and kill Kane if he attacked them. One of the other boys spoke up. "He's kinda crazy. You ought to just forget this and leave him alone."

When Kane pointed to the shooter and asked, "What's his name?" the boy responded, "Joe DeAngelo." The group of three took off. Kane was angry at being shot at and determined to find his shooter. He recalls, "The next day, I started out trying to find him. I'm looking at all the hangouts. McDonald's, the bowling alley, and different places. I heard he worked at the base at the swimming pool. I went out there, but it was his day off. I was trying to catch him when he didn't have a gun and . . . I could just lay into him."

While hanging out at the bowling alley later that day, Kane felt a tap on his shoulder. Turning around, he saw DeAngelo, who put his hands up and said, "I apologize for the other day, what I did. And if you wanna fight me, it's all right. We can go around back and have it on. But if you wanna be my friend, I would like—I would like you to be my friend. I've got a car over here."

Kane responded, "Okay. I'll accept your apology."

DeAngelo answered, "Well, come on. We'll go down to the river and we can ride." Kane had never had a friend with a car. They went cruising in DeAngelo's Chevy Bel-Air. Over the summer and into the following year, they became friends. Kane noticed that DeAngelo would repaint the Bel-Air a different color every few months to avoid getting recognized and caught by the police. For the first few weeks, they spent their time swimming in the river and taking DeAngelo's rifle and handguns out to the local landfill to shoot target practice. But as the summer progressed, DeAngelo introduced Kane to increasingly delinquent behavior that foreshadowed what was to come in the ensuing years. The bad seed was thriving in the fertile grounds of Sacramento.

One evening in late summer, DeAngelo and Kane rode their bicycles around the Cho looking for a house with an open garage door and a freezer or refrigerator inside. DeAngelo had been breaking into garages for months and wanted to introduce Kane to the thrill of doing so. After spotting a garage with its door open, they parked their bikes around the corner and returned on foot. As they got halfway up the driveway, a large German shepherd came running out of the garage and barked at the intruders. As the dog advanced, DeAngelo tripped over his own feet backing up, and Kane pulled him up as they retreated toward the street.

More angry than hurt, DeAngelo seethed. "I'm gonna kill that dog!"

Kane immediately pleaded, "No, man. That dog's doing its job. He owns that property. He's protecting it. He's a good dog."

But DeAngelo only muttered, "No, I gotta get him. I'm gonna get him!"

Trying to calm him down, Kane said, "Don't do anything to that dog. Come on."

According to Kane, DeAngelo reached into his pocket and pulled out a Cherry Bomb M-80 firecracker, lit it, and threw it in the garage. It landed under the dog and exploded. The animal died from its injuries. A few weeks later, during Halloween, Kane escorted his little brother and sister to trick-or-treat through the neighborhood. When they walked up to the house, the homeowner handed the kids candy and mentioned that their dog had been killed when someone threw an explosive into their garage. She asked if they knew who had done it. Nearly six decades later, Kane described the memory to an investigator, the regret obviously still fresh in his mind. "I felt so guilty, so horrible down in the pit of my stomach. And I just shook my head no. I said, 'I don't know nothing,' and walked away."

DeAngelo and Kane broke into more garages, where DeAngelo would steal meat from the freezers and an occasional drill that he would resell for money. During one of the burglaries, DeAngelo found a beautiful hunting knife in a leather sheath. He handed it to Kane and told him to take it home. Kane's father found the knife hidden in the garage and confronted his son, who claimed he had found it by the river. His father ordered him to bring it back to where he found it and told him he didn't want any more stuff showing up at the house.

Around the same time as the German sheperd incident, DeAngelo and Kane were prowling behind the Sierra Madre Apartments in Rancho Cordova. Young DeAngelo enjoyed spying on people. As Kane recalled,

"We heard a big commotion going on, coming out of one of the apartments. People yelling and screaming and stuff like that. And we looked in the kitchen window, and there was a bunch of naked people, slapping each other on the butt or something. Some crazy stuff was going on in that apartment."

DeAngelo spotted a huge bowie knife sitting on the kitchen table and said, "I gotta have that bowie knife." Kane thought that his friend was insane as there were grown men and women inside the house, but DeAngelo went up to the front door, which was unlocked, and opened it. He snuck inside, ran into the kitchen, grabbed the knife, and ran out of the house. One of the men wrapped a towel around his waist before chasing the boys, yelling, "I'll get you guys!" According to Kane, DeAngelo clearly enjoyed the excitement and danger of the moment as they were escaping.

The birth of the Visalia Ransacker thus occurred in the small homes and garages of the Cho. As a teenager, DeAngelo displayed an adeptness at breaking into homes by pushing a butter knife or sharp screwdriver against a door lock and jimmying it open. The two boys also burglarized homes in Carmichael and Citrus Heights, locations where he would later commit rapes as the EAR. Kane noticed that his partner in crime enjoyed stealing items that had little monetary value but had sentimental value to their owners. For example, he took pleasure in stealing record albums. People's taste in music and their record collection were personal in nature. Stealing those items along with trinkets of jewelry seemed to excite DeAngelo, but the burglaries began to weigh on Kane's conscience. As they progressed through high school, they began to grow apart; Kane was one year behind DeAngelo, who did not want to associate with a lower classman. When Kane broke his ankle and had limited mobility, they saw less and less of each other. DeAngelo graduated and enlisted in the United States Navy in September 1964. The two friends never saw each other again.

DeAngelo completed basic training at the US Naval Center in San Diego and reported to duty aboard the USS *Canberra* in December 1964. From January 1965 to June 1967, DeAngelo deployed three times to Vietnam. The vessel shelled artillery on North Vietnamese troops from a safe distance, and DeAngelo mostly remained on the boat. In June 1967,

DeAngelo transferred to the USS *Piedmont* while the ship patrolled the coast of Vietnam. On June 22, 1968, DeAngelo accidentally amputated the tip of his left index finger when he failed to pull his hand out of the way of a rolling drum. He recovered from his injury and returned to San Diego in July 1968. After declining reenlistment, he left active duty in August 1968 and enrolled at Sierra Community College, about thirty minutes outside Sacramento.

From 1968 to 1970, DeAngelo attended Sierra College, where he earned an associate's degree in police science. During his time there, he met and dated another student, an eighteen-year-old sophomore named Bonnie Colwell. From a family of academics, she excelled in school and was working as a lab assistant. She had lived a sheltered life, and DeAngelo seemed experienced in the ways of the world, especially as a veteran. He lied and told her he had lost the tip of his finger fighting in the jungles of Southeast Asia. To Colwell, he seemed confident and bigger than life, and they quickly started dating. He projected the bad-boy image she saw in the movies and in books. He taught her how to shoot a gun, hunt, and scuba dive.

But there was a dark side to DeAngelo. He enjoyed taking risks and breaking rules and always had to be in control. He liked to speed through the foothills of Sacramento on his Honda motorcycle with Colwell holding tightly onto him. The more scared she became and the tighter she held on, the more excited he got. Bonnie valued rules, but DeAngelo felt they didn't apply to him; they applied only to ordinary people. Rifle in hand, he made her jump over fences and trespass on private land to go hunting. He hunted deer offseason on other people's property, acting as if everything belonged to him and he belonged everywhere. Another time, he pulled out a rifle and shot a vulture out of the air for no reason other than to show his power over another living creature.

After DeAngelo's arrest, we tried to retrace every step of his life. When investigators tracked Colwell down, I asked them to interview her and ask for details of her relationship with the future East Area Rapist. In particular, I wanted to see if he had exhibited any sexual proclivities with her that bore the markings of the EAR. Colwell revealed she had been a virgin when she first started dating DeAngelo. Once they started having intercourse, she described his sexual appetite as insatiable. He would climax up to five times over a three-hour period and seemed completely indifferent to any pain or exhaustion she endured. This mirrored the characteristics of the EAR, who raped his victims multiple times over the course of several hours.

In May 1970, DeAngelo proposed to Colwell, and she said yes. He gave her a half-carat solitaire diamond ring, and though she was suspicious as to how a student could afford such an expensive item, she nonetheless wore it and waited for a wedding date to be set. But one never came. In February 1971, they started attending Sacramento State together. Later that spring, DeAngelo was failing a psychology class he took with Colwell. As a criminal justice major, he needed to pass this prerequisite class, so he asked her to help him cheat on a test, wanting to look over her shoulder and copy her answers. But with a mom who was a teacher and a dad who was a school principal, she wouldn't help him. It violated everything she believed in. Incensed, DeAngelo berated her constantly and told her she needed to support her future husband. He wouldn't let it go, pressuring and cajoling her every chance he got. But she never gave in.

Colwell had had enough and asked DeAngelo to stop by her house. Sitting in her living room, she called off their engagement. He begged her to reconsider and professed his love for her, but she had made up her mind. "We're not a good fit," she told him and handed back the diamond ring. She saw him toss the ring into a field behind the house as he left.

But that would not be the last time Colwell saw her ex-fiancé. A couple of nights later, he returned and knocked on her window. When she opened up her curtain, she saw him outside with a pistol in his hand. He told her to get dressed because they were heading to Reno to elope. She knew he wanted to control her as well as what he was capable of. Terrified, Colwell ran to her parents' room and woke her father, Stan, a World War II veteran. When his daughter told him that DeAngelo was waiting outside with a handgun, ready to kidnap her to Reno, he told her to lock herself in the bathroom. He calmly walked outside and spoke to DeAngelo in the dark. He didn't return for almost two hours. What was said between them has been lost to the passage of time. Regardless of the words spoken, Stan Colwell convinced him to leave. DeAngelo never returned.

After the arrest of the East Area Rapist, the media found Bonnie Colwell and hounded her mercilessly. Over the years, some have theorized that the EAR committed his rapes because Colwell had broken his heart, but that kind of speculation is wholly unfair and inaccurate. The atrocious acts of a fiend rest solely on the shoulders of that fiend, and not the conscience of any other person. Evil does not get to point its finger at anything else but itself. Ultimately, whether it's nature or nurture, whether it's in our predetermined genes or, as William Ernest Henley wrote, "in the fell clutch of circumstance," the ultimate responsibility lies in the palm of our hand.

On June 9, 1972, Joseph DeAngelo graduated from Sacramento State with a Bachelor of Science degree in criminal justice. Forty-eight years later, he would return to the same place—but not as a student. The Exeter Police Department hired DeAngelo on May 18, 1973, after he completed the Basic Police Academy at the College of the Sequoias. In the 1970s, the Exeter force had only about seven to ten officers on staff. Overeducated and overtrained, DeAngelo stood out and felt out of place. Fellow policeman Farrell Ward described conversations with DeAngelo as strained and overly serious. During downtime, the officers enjoyed meeting up and talking. Although he tried to join in, DeAngelo came off as aloof, rarely speaking about his personal life or background. Regardless, he rose quickly through the ranks and was promoted to police sergeant in November 1975, two months after the murder of Claude Snelling. DeAngelo married Sharon Huddle at the Auburn First Congregational Church on November 10, 1973.

Less than a year after DeAngelo began his career as a cop, the Ransacker began breaking into homes ten miles to the east, in Visalia. With a badge, he felt even more invincible and untouchable. He enforced the laws, but they didn't apply to him. What started on hot summer nights in the Cho with his friend Fred escalated and evolved. After the murder of Snelling and the attempted murder of Officer Bill McGowen, DeAngelo began looking to move back to Northern California and spent time traveling back and forth from his home in the Central Valley and the Sacramento region. In August 1976, the Auburn Police Department hired DeAngelo.

Former Auburn Police Chief Nick Willick described DeAngelo as an "average cop." Located in the foothills of the Sierra Nevada mountain range, Auburn was a short drive to the bustling and sprawling suburbs of Sacramento. About double the size of Exeter, the Auburn PD employed about seventeen officers during that time. Small departments tend to be tightknit. Again, DeAngelo stood out as professional but aloof and different. Chief Willick described the first and only time he visited DeAngelo's house in Auburn. Providing his boss a tour of the tiny home, he pointed out his wife's bedroom and then a separate room where he slept, identifying it as the one in which they would consummate their relationship. Willick found it strange that a young couple slept separately. The chief also noticed a lot of unwrapped drill sets, tools, and other miscellaneous merchandise strewn about the house.

In July 1979, Ronald Stillwell was working at the Pay 'n Save store in Citrus Heights when he saw a customer shoplifting dog repellent. As the employee approached, he could see something in the man's pants. When confronted, the thief ran out the front door, and Stillwell and another employee gave chase. After tackling the suspect, they found a hammer in his pants and saw he had defecated on himself. They restrained him, dragged him upstairs, and tied him to a chair before calling the police. It turned out that the shoplifter was a cop: Joseph DeAngelo.

After DeAngelo's arrest for petty theft, Chief Willick fired him for bringing dishonor to the department and violating the public's trust. In a released statement, he noted, "It is very important that the community have the utmost trust and faith in its officers' integrity; when this trust and faith has [*sic*] been compromised, officers can no longer effectively function in the community." DeAngelo took the petty theft case to trial in October, testifying in his own defense and denying any intent to steal. The jury convicted him, and the judge sentenced him to six months' probation and ordered him to pay $130 in fines or do three days of community service.

DeAngelo also filed a lawsuit against the Auburn Police Department and made a disability claim seeking stress leave. During a mandatory therapy session, DeAngelo admitted that he had gone to the chief's house, armed with a gun and an intent to kill his boss, and peered through the windows trying to find his boss. Initially, the chief disregarded the potential threat until one night, his four-year-old daughter climbed into his bed. She said she was scared because she had seen a man looking into her bedroom window with a flashlight the night before. The law was catching up with DeAngelo, but not soon enough.

In fall 1979, Sharon Huddle started attending McGeorge School of Law in Sacramento. DeAngelo, on the other hand, was watching his life spiral out of control: fired from his job; convicted of theft by a jury; his lawsuit dismissed; and no discernable income. With his wife attending law school full-time and no children to care for, DeAngelo was left alone to his own deviant devices. Three weeks before his trial, DeAngelo terrorized Catherine and Anthony in Goleta. In late December, two months after his conviction and sentencing, he returned to Goleta to murder Robert Offerman and Debra Manning. He continued his rampage in Ventura in March 1980, murdering the Smiths; his brutal slayings of the Harringtons in Dana Point followed five months later. With more time on his hands, he returned to Orange County in February 1981 to rape and murder Manuela Witthuhn. Finally, in late July 1981, he viciously killed Cheri Domingo and Greg Sanchez in Santa Barbara, capping a terrifying streak of death and destruction since his arrest for theft two years before. His subsequent dismissal from the force gave him the time and the motivation to roam, stalk, and kill.

But just as DeAngelo reached the dizzying heights of his wave of terror, he stopped. The rapes and murders simply ceased. He had invaded and assaulted and murdered without regard, leaving behind his semen at each crime scene, not knowing that forensic DNA would be used in future criminal investigations. If he had committed more heinous crimes, we likely would have had evidence of it—but nothing more has been found thus far. So why did he stop?

To understand the reason, we need to go back a few years. In July 1977, DeAngelo and Sharon Huddle bought land on Canyon Oaks Drive in Citrus Heights. They later completed construction of a home on the property in 1979 but didn't move in until April 1980. A year and a half later, they welcomed the birth of their eldest daughter in September 1981, just two months after the murder of Cheri Domingo and Greg Sanchez. With Huddle still attending law school, DeAngelo needed to take care of his daughter and start looking for a new job to support the growing family. That fall, he enrolled in mechanics classes at American River College. With a newborn in the house, he could no longer disappear for hours and drive to distant locations to commit his crimes. Tethered to family life, he had to stop his predatory ways—for the time being.

In 1982, Huddle graduated from law school, passed the bar exam, and began working as a lawyer. After DeAngelo earned his degree in diesel equipment mechanics in January 1984, the family moved to Southern California. While Huddle practiced law, DeAngelo worked as a mechanic for a trucking company named ProExpress, located in Montebello, just east of downtown Los Angeles. They continued to live in the cities surrounding L.A., bouncing between Whittier and Long Beach. During those years, the monster remained hidden from the public. But in early May 1986, the Golden State Killer reappeared and struck again, brutally murdering eighteen-year-old Janelle Cruz in Orange County. A few months later, in November 1986, DeAngelo and Huddle's second daughter was born in Los Angeles. Cruz's murder marked the official end of the Golden State Killer's reign of terror.

Many people have asked me why the Golden State Killer stopped killing in 1986. My response is, "What makes you think he actually stopped?" The three years between the birth of his second child until his return to Sacramento in 1989 remain shrouded in mystery. Did he spend his time as a doting father, attending soccer practices and dance recitals? Did he put away the mask, lock up the gun, and put the knife back in a kitchen drawer? How could he have abstained permanently from preying on the innocent after all those years? How did he ignore his sadistic need for the taste of blood and lust?

We knew that as the Visalia Ransacker, he had morphed from a peeping prowler and voyeur to a perverse cat burglar who left behind his semen. He became a sexual predator who tried to kidnap a young Beth Snelling and killed her father, Claude, out of necessity. He evolved into a methodical and prolific rapist who enjoyed dominating and intimidating his victims as much as he wanted the sexual gratification. Finally, he mutated into the ultimate hunter, who stalked, pounced, raped, and murdered his victims, leaving behind no witnesses to his evil deeds. Predators can evolve. The Golden State Killer without a doubt did so.

With over eight million residents in the late 1980s, the Los Angeles Basin presented a vast potential killing field for DeAngelo. Like Lonnie David Franklin Jr., a.k.a. the Grim Sleeper, who was convicted and sentenced to death in 2016 for killing nine women and one girl from 1984 to 2007, did DeAngelo change his standard operating procedures and target people living on the margins of society? Was he able to pick them off the street, torture them with his depravities, and dump them in the Angeles National Forest? Knowing that law enforcement started employing a new tool, DNA, did he make sure that all evidence of his crimes—semen, blood, clothes, shoelaces, and the victims themselves—disappeared? We may never know the answers to these questions.

DeAngelo and his family returned to Sacramento in 1989, and he started working as a mechanic for the Albertsons/Save Mart grocery chain. Huddle started her own practice specializing in family law cases. Their third and final daughter was born almost three years to the date after Cruz was raped and murdered. They settled back into their home in Citrus Heights. In December 1990, DeAngelo and Huddle separated, but the divorce was not finalized until after his arrest in 2018.

Several times over the years, people have asked me whether Huddle had any inkling that her ex-husband was the East Area Rapist. To answer that question credibly, one would need to examine their relationship thoroughly. Even as a young couple, they slept in separate rooms. Throughout most of their relationship, they lived different lives with different focuses. While he worked as a police officer, she gave little thought or care to his erratic schedule. After his firing from the Auburn Police Department, she focused on attending law school and building her legal career. Then the children came, followed by new jobs and a return to Sacramento. I honestly believe that Sharon Huddle was so fixated on her own life that she never realized she was married to the Golden State Killer. The surprise and shock of his arrest left her reeling.

Although their identities can be found in open-source materials and is publicly available, I will not provide the names of his daughters. Like all of us, they did not pick their father or the family into which they were born. The sins of the father should never be cast upon his children. I view them as victims of the Golden State Killer. I will, however, note a few facts that show the strange ways in which the universe connects us all. One of Joseph DeAngelo's daughters, a physician, was employed by the same hospital as the son of Dr. Robert Offerman, also a doctor. Detective Sergeant Kenny Clark served as the main Sacramento Sheriff's Investigator after DeAngelo's arrest and led the interrogation of the GSK. A year before DeAngelo's arrest, Kenny suffered a heart attack and was treated at the same hospital at which DeAngelo's daughter worked.

As I investigated the case, pulling away the mask to reveal the monster behind it, I created a pinned wall of visuals and information much like the ones shown in detective shows. Early on, I pinned two pictures: One depicted a map with all the locations of DeAngelo's crimes, with red dots representing both incidents and victims. The other was a picture of Brian and Katie Maggiore on their wedding day. It was a fortuitous drive to the Cho in 2012 while preparing for a murder trial that brought me to where the Maggiores had been murdered; and their picture reminded me of their lives cut short and forever frozen in time.

9
Connecting the Dots

Summer 2018

Within law-enforcement circles, many questioned whether the same person who had terrorized Sacramento as the EAR, who tore through Santa Barbara and Ventura as the Original Night Stalker, and who swept across Orange County as the Golden State Killer was also the shadowy figure known as the Visalia Ransacker. Fully engrossed in every last fact and detail of the crimes committed in Sacramento, Contra Costa, and Santa Barbara Counties, I could barely breathe, much less dig into a series of some 120 burglaries in Visalia. I heard about the killing of Professor Snelling and the near capture of the Ransacker by a Visalia officer through the excited rants of Sergeant Kenny Clark.

"It's him! The Visalia Ransacker is also the EAR!" Kenny stated as he pounded my desk with his fist.

"Kenny, you also told me recently that the EAR was the Cordova Cat Burglar, who committed a string of burglaries in Rancho back in the early seventies," I retorted. "And you believed he was also a retired phone company employee who drove cross-country in an RV."

As Detectives Peters stood grinning at the door, Kenny responded confidently, "I went through thousands of burglary reports from the 1970s that occurred in the Cordova area. The same MO is there as with the EAR, absent the sexual assaults, and the Ransacker too. Do you know how mind-numbing it was reading all those reports?"

"I can only imagine," I nodded, admiring Kenny's tenacity and dedication, and logged Kenny's comments in the back of my mind.

Orange, Santa Barbara, and Ventura Counties all filed separate criminal complaints in their own Superior Courts, charging DeAngelo with the murders he committed in their jurisdictions. Two outstanding issues remained: First, would Tulare County join the prosecution team by charging DeAngelo with the murder of Professor Snelling? Second, where would the People vs. the Golden State Killer case be tried?

In July 2018, Tulare County DA Tim Ward and his Chief Deputy David Alavezos traveled three hours north to Sacramento. Noemi scheduled the meeting for 9:30 a.m., before the blistering summer sun cast its unforgiving heat on us. DA Schubert, Rod Norgaard, Chief Deputy Steve Grippi, Amy Holliday, and I all attended the meeting. With short brown hair and an easy smile, Ward looked like a professor at the College of the Sequoias. Speaking with an accent that could be from anywhere and everywhere, he possessed the ability to make everyone feel comfortable. Alavezos was athletic and fit, with thinning light brown hair framing a square jaw. I later found out he spent his weekends long-distance cycling. He's a grinder, a worker, someone who simply puts his head down and does the job. You want someone like that in the trenches with you.

They came to present the proposition that the Visalia Ransacker murdered Professor Snelling and then later evolved into the East Area Rapist and eventually the Golden State Killer. They wanted to join the prosecution team. As Alavezos spoke, I could tell immediately that he possessed a wealth of experience. A courtroom veteran, he had tried multiple death-penalty cases and well over a hundred jury trials in his career—in short, a legit trial lawyer.

Alavezos recounted the compelling evidence supporting their theory. "DeAngelo joined the Exeter Police Department in May 1973, and in less than a year, the Visalia Ransacker started breaking into homes in a three-mile square radius around the College of the Sequoias." He projected a map of the area on the screen. "His MO was consistent: After coming into the house through the garage or the back door, he would turn off the air conditioning unit so he could hear if someone came home; set glasses by the door as an alarm system; ransack through the house, eating their food and drinking beer; he would lay women's clothing on the bed, masturbate, and leave behind semen; and take small trinkets like coins, stamps, and a single earring from a pair," Alavezos continued.

I sat up in my chair when I heard about the Ransacker turning off the air conditioning and creating a makeshift alarm system. Kenny had told me the same thing about the Cordova Cat Burglar's modus operandi. Just like the EAR, the Ransacker also took a single earring from a pair, leaving behind the other one to remind the victim of what was taken. Alavezos recounted the fateful night of September 11, 1975, when the Ransacker tried to kidnap Beth Snelling and killed her father, Claude. My mind jumped ahead of the presentation. How did we know it was in fact the Ransacker who kidnapped Beth and killed Claude Snelling? As if reading my mind, Alavezos stated, "A little over a week before the Snelling murder, the Ransacker stole a Miroku handgun during a burglary. The gun owner had gone to target practice and fired multiple rounds from the pistol into a tree stump. Investigators later recovered the bullets from the stump and compared them to the one removed from Snelling, and it was a perfect match."

I nearly jumped out of my chair when I heard Miroku. I knew it was an uncommon pistol. I had just read in the Maggiore investigative file that the bullet removed from Brian's body had been analyzed by the Crime Lab's ballistics expert. From his examinations of the striations and markings on the bullet, he speculated that it had been fired from either a Colt or Miroku pistol. Without DNA evidence connecting DeAngelo to the Maggiore murders, I needed every piece of circumstantial evidence I could find.

Alavezos explained that during a sting operation set up by the Visalia PD, Officer Bill McGowen encountered the Ransacker and cornered him in a backyard by firing a round into the ground. The fugitive pleaded in a high-pitched, effeminate voice, "Please don't shoot me." The Ransacker then turned around, pulled out a handgun with his left hand, and shot at McGowen. The bullet struck the officer's flashlight and knocked him to the ground, allowing the Ransacker to escape. Again, I was reminded that several of the EAR's rape victims had described him speaking in a high-pitched voice when under stress, and one of the EAR's early victims saw him wearing a utility belt with a gun in the holster on the lefthand side. DeAngelo was lefthanded, just like the Ransacker.

The story got even more interesting. "When the responding officers asked McGowen what the Ransacker looked like, he said that the shadowy figure they had been chasing looked familiar. While he could not put a name on the face, he had seen him before. . . . Joseph DeAngelo was a sergeant at the Exeter Police Department, a few miles away from Visalia. From time to time, he had assisted in the search for the Visalia Ransacker. And he was the Ransacker," Alavezos concluded with a dramatic tone to his voice.

I blurted out, "Wow! That's like something out of a true-crime movie."

Alavezos ended his presentation by projecting a sketch of the Ransacker next to a picture of DeAngelo from a wedding. The round baby face, chubby cheeks, and receding hairline looked eerily similar. At the time of Snelling's murder, the death penalty in California had been ruled unconstitutional by the courts. Therefore, Tulare County could not file a special circumstance murder and seek the death penalty in its case. By the time that Brian and Katie Maggiore were murdered in February 1978, the death penalty had been reinstituted in California.

After Ward and Alavezos set off on their long drive back home, we sat around the conference table to discuss the case. DA Schubert shook her head and expressed doubt as to whether DeAngelo was in fact the Ransacker. Amy and I harbored concerns regarding the admissibility of certain evidence.

Amy mentioned, "Officer McGowen passed away, and his account of that night would be hearsay."

"Well maybe we can get it into evidence as an excited utterance," I offered, referring to a statement made by a witness during or immediately after a shocking event, making it potentially admissible as evidence. Litigation represents the ultimate game of chess, requiring us to always think several moves ahead.

I found the possibility compelling. When DeAngelo started working at Exeter PD, the Ransacker series started; and when he left Exeter after the McGowen shooting, the Ransacker series suddenly stopped. When

DeAngelo started working at Auburn PD, the EAR series started; when the police released the "Robin Williams sketch" to the media after the Maggiore murders, the EAR never returned to Sacramento. The Ransacker used a Miroku handgun to murder Snelling; the Miroku was one of two possible types of handguns used to kill the Maggiores.

Although the sexual proclivities of the Ransacker did not match that of the EAR, predators do evolve over time, ratcheting up their depravity with each new crime to trigger the desired stimulation. I smiled as I thought of Sergeant Kenny Clark's rant earlier in my office. He was right, as it turned out. But ultimately, the decision to file the charges and allow the Snelling murder charges to join our case was not mine to make.

— — —

As line prosecutors, who handle and prosecute cases rather than supervise the administrative duties, we deal with the facts and the law. However, the elected district attorneys are responsible for navigating complicated relationships and a minefield of egos and political pitfalls. Watching from afar, I was glad to stay away from the ugly mess above me as I focused on the more simple mission of bringing justice to the victims. I preferred the strategy of litigation, figuring out what evidence to admit, how to weave a compelling story, and staying several moves ahead of my opponent. *Why would anyone want the job of DA?* I thought to myself.

Prosecuting cold cases creates certain challenges. Many questioned how much longer DeAngelo, now seventy-two, would live. Our survivors and witnesses ranged in age from their early fifties to their nineties. With the most incidents but no DNA in any of our cases, Sacramento needed more than any jurisdiction to have all the charges from all the counties tried at the same time and in the same courtroom. Neither DeAngelo nor many of the victims would live to see a second trial. Everyone felt we only had one chance to prosecute the Golden State Killer.

Possession is nine-tenths of the law. DeAngelo sat securely in the Sacramento County Jail thanks to the order that I'd written and Judge Steve White had signed, which prohibited the removal of DeAngelo from

Sacramento. We held all the leverage. But DA Schubert did not want to act unilaterally on this issue, and that was the right call. With Santa Barbara, Ventura, and Sacramento Counties united in our position, the case would never be tried in Orange County. Instead, the People vs. the Golden State Killer remained where it always belonged: Sacramento. But now, they had to break the news to Orange County DA Tony Rackauckas.

To provide him with some political cover, the other elected DAs decided to hold a press conference in Orange County to announce that the GSK case would be tried in Sacramento. Rackauckas would lead the press event, allowing him to frame the narrative while the other DAs lavished praise on him. The event would be carefully choreographed, with Rackauckas standing at center stage, framed by the flags of the United States and California and flanked by DAs from throughout the state. The press conference started in the late morning of August 21, 2018. In a coordinated plan, I walked over to the Sacramento Superior Court a couple of hours before it began and filed a First Amended Criminal Complaint, adding all the murders in Southern California to the killings of Brian and Katie Maggiore. But Count One of the new complaint charged Joseph DeAngelo with the murder of Claude Snelling. His daughter, Beth, had waited forty-seven years, eleven months, and twenty-one days to know the face and name of her father's killer. On this day, she would finally move a step closer to justice. Following up on the research I had done on using the charge of aggravated kidnapping for robbery, we also filed nine additional charges from Sacramento and four from Contra Costa County related to the rapes.

OC DA Tony Rackauckas kicked off the press conference. "This human predator, DeAngelo, took a path through all of these counties in our state, and wherever he went, he left terror in his path. He committed vicious and violent crimes throughout all of these jurisdictions. We've been meeting and working together to work on the management of this case, to determine the best place to conduct the case and how best to handle it. We've been, as you know, our team has been working for decades to try and capture this person. And this individual created such a terror throughout the state . . . Each of these DAs has taken into account various things to determine how and where to handle this trial: the location and the complexity, the length of the evidence associated with the charges, where the offenses occurred, the rights of the defendant and the People, and the inconvenience and hardship to the various victims and witnesses that are likely to appear in the case. All these things are factored in. So as a group, we've determined that the trial should take place in Sacramento," he declared.

Ventura County District Attorney Greg Totten then spoke, emphasizing the theme of unity. "The complaint filed today in Sacramento Superior Court against Joseph James DeAngelo reflects the sheer criminal breadth, geographical scope, and the generational impact of this very significant case. It is a case that began more than four decades ago and profoundly altered the lives of countless individuals across multiple jurisdictions from Southern to Northern California. Bottom line, we are united, we are together, and we are going forward with an ideal determination to have a successful result in this case."

Santa Barbara DA Joyce Dudley was next to state her perspective on the proceedings. "We know criminal justice does not feel just to those who have waited decades for justice. We also know that we can never give those victims and those victims' loved ones those decades back. And we know that because we've always known that 'Justice delayed is justice denied.' Therefore, we concluded that more than anything else, the still suffering victims and their loved ones needed this injustice to end. Step one was clearly the arrest. Step two has to be taking this case to trial as soon as possible in Sacramento, where we can combine all of our cases and where the defendant now resides. We now have an opportunity to have a single comprehensive, speedy trial for all the victims, and that was an opportunity that none of the district attorneys wanted to pass up."

Keenly aware of the need for diplomacy, Dudley heaped praise on the OC DA. "A special thank you to Tony Rackauckas. Tony has had great insight into our criminal-justice system. He has done this for decades. He understands how victims feel; he understands how the loved ones of victims feel; and he wants very much justice for all."

Tulare County DA Tim Ward spoke next about the impact of this day for the Snelling family. "There is one count in the amended complaint filed this morning that reflects crimes occurring in Tulare County, and I believe it is actually Count One of the complaint. It correlates to the murder that occurred in the City of Visalia in the fall of 1975. And I stand here today representing a family that was impacted by tragedy." He continued with the message of unity, adding, "I, along with the Visalia police chief, agree and fully support the consolidation of this case and the prosecution going forward in Sacramento. We have full faith and confidence in not only DA Schubert, but also faith in the men and women of that office, that they will spearhead what should be and will be a successful prosecution and obtain justice for victims across the state."

As with the other speakers, he then lauded praised on the host. "Last but certainly not least, I want to thank Tony Rackauckas and the men and women of Orange County. Sir, I've been humbled and will continue to be forever in your gratitude for what you and your amazing team of professionals and experts have brought to the table. We are here today in Orange County in no small part because of what you have done and provided."

A former judge, recently appointed Contra Costa County District Attorney Diana Becton had yet to develop some of the relationships that the other DAs on stage had fostered. She kept her remarks simple and direct. "I can announce this morning that the Contra Costa District Attorney's Office is able to charge four separate cases against Joseph DeAngelo for the crimes in our county. For decades, he invaded and devastated communities across California. We thank District Attorney Schubert for her role in handling all of these charges statewide, which will promote efficiency of our resources, and hopefully swifter justice for all of our victims. My office will remain in close contact with DA Schubert's office as we work together to prosecute these cases." Regardless of the criticism she faced from inside or outside the office regarding her leadership abilities, Schubert deserved tremendous credit as a major force behind the capture of the Golden State Killer. She approved the necessary resources and, like many of the other members of the law-enforcement family, she refused to give up on that pursuit of justice.

As I sat in Sacramento watching the press conference being livestreamed, I listened carefully as DA Schubert took her turn at the podium. She, too, continued with the theme of unity. "I am honored and humbled, and I'm certainly proud to stand up here with my colleagues today. We stand united, we stand together, as I have often called our team, 'Team Justice.' This morning around ten o'clock, in Sacramento Superior Court, my office filed an amended felony complaint alleging all crimes for all counties, in one felony complaint: twenty-six counts; thirteen murders, twelve of which carry special circumstance allegations; and thirteen charges of what we call kidnapping for robbery, which at the time in the seventies was what we called a life term, which allows us the opportunity to now file those charges."

Sticking to the script, she praised her colleague from Orange County. "I also want to thank Mr. Rackauckas, because for those who don't know, he has a nationally recognized DNA Unit that is second-to-none. They have the knowledge and expertise to do one thing—finding the truth through the use of forensic DNA evidence. There is no doubt that this unit and his prosecutors and his investigators and all those folks together will continue their role in this prosecution." She concluded, "It is very fitting that this journey for justice ends in Sacramento. I'm proud to be standing with my colleagues and I look forward to ending this journey for justice."

— — — — —

Fall/Winter 2018

How do you eat an elephant? There were so many victims, so many witnesses, and so much evidence to go through. Whenever I stopped for a moment to reflect on the magnitude of the case, my breathing became shallow, my heart rate increased, and my mind raced. The cases, the names, the places—they all seemed to blur together. Where do we start? How do we organize a case with decades of investigation poured into it? Feeling and acknowledging that sense of panic, I simply closed my eyes, took a deep breath and reminded myself: one bite at a time.

I devised an organizational system: Each county remained responsible for gathering their own police reports, photos, and videos and assigned unique identifiers to each piece of evidence. The designated main prosecutor for each of those counties would then send the materials directly to me. As the lead prosecutor, I would be responsible for logging the materials into Sacramento's case-management system before redistributing them to all the other counties and to the defense attorneys. As the hub for all the information, I would read, see, and hear every piece of evidence. The survivors and main witnesses needed to be reinterviewed, their memories refreshed, and their accounts verified; and all the corroborating evidence needed to be located and catalogued. We tasked one set of investigators with the reinterviewing. A second group retraced DeAngelo's life, and the final group worked on the Maggiore murders and any other investigation we needed.

When our ancestors navigated across vast expanses of ocean or through mountain passes or sweeping savannahs, we always looked to the stars and used true north to guide us. For prosecutors, our victims represent our compass guiding us to the green plains of paradise where justice stands waiting. Everything starts and ends with them. We needed a great investigator to make contact with all of our victims.

For nearly two decades, Kevin Papineau worked as a detective for the Elk Grove Police Department. Only fifteen miles south of downtown Sacramento, it started as a small farming and ranching town before becoming the second largest city in the region. I first met Detective Papineau about a decade earlier when he solved a child-molestation case by tracking down and locating the victim. The National Center for Missing & Exploited Children (NCMEC) forwarded him videos and pictures of what appeared to be a ten-to-twelve-year-old girl being assaulted. Her abuser videotaped the attack and posted pictures and videos online for other pedophiles to view. NCMEC contacted Elk Grove Police because in one of the photos, the city's logo was visible on a garbage can in the yard of an unidentified house.

Papineau realized that the molester posted the pictures intermittently, mostly on weekends. He concluded that the child lived primarily somewhere else and saw the abuser only periodically, perhaps in connection with visitation rights. He expanded the geographical scope of his search. In one of the photographs, the victim wore a Girl Scout uniform. Detective Papineau cropped a picture of her face and contacted all the Girl Scout groups he could locate online within a two-hour radius of Elk Grove. A troop leader contacted him, identifying the girl. Fearing that her biological father was molesting her during his visitation periods with her, Papineau zeroed in on the suspect. Examining the father's credit and property history, the detective identified several properties and visited them. He eventually found the exact yard where the photo of the garbage can was taken. I was assigned to prosecute this sexual predator, and he was given a life sentence in federal prison. After receiving extensive counseling, the victim eventually married and started a family of her own.

Papineau was tall, thin, and clean-cut, like a detective in a 1950s television show. Meticulous, calm, and unrelenting, Papineau also led the investigation of the Moses Valdez homicide case, which I tried just a few months before DeAngelo's arrest. After the completion of that trial, he left the Elk Grove PD to join our office as an investigator, and I asked that he assist us on the GSK case. Sergeant Michelle Hendricks, who spoke to DeAngelo in the interrogation room, would partner with Papineau to reinterview all the victims from the charged Sacramento and Contra Costa cases.

Settling into the GSK case, Amy Holliday and I began the process of meeting with the survivors. We met with Trish privately in our office. She seemed physically small and frail. After punching Trish in the face, DeAngelo had moved her to the side of the house. She looked a little caught off guard when we told her that her case could be charged as an aggravated kidnapping. Sitting in the chair, her shoulders slouched and her hands shook from the weight of forty years of anguish. I sensed a deep sense of apprehension and uneasiness from Trish as she tried to sort through her emotions. She told us she'd suffered a nervous breakdown after DeAngelo's arrest. Amy's eyes began to well up as we listened to Trish talk in a quiet voice about her struggles. It was in these moments that we realized just how much we cared not only about obtaining justice for the victims and survivors, but also about their emotional and psychological well-being.

In between our meetings with the survivors, Noemi came by and told us that someone was here to see us. As we stepped into the lobby, retired Undersheriff Carol Daly greeted us with a warm smile. After the third attack, Carol was named one of the lead detectives on the East Area Rapist case. She pursued the EAR for so long—she retired in 2005—and was never able to leave the victims behind. Time etches its marks on all our faces, but pain and sorrow leave even deeper marks upon our souls. The gun-toting detective who rose to become the first woman undersheriff in Sacramento County history was now a loving and gentle grandmother who doted on her family. But some things never change. Carol still exuded the timeless class she had exhibited as Detective Carol Daly. Her gentle eyes beamed brightly. She wanted to talk to us about the case. "It's been a long time coming. I never forgot those victims," she said quietly, holding back tears. "Those victims never left me." Carol had absorbed so much sin and pain. The responsibility of catching the East Area Rapist weighed upon her, as the lead detective on the case, for so many years. She also carried the guilt of not being able to catch him. Even though his arrest lifted that burden, it still left its mark.

Looking down at the ground, she added sheepishly, "I don't remember everything I did in the case. I hope we did everything the right way." We reassured her that our research had shown that her investigation, especially the way in which she had treated the victims with empathy, represented the best of law enforcement. Worried that she would misstate or misremember something, she asked for a copy of all her police reports so she could study and prepare for her testimony. The consummate professional, Carol was determined to see this through to the very end.

— — —

Traveling east from Sacramento, the roads ascend into the clouds as they hug the mountainside dotted with pine trees. As summer grew into fall and the leaves turned yellow and red, my family headed east up to Apple Hill. I looked forward to glasses of apple cider and slices of sweet apple pie wrapped in buttery dough that melted in your mouth. It was an annual tradition that marked the start of the holiday season for us. We usually made the drive on the first Monday in October, a state holiday in California. In between the hot dogs and dessert, my cell phone began to buzz. I snuck a peek as my wife gave me yet another death stare. And again, it was Detective Rob Peters. Trying to be sly but utterly failing at it, I texted Peters that I would call him back.

He quickly responded, "It can wait until Tuesday." I hated text messages like that as curiosity would burn a hole in me the rest of the day, but I needed to turn my attention back to my family and that apple pie sitting on the table.

Sergeant Kenny Clark and Detective Rob Peters led the team of investigators focused on the Maggiore murders and whatever else the prosecution needed. They both showed up right at 8 a.m. at my office the next morning. Wearing his characteristic bowtie and thick, black-rimmed glasses, Peters stood in the doorway grinning sheepishly. I knew something was up.

Sergeant Clark was looking at the ground, rocking back and forth. "Umm, uhh . . ."

"Okay Kenny, what the hell is going on now? I got Rob calling me on my day off," I questioned, my blood pressure beginning to rise.

"Day off? I thought you're always working," Peters said sarcastically, still grinning. I was in no mood to joke this early in the morning and sensed bad news coming my way.

"The bullet recovered from Brian Maggiore that you asked us to find . . ." Kenny began.

"Yes, I want it reexamined using today's technology. Maybe we can prove definitively that the same gun killed both Snelling and Maggiore," I said.

"Well, there's a problem," Kenny continued. "The bullet was examined decades ago and so, well, we can't find it."

My jaw dropped. "What the fuck? Of all the fucking murder cases, how the hell did we lose the bullet from that case? First, we threw away all the DNA evidence from the East Area Rapist's assaults after the statute of limitations ran out. Then we couldn't track down the pretied shoelaces found next to Maggiore's body. And now, we lost the goddamn bullet?"

Peters replied, "We looked everywhere at the Sheriff's property warehouse, where all the EAR evidence was stored. It's not there. We've looked for it under all the other case numbers as well, thinking it had been mislabeled. But nothing."

I felt disbelief mixed with anger and frustration. Steam was about to blow out of my ears. But I looked over at the picture of the Maggiores on my wall, closed my eyes, and took a deep breath. Suddenly, a strange sense of calm came over me, as if Brian and Katie themselves had reassured me that we would find it.

"It must be at the Crime Lab," Kenny Clark suggested.

"You're right, Kenny. This case is over forty years old," I admitted. "Naturally, we're going to lose and misplace things. It's probably at the lab, in a bag inside a box sitting in some corner. We've got the best Crime Lab in the world. Hell, they worked overtime to confirm DeAngelo's DNA. If it's at the lab, they will find it." The science of firearm ballistics can make or break a case. When a bullet is fired from a handgun, its rotation as it is propelled through the barrel and exits the gun leaves distinct markings and striations on the projectile. Bullets can thus be compared with each other to see if they have similar markings, indicating they were fired from the same pistol. Additionally, a recovered projectile can be compared with a bullet test-fired from a gun. To make any evaluation, we first needed to find the bullet.

— — —

Fear can cripple your spirit, and it can motivate you to move mountains. But no one can truly escape their fears until they face them. Every great trial lawyer feels the fear of losing in the pit of their belly as they step into the arena to argue their case. When fear is selfishly focused on your own ego and personal interest, it lacks the power to inspire and motivate. By turning the focus outward, however, it can change the emotion entirely—the fear of letting someone else down, of failing to accomplish a greater good, of righting a wrong. Fear can then transform and infuse your actions with undeniable purpose.

To the world, Joseph James DeAngelo was the Golden State Killer. But to Sacramentans, he will always be known as the East Area Rapist, the masked bogeyman who raped fifty women and murdered a young couple in Rancho Cordova. Conducting the trial in Sacramento meant that Brian and Katie Maggiore's murder would be front and center. Regardless of the difficulties and challenges, justice would be theirs, one way or another. Failure was not an option. I had never lost a homicide case, and I certainly would not lose this one. Nevertheless, I felt the full weight and measure of that responsibility on my shoulders.

DeAngelo's own words provided the most compelling evidence that he had killed the Maggiores. The guttural whispers he spewed during breaks in the interrogation, as he sat alone in the room, represented the linchpin of my case. After Sergeant Kenny Clark and others showed him photos of the Maggiores and the Smiths and asked if he had killed them, he denied it at first, but left to himself, he began to confess. "I did all that. All these years, I was too weak. I was too weak, to stand up to [Jerry]. I don't remember any of it. . . . I did all that. . . . I didn't have the strength to push him out. He made me. He went with me. It was like, in my head, I mean, he's a part of me. I didn't want to do those things. I pushed Jerry out and had a happy life. I did all those things. I've destroyed all their lives . . . I raped. So now I gotta pay the price."

Although DeAngelo's own words incriminated him, they also created a conundrum. He seemed to be claiming that he had multiple personalities within him. Dissociative identity disorder, also known as multiple personality disorder, is a psychological condition that first captured the imagination of forensic psychologists, defense attorneys, and even Hollywood thanks to *Sybil*, Flora Rheta Schreiber's 1973 book about the treatment of Shirley Ardell Mason, a.k.a. Sybil Dorsett, for multiple personality disorder by her psychoanalyst, Cornelia B. Wilbur. In the book, Wilbur described Dorsett's various personalities or "alters," which included a sophisticated young French girl named Victoria, a talented musician named Vanessa, a carpenter named Mike, and a baby named Ruthie. Although Mason later recanted her story, saying, "I do not really have any multiple personalities. . . . I have been lying in my pretense of them." Nevertheless, the book became a bestseller and spawned an eponymous television movie starring Sally Field.

In fall 2018, Orange County prosecutor Deborah Lloyd and I regularly discussed DeAngelo's mental state. We both expected the defense to mount some sort of defense around this. "We need to hire an expert, like, yesterday," she suggested to me over the phone.

"Who are you thinking of, Debbie?" I asked.

"Kris Mohandie, of course. He's crazy expensive but he's one the best around," Debbie responded immediately.

Dr. Kris Mohandie's salt-and-pepper gray hair, eternally tan skin, and sharply tailored suits reminded me of the actor George Hamilton. But he was no shallow expert witness. When it came to forensic psychology, his knowledge and stellar reputation warranted his high fees. Hiring an expert witness in this area would accomplish several goals: provide a professional analysis of the defendant's true mental state, postulate possible defenses, give advice on strategies to counter the opponent's claims, and prevent said expert from being hired by the other side.

I agreed with Debbie. "I don't like shrinks, but I like him, and the jurors love him too. Let's hire Mohandie and send him DeAngelo's interview."

— — —

"I have good news and bad news. Which one do you want to hear first?" Sergeant Clark asked me one early December morning.

Shaking my head, I requested, "Give me the bad news first, Kenny."

"Why do people always want the bad news first?" Detective Peters jumped in.

I reflected on it for a moment, then offered, "It's evolutionary, Rob. If you are trekking through the Himalayas and someone comes up to you and says, 'I got good and bad news. Which one do you want first?' You're going to say, 'Give me the bad news first, in case it's about an avalanche or a storm bearing down on me.' So just give me the fucking bad news."

"The *good* news is that the Crime Lab found the bullets recovered from both Brian and Katie Maggiore," Sergeant Clark reported. I took a deep breath to prepare myself for the worst. "The bad news is that the bullets are in such bad condition that it's really difficult for the criminalist to definitely conclude, or exclude, that it was fired from a Miroku."

I breathed a sigh of relief that we were no worse off than we were before. "Well, that makes his confession all the more important."

With his usual grin, Rob remarked, "You mean that 'Jerry made me do it' routine?"

"We hired the best expert in the business to debunk that defense. Besides, DeAngelo tried the same thing back in 1979 when he got arrested for petty theft," I said.

The circumstances surrounding what precipitated the Maggiore murders were shrouded in the darkness of that night, lost to time. Only Joseph DeAngelo could say for sure. Some hypothesized that the violence resulted from a chance encounter when Brian confronted a man peeping through a window, as described by the jogger witness Benny Pickett. Just like Claude Snelling's murder, DeAngelo needed to escape. On the other hand, the murders in Southern California were sexually motivated crimes steeped in sadism. In all the cases, whether in Visalia, Sacramento, or Southern California, he killed to eliminate witnesses that could identify or stop him.

— — —

Looking at my phone, I saw it was Orange County prosecutor Deborah Lloyd calling me. I had told her about the recent reexamination of the bullets from the Maggiore murders.

Debbie knew her way inside a courtroom, having litigated a long list of homicide cases. For years, we had both battled expert witnesses paid to push their client's agenda, even if it meant trading in the truth. We quickly struck up a friendship and deep respect for the years of toil we each spent fighting for justice. She is a relentless fighter for her victims and an unapologetic defender of her office. If I were the DA, I would want someone in my corner like Debbie.

She never came right out and said it, but I could read between the lines. From a proof perspective, her cases were rock solid. The Orange County murders of the Harringtons, Manuela Witthuhn, and Janelle Cruz involved tremendous violence. DeAngelo bludgeoned them to death and sexually assaulted the female victims. DNA definitively connected him to each of those crimes, making them unquestionably strong cases. The Maggiore murders, on the other hand, with a lack of DNA evidence, was a real challenge. There was not a doubt in my mind that the EAR murdered Brian and Katie. I just needed to prove it, and DeAngelo's confession gave me that chance. However, a defense of insanity, even made up, was nonetheless a defense. I could sense that Debbie was worried that while his statement was absolutely necessary to prove my case, it could also create a problem in hers. Working together, we focused on undermining any insanity defense based on dissociative identity disorder.

Dr. Mohandie saw through the fake insanity defense, especially with DeAngelo's admitted history of malingering, or pretending to be ill. According to our expert, dissociative identity disorder was an extremely rare condition, and people suffering from it usually displayed specific symptoms: amnesia or gaps in memory regarding daily activities and personal information; significant inability to function in social situations, at work, or at home; and other mental health symptoms such as anxiety, delusions, depression, substance use, and suicidal ideations.

A third team of investigators was assigned to build a profile of DeAngelo by interviewing his family, friends, neighbors, and former coworkers. Sharon Huddle filed for divorce from DeAngelo in August 1993, citing irreconcilable differences, and requested physical custody of the children. However, she did not finalize the divorce until after his arrest in 2018. He continued to live at the Citrus Heights address and worked at the Save Mart supermarket as a mechanic. In November 2010, DeAngelo retired but later returned to work part-time.

Grant Gorman grew up in Citrus Heights, and his family home shared a fence with DeAngelo. He remembered DeAngelo had threatened to kill their family dog for barking too loudly, leaving a message on their answering machine, "Shut that dog up, or I will bring a load of death to your home." Gorman also recalled DeAngelo talking to himself in the backyard, cursing at himself and yelling about death and killing. The neighborhood kids referred to him as the angry old man. In fact, every person who dealt with DeAngelo on a personal basis gave fairly consistent statements that undermined any insanity defense, especially one based on dissociative identity disorder. They never observed or heard DeAngelo complain about amnesia or gaps in his memory. No medical record or witness account showed any experience with depression, anxiety, or suicidal ideation. For people suffering from this condition, the effects are tremendously debilitating and result in patients who cannot hold a job or interact normally with others. Yet DeAngelo held multiple jobs for years, including as a police officer.

First and foremost, we strongly believed that his "Jerry" routine reflected nothing more than a poor attempt at malingering. He demonstrated a history of doing so. He wanted to be a modern-day Sybil. As Debbie and I regularly discussed a potential insanity defense, we always returned to the M'Naghten Rule. In California, it considers someone legally insane if they either did not understand the nature of their criminal act or did not understand that what they were doing was morally wrong.

"Debbie, that's where DeAngelo is screwed. Even if you believe for a moment that he actually has dissociative identity disorder and isn't faking, he can't get pass M'Naghten," I told her over the phone on my drive home.

"Yes, he knew right from wrong, and he knew that what he was doing was wrong," Debbie emphasized further.

"DeAngelo thought he was being clever in the interrogation room by using the split personality defense, but he didn't know the law," I pointed out. Without question, DeAngelo knew his actions were morally wrong. Assuming for a moment that Jerry existed as an "alter" inside the GSK, Joseph DeAngelo's own words showed his true mental state. While mumbling, he admitted, "He's evil [unintelligible] self. It's so shameful [unintelligible] I did all that. All these years, I was too weak. I was too weak to stand up to him. I don't remember any of it." DeAngelo acknowledged that Jerry was evil and what he did was shameful. He talked about pushing Jerry out, demonstrating that he was aware of his moral corruption.

He later admitted he knew he had to "pay the price" for his evil acts. His own words defeated any such possible defense. Confident in our ability to admit his confession and fend off any fake mental defenses, we turned our attention to the decision of whether to seek death.

10
The Decision

Spring 2019

The death penalty evokes strong emotions and controversy on both sides of the conversation. Many believe it to be an inhumane and barbaric practice of the past, while others object on religious grounds. Among its supporters, some feel it deters heinous crimes, and many believe that certain crimes shock the human conscious to such a degree that it warrants death. Losing a loved one is devastating enough, but having that life cut short in a cruel and vicious way might compel us to invoke the highest form of punishment the law allows.

I believe that the most serious crimes deserve the most serious punishment. I share the concerns of many regarding the problematic history of the death penalty, especially in certain parts of the country and as it relates to people of color. However, I do believe that the extreme crimes committed by the likes of Oklahoma City bomber Timothy McVeigh and serial killer Ted Bundy warrant the imposition of death. In California, Penal Code section 190.2 sets forth the factual situation or "special circumstances" under which prosecutors can seek the death penalty or life without the possibility of parole. To receive the death penalty, a defendant must have committed first-degree murder under at least one of twenty-two special circumstances, including during the commission of rape, sodomy, kidnapping, residential burglary, robbery, or the commission of multiple murders.

A death-penalty case is separated into two phases, guilt and penalty. During the guilt phase, prosecutors must obtain a guilty verdict from a jury for first-degree murder with an affirmative finding that the defendant committed the act under one of the twenty-two special circumstances. Next, Penal Code section 190.3 requires the same jury to consider certain "aggravating and mitigating factors," factors A–K, that determine the nature and circumstances of the present offense, any prior violent felony conviction, and the defendant's age, character, background, history, and mental and physical condition.

Seeking death is a solemn decision, the gravity of which requires the most thorough investigation and analysis and the utmost thoughtful balancing of the scales of justice. We combed through DeAngelo's entire existence, from the moment of his birth through his childhood, teenage years, military service, work, and family life. I reexamined every piece of evidence, reinterviewed every witness, and uncovered new evidence in the Maggiore murders. We left no stone unturned; but we had one more place to go and one more thing to do.

For me, it always started and ended with Brian and Katie Maggiore. They grew up in the Central Valley, the breadbasket of the Golden State, among the rolling farmlands and cattle ranches just outside Fresno. Only a year apart in age, Brian and Katie grew up in Fresno and went to different high schools only a few miles away from each other. They married in July 1976 and looked forward to starting a family. After Brian joined the US Air Force, the couple moved to Alaska, where Brian was stationed, then to Rancho Cordova when he was reassigned to Mather Air Force Base. They had their whole life before them. We needed to go see their family. No decision on seeking death could be complete without consideration of those who loved the victims and felt their loss most deeply. The families' opinion on seeking death heavily factored into my recommendation.

Amy Holliday, Victim Advocate Mailyn Chuong, and I drove down to Fresno to meet with their families. Along with my notepad, I brought a wedding photograph of them with me. I'm not sure why, but it just felt like I needed to keep them close. I tossed and turned and hardly slept the night before the trip. When I did slip into my dreams, I saw Brian and

Katie standing on a dark street with their dog. They stood in the shadows, staring at me in silence. Then the scene flashed to some blue pretied shoelaces, the same kind the EAR had carried with him to crime scenes, lying on the wet grass next to Brian. I woke up and looked at my phone to check the time. I love the time between 3:00 and 4:00 a.m., which is sometimes called "the hour of the wolf." Everything is quiet. The streets are empty. People are in bed, and even the birds are asleep. It feels like the world stops spinning and remains completely still. That night, I just stared at the ceiling.

On the drive down, Amy, Mailyn, and I talked about Brian and Katie as long stretches of land flashed by the car window. Those final moments as they ran for their lives must have been horrifying. One minute, they were enjoying a leisurely walk; the next minute, their hearts were literally pounding out of their chest as they sprinted away from death. For Katie, those last few seconds were soaked in terror as she saw her husband gunned down. She ran frantically, only to come upon a locked gate. Trapped and alone with the monster, Katie could not escape death that night. The pain of being told that your child is dead never leaves. Never. I can only imagine what their parents went through that day in early February 1978.

We pulled up to a one-story house in a quiet neighborhood just outside Fresno to see Katie's brothers. As we walked up to the door, I could hear a small dog yelping and barking. "Hi, I'm Ken. Please come in." Ken Smith, a big man with white hair, a neatly trimmed handlebar mustache, and kind, sad eyes, came out and shook my hand.

Being Asian, I always have the natural instinct to remove my shoes before going into someone's house, but I noticed that Ken walked around his house with his shoes on. So I kept mine on. Stepping into the living room, I was greeted by Keith, Katie's youngest brother. He stood at least six-foot-three, and his bearlike hand reached out to shake mine. A police officer who lived up in the Pacific Northwest, he had come back home for this meeting. We all sat down at the kitchen table as the little dog that had greeted us with its bark hobbled around. Ken told us the dog was blind but still very protective of its home. It walked by and brushed up against my leg before falling asleep in the corner.

Ken had retired as a prison guard at Corcoran State Prison, having worked more than two decades in law enforcement, while Keith was looking forward to his impending retirement. Both men had dealt with crime and criminals all their lives, and they talked with the bluntness of cops, never mincing or wasting a single word. Their tough exteriors were hardened by decades of work, but as soon as they started talking about their big sister, their hands began to tremble and their voices quavered. They loved and missed Katie.

A couple of years younger than his sister, Ken was a junior in high school looking forward to the upcoming baseball season when Katie was murdered. Keith, the youngest sibling, was ten years old—half Katie's age—and adored his sister. The morning after Brian and Katie's death, air force officers arrived at their father's work and told him about the murder. He couldn't believe that his only daughter had been killed. Stunned and shocked, Katie's father simply shut down. Ken recalled, "After my sister's murder, my father stopped celebrating birthdays, Christmas, and any anniversaries or holidays. My dad used to love fishing and hunting, but that all ended too. He stopped living." Losing his daughter made him lose all joy in life.

"How did your mom react to Katie's death?" Amy asked both men.

Keith responded, "My parents both passed away several years ago. While my dad never wanted to talk about Katie's death, my mom was the complete opposite. She would tell everyone about it. She would stop random strangers at the grocery story to tell them about Katie's murder. After a while, I didn't even want to go shopping with her anymore. But it was her way of coping." As children living at home, they saw the devasting effect of her death on their parents, who died never knowing who had killed their only daughter. "Katie had just turned twenty a few days before she died," Ken said, his voice trailing off. Forty years had passed, but it was obvious that the pain of her death still cut deeply.

There's never a good time to talk to people about seeking the death penalty for their loved one's case. But that was the reason we had come. "The defendant is eligible for the death penalty. How would you feel if we sought the death penalty against Brian and Katie's murderer?" I asked.

"My kids never got the chance to meet their aunt and uncle," Ken replied. "Brian and Katie had their whole lives in front of them, and he took that away from them. He deserves the death penalty."

"I agree," Keith added. "He already got to live forty years of his life as a free man after killing them. He doesn't deserve to live."

Society often views those in law enforcement as tough, jaded, and emotionally closed off. But we sat with two grown men fully in touch with their emotions, who broke down in tears as they discussed the heart-wrenching impact of their sister's death on them, their parents, and the rest of their family. There was not a single dry eye at that kitchen table.

I explained that we would take their wishes into consideration as we made our final decision on whether we would pursue the death penalty; and that we would let them know before announcing it publicly. With the volume of evidence involved in the case, I warned them that the preliminary hearing would likely not occur until later that year or early the following year. As officers, they both knew that a preliminary hearing was when prosecutors called witnesses and presented evidence before a judge to demonstrate that we had sufficient evidence to proceed to trial. It's a screening process required by law, but it also serves as a way for us to preserve evidence in case witnesses later pass away or become otherwise unavailable. I told them a homicide case was like a marathon and not a sprint and that they needed to pace themselves for the long road ahead.

After leaving Ken and Keith Smith, we drove a few miles over to see Brian Maggiore's mother, Loretta. When we rang the doorbell, Brian's nephew greeted us. A picture of the young couple on their wedding day sat on a small table in the hallway. Loretta turned to greet us when we entered the family room. She remained seated, not having the strength to stand. I immediately walked over, shook her hand, and introduced myself. Her hands trembled. We sat on the large couch across from her.

We spent the first ten minutes chatting with her about her lovely home, the neighborhood, and how Fresno had grown so much over the years. We avoided turning the discussion immediately to Brian and Katie. It's always important to ease into these sorts of conversations. Whether the murder happened yesterday or forty years ago, the pain remains.

"I think of Brian every single day," she began.

"It must have been hard to find out all those years ago that Brian and Katie had been murdered," I said gently.

"When I was told they had been murdered, I couldn't believe it," Loretta looked down as she told us. "We always wondered what he would have become." At the time of our meeting, Brian would have been sixty-one, had he gotten the chance to grow old.

"Well, Loretta, as you know, we are prosecuting Joseph DeAngelo for capital murder, which makes him eligible for the death penalty," I explained and started to lay out the charges. "We're also prosecuting him for several sexual assault incidents in Sacramento and Contra Costa, along with eleven other murders and rapes in Southern California."

Getting straight to the point, she asked, "Are you seeking the death penalty?"

"We want to get your thoughts and opinion," Amy replied. "How would you feel if we sought the death penalty against Brian's killer?"

"In my mind, I always thought my son's murderer was dead. I think he should get the death penalty," she told us without any hesitation. "He deserves it."

I reached out and placed my hand on hers. "Loretta, thank you for sharing your thoughts with us. It means a great deal to us."

I gave her my usual "marathon" speech, but with a twist. "This case was always going to be a marathon, but if we seek the death penalty, it will turn into an ultramarathon. It's going to take a long while to get across the finish line."

"It doesn't matter how long it takes. I'll be here with you to the end!" she told us with a confident smile. I could sense her steeliness and toughness.

We didn't talk much on the drive back to Sacramento. As the fields rolled by, I was still absorbing all the emotions from that morning. You open yourself up to be present, listen, and receive all that a victim's family pours out. They share with you all their emotions and all their pain. With great anguish, they reveal how their dreams were forever dashed in a single moment of fate. It was a lot to take in, and it left me feeling raw and vulnerable. Having met with Brian and Katie's family, I felt closer to them. We were now ready to give our recommendation regarding the death penalty.

— — —

I read through countless pages of reports regarding all the rapes in Northern California, the Maggiore murders, and the Santa Barbara crimes. The task of litigating those cases fell upon Sacramento. The murders of Robert Offerman and Debra Manning, along with the killing of Cheri Domingo and Greg Sanchez, reflected DeAngelo's escalating brutality. He left behind his semen and DNA when he sexually assaulted Domingo. Like the Orange County crimes, the evidence in that case seemed particularly strong. A prosecutor would cap off the case with the DNA collected from the crime scene, irrefutably incriminating the defendant.

The other Santa Barbara case presented a different, more difficult set of challenges. Offerman broke free from his bindings and charged at his assailant, causing DeAngelo to fire multiple rounds of his gun and kill the victim. He then walked over and executed Debra Manning. The Golden State Killer didn't leave his DNA at this crime scene, just his signature MO. That case required careful and proper placement within this serial killer's entire scheme, connecting it with all of the GSK's other crimes. I offered Amy Holliday an opportunity to choose which of the Santa Barbara cases she wanted to present at trial. She chose the Domingo-Sanchez murders. That meant I would handle the Offerman-Manning murders along with the attempted rape on Queen Anne Lane. I welcomed the challenge.

Before reaching trial, we had to resolve one key issue. Every district attorney's office creates its own set of protocols to decide whether or not it seeks the death penalty. For Sacramento, the trial attorney is responsible for applying the "A–K Factors" of Penal Code section 190.3 and then making a recommendation to the elected district attorney, the chief deputy (second-in-command), the assistant DA (third-in-command), and the homicide chief. At the discretion of the DA, the trial attorney conducts a formal presentation setting forth the facts of the case and an explanation for their recommendation. Considering the magnitude of this case, we had to present the death-eligible charges before all the participating jurisdictions' district attorneys and their leadership teams. For the presentation, Sacramento covered the Visalia Ransacker series, the Sacramento crimes, the rapes in Contra Costa, and all the rape-murders from Santa Barbara. Ventura County Chief Deputy Cheryl Temple was to present the murders of Lyman and Charlene Smith, while Deputy District Attorney Deborah Lloyd would cover the Orange County crimes.

We had worked tirelessly toward this point for the last year, gathering the evidence and exploring all facets of DeAngelo's life and those of the victims. I carefully laid out the order of the presentation: I would open by covering the Ransacker's crimes, then move on to the assaults in Sacramento and their culmination with the Maggiore murders. Next, I would describe how the EAR's reign of terror spread like a plague through Contra Costa County and Northern California, followed by an explanation of the evolution of this monster as he swept into Santa Barbara County with his thwarted attack on Queen Anne Lane and the murders of Offerman and Manning. Prosecutor Holliday would then cover the Domingo and Sanchez murders before going through the factors in aggravation justifying the death penalty. Finishing our portion of the presentation, I would then cover the factors in mitigation, including DeAngelo's background, and conclude with our formal recommendation before turning it over to Ventura and Orange Counties for their respective cases.

We scheduled the death-penalty presentation for 9:30 a.m. on April 10, 2019. We allotted the three counties time to make their case before the elected district attorneys, who would then retire to a private room and finalize their collective decision. Court was scheduled for 1:30 p.m. that afternoon. This gave us just enough time over the noon hour to inform the victims' families of our decision.

I spent days drafting my presentation, carving it down bit by bit, like a sculptor chipping away at the marble, removing the inessential pieces of stone to reveal the figure underneath. Every word had its place and purpose.

The master thespian Anthony Hopkins once explained his secret for great acting: preparation. He claimed he read his script out loud 250 times until it became ingrained. Once I completed the script, I created a

PowerPoint deck to supplement my words. I went to our large conference room and practiced it over and over again until it became second nature. Although I did not rehearse it 250 times, I did it enough times to nearly lose my voice. Since the meeting wasn't until the following Wednesday, I had the weekend to let my voice recover.

On the day of the death-penalty presentation, I was at my desk by 6 a.m.; the meeting was scheduled for 9:30. I completed a final check of the PowerPoint deck right as Contra Costa DA Diana Becton walked in with Chief Assistant Venus Johnson. Ventura DA Greg Totten came in with Chief Deputy Cheryl Temple. "Good morning, Thien. Today is going to be a great day!" she beamed and handed me a thumb drive containing her slides.

As usual, Orange County came with a large contingent of prosecutors, but many things had changed since Tony Rackauckas took the stage back in August to announce the joint prosecution in Sacramento. He had lost his reelection campaign in November to County Supervisor Todd Spitzer, ushering in a new regime. The newly elected DA Spitzer walked into the room with an electric energy around him. He had a big voice and personality, making his presence felt wherever he went. Upon taking over, he brought in Pat Dixon as his special advisor. Dixon worked for thirty-seven years at the Los Angeles County District Attorney's Office under Steve Cooley, rising to the rank of Assistant DA in charge of central operations, with supervisory authority over 400 attorneys handling vertical prosecutions. With silver hair and a Brooks Brothers suit, Dixon exuded the fashion sense of someone from Martha's Vineyard or Balboa Island. When he spoke, his words were never sharp; rather, they landed with round edges, seeking to create consensus.

Although Debbie had prepared the slides, a new prosecutor, Matt Murphy, was brought aboard to litigate the Orange County cases. Everyone called him Murph. He had tried over one hundred cases as a prosecutor, including the infamous Dating Game Killer, Rodney Alcala, in 2010. After Alcala's case had been reversed two previous times, Murph obtained a conviction with a death-penalty verdict. Tall, thin, and good-looking, Murph spent his free time surfing on the beaches of Southern California, Indonesia, and around the world. Regularly featured on *20/20* and other shows, Murph possessed the credentials of a true trial lawyer. In a phone call about a week before the presentation, Debbie told me that Murph was joining the team. Regardless of whom Orange County added or removed, I knew that Debbie was the heart and soul of their team, having worked the case from the beginning.

Santa Barbara DA Joyce Dudley entered with Kelly Duncan. Over the last several days, I'd made sure that my recitation of the facts of the Offerman-Manning case reflected Kelly's understanding of that incident. Despite working intensely on the MS-13 gang case, she always found time to take my calls and thanked us repeatedly for handling their cases.

DA Dudley represented the wild card. While not legally required, all the district attorneys with capital murder charges needed to unanimously agree to seek death. There could be no dissension. If three of the four offices sought death but one did not, the jurors would be left wondering how they were supposed to agree if even the prosecutors couldn't. We needed to proceed with unity. Dudley had repeatedly refused to seek the death penalty in many homicide cases in Santa Barbara and expressed great reluctance to do so even in this case. She knew her community did not generally support its use. Would she change her usual course of action and seek death against the Golden State Killer? As we took our seats, no one knew the answer to that question.

I kicked off the session. "The scope of Joseph DeAngelo's crime spree is simply staggering, encompassing thirteen known murders, fifty rapes, and over one hundred burglaries between 1974 and 1986. His monikers reflect the sweeping geographical impact of his crimes: the Visalia Ransacker, the East Area Rapist, the Original Night Stalker, and the Golden State Killer. Today, he faces thirteen counts of kidnapping for robbery and thirteen counts of murder with eighteen special-circumstance allegations. Eleven different counties have felt the brunt of his crimes, starting with Tulare."

I then proceeded to talk about the Ransacker. "From 1974 to 1975, Visalia experienced 120 residential burglaries, in which the homes were ransacked in distinctively similar ways. He laid women's clothing out on the bed and left his semen behind to mark his territory. Small items like a single earring, coins, and hand lotion were taken; makeshift alarms were used to detect if someone suddenly came home; and the suspect ate the homeowners' food and drank their beer. He was dubbed the Visalia Ransacker."

After describing in detail the attempted kidnapping of Beth Snelling and the murder of Claude, I spoke about the near capture of the Ransacker by Visalia Police Officer Bill McGowen. I noted that after his face was seen, DeAngelo left the Exeter Police Department, and the Ransacker burglaries suddenly stopped. "Just as the defendant moved to the Sacramento region, the East Area Rapist began his reign of terror here." In discussing the EAR series, I stated, "He was prolific; the fear was pervasive; and the community was paralyzed."

With black-and-white aerial photographs of Rancho Cordova in 1978, I went through in great detail the murder of Brian and Katie Maggiore. Everyone sat in complete silence as I said, "On that seemingly peaceful and quiet night, it is believed that Brian and Katie encountered DeAngelo, who was prowling the area looking for his next victim."

I described Katie's final moments. "While her husband was being gunned down, Katie fled down the east side of the house, screaming for help. Just as Katie reached the gate, the defendant caught up and shot her from behind to the top of the head. When the deputies arrived on scene, Katie tried to talk but was unable to do so. She died on the way to the hospital."

Connecting Brian and Katie's murder to the EAR, I explained, "Twelve homes in the immediate area reported incidents in the days and hours leading up to the murders that were classic East Area Rapist prowling activities. On the night of the murders, just around the corner, someone tried to break into a woman's home, but a second lock on the sliding door prevented it. A week before, a real-estate agent noticed that someone had broken into a house for sale across the street from the murder scene. The agent had seen a ten-speed bicycle parked by the front door. The East Area Rapist was known for using stolen bicycles to arrive at and escape from his crime scenes. Brian and Katie were killed within a mile of these other Rancho Cordova rapes."

Making my case, I noted, "Pretied shoelaces were found just a few feet away from Brian's body. The homeowner, Nicholas Ottlinger, now eighty-eight years old, told the deputies that the shoelaces did not belong to him.

These shoelaces were pretied with a granny knot, allowing for quick cinching, a common technique and knot used in many of the East Area Rapist incidents." Connecting the Maggiore murders to Contra Costa, I talked about Mia's rape on June 11, 1979. "Both Mia and her husband, George, were bound with pretied shoelaces. Approximately half a mile away from their residence, a bicycle was stolen from another house that same night. Next to where the bike was taken, officers recovered white pretied shoelaces that had been left behind. Around the time of Mia's rape, a neighbor saw a prowler leaving the area near her house on a bicycle. DNA evidence from her vaginal swab matched the defendant's profile."

I went on to connect the entire series of crimes. Projecting the "Robin Williams sketch" on the screen, I stated, "Just as with the Ransacker cases, when DeAngelo's face was exposed and a composite sketch released to the public, he never committed another rape in Sacramento. The distinctive EAR crimes stopped in our county. Instead, he brought his brand of terror to the Bay Area and Contra Costa County."

I then launched into the initial Santa Barbara crimes on Queen Anne Lane and the Offerman-Manning murders. After going over the gruesome details of the crimes, I pointed out that "shoe impressions outside of Dr. Offerman's condo appeared similar to the star-pattern impressions found during the investigation of the incident involving Catherine and Anthony on Queen Anne Lane, which was located about half a mile away through San Jose Creek. The neighbor who heard the gunshots also reported that her son's ten-speed bicycle had been stolen during the night." Again, every little nugget and fact connected DeAngelo to the entire pattern of criminal conduct cases.

I then turned it over to Amy Holliday. She went through the murder of Cheri Domingo and Greg Sanchez before analyzing the factors in aggravation. I then returned to the front of the conference room to cover DeAngelo's life, the factors in mitigation, and his confession.

Finally, I gave Sacramento's official recommendation. "The death penalty is a fitting punishment for individuals who have ripped at the very fabric of our community with the heinous crimes they commit. Originally, we were asked to weigh the factors in aggravation and mitigation as it related to just the Maggiore murders. On those counts alone, we would seek the death penalty. While there may be some underlying mental aspect to his rapes, when he killed Brian and Katie, DeAngelo made cold, calculated decisions to evade capture and to escape responsibility for that crime. Recently, we were asked, out of great deference to Santa Barbara County, to incorporate a recommendation as to their murders, which are an important linchpin this case. What we have here is an evolution of a monster, a predator who, by the time he arrived in Santa Barbara, was determined to rape and then leave no witnesses behind. A hunter kills his prey quickly so as not to prolong the pain and suffering. This hunter chose to torture and taunt his prey. No words can adequately capture the depravity and devastation of Joseph DeAngelo's crimes. Therefore, we would respectfully recommend capital prosecution for the Santa Barbara murders as well."

I handed over the presentation to Cheryl Temple to present the Ventura crimes. Without any notes and with absolute precision, she set forth the timeline of Charlene and Lyman Smith's death, even explaining the timing based upon the contents of their stomach and what they had for dinner the night before. In chilling detail, she discussed the sexual assault and bludgeoning death, especially in those horrifying last moments when DeAngelo forced Charlene to listen to her husband's murder. After analyzing all the factors, Cheryl also recommended the death penalty.

Murph then walked to the front of the conference room to present DeAngelo's particularly violent and bloody crimes in Orange County. A sense of sadism pervaded everything at these scenes. Words alone could never adequately describe the level of violence as Murph clicked through the slides. Having been brought in at the last minute, he went through the facts of each case as laid out by Debbie. After going through the factors in aggravation and mitigation, Murph gave his recommendation. "It's a no-brainer that we should seek death."

For me, the decision was a "no-brainer" as well, but when Murph uttered those words I could hear Santa Barbara DA Joyce Dudley audibly groan. She had strongly opposed the GSK case being tried in Orange County, and now one of their prosecutors unknowingly dismissed her struggles with an offhanded comment. Having just joined the team, Murph was understandably unaware of its internal dynamics. In presenting my final recommendation, I had used words such as "out of great deference to Santa Barbara" and "we would respectfully recommend capital prosecution for the Santa Barbara murders as well." All it took was a single no vote to derail a decision to seek death.

After Orange County's presentation, we opened up the meeting for comments and questions. Whether by design or accident, the elected DAs remained relatively quiet as they would soon deliberate privately among themselves. On the other hand, their executive teams spoke up. Sacramento Chief Deputy Steve Grippi spoke first in measured terms, "The decision to seek death should never be rushed or casually made. The breadth of his crimes is staggering, and perhaps unprecedented in California. If not him, then who should receive death?"

Pat Dixon from Orange County spoke up from the back of the room. "I served under Steve Cooley in L.A. for over thirty years. We sought death against violent gang members for indiscriminately killing people on the streets of East L.A. and Compton. Now, we have one of the most prolific serial killers and rapists I've ever seen, who committed many of his crimes while wearing the badge of an officer. How can we justify death in other cases but not this one?"

Joyce Dudley stirred in her seat. I sat and listened intently to the comments. Contra Costa DA Diana Becton, the first African American district attorney in her county's history, was considered a progressive prosecutor, which made some question whether she would support the death penalty for DeAngelo. For the most part, I found her to be measured and calm in her approach to justice. A former judge, she brought a unique perspective to the proceedings. She said, "We obviously don't have any death penalty–eligible crimes in Contra Costa, but one thing to keep in mind is the age of the case and the defendant. Many of our victims and witnesses are elderly. A long and drawn-out trial may not be in our best interest. His crimes, without question, are incredibly heinous and deserve punishment to the fullest extent of the law." She left room for interpretation as to her actual position regarding the death penalty, especially as her county would not be a part of that conversation.

Tulare County DA Tim Ward spoke up next. "The death penalty was not in effect at the time of the Snelling murder. He started in Visalia and just cut a path of death across the state." Without saying it, I knew where Ward stood on the issue since his office had sought capital prosecution on many occasions.

I looked over at Joyce Dudley for any clues but saw none. The other DAs could push their point, but if they pushed too hard, that strategy could backfire. With California divided into fifty-eight different counties, each with its own district attorney, each one ruled their kingdom independently from the others.

DA Schubert announced, "We are going to head into the other conference room and work it out." We watched the DAs from Sacramento, Ventura, Orange, and Santa Barbara Counties file out. The room fell into a nervous silence.

I walked over to Cheryl and asked, "What do you think Santa Barbara will do?"

"Not sure," she replied. "I hope they go with the rest of us and seek death. We need to be united." We both wanted to get some insight about Joyce's position from Kelly Duncan as she knew her boss best, but we didn't want to put her on the spot. I checked in with Debbie as well. The transition to a new administration weighed on her as she was particularly close to Tony Rackauckas. However, like most soldiers, you move forward toward the enemy lines, regardless of which general issues the command. Murph walked over, and I welcomed him to the team with a hearty handshake. With so much to take in, the last week had flown by in a whirlwind of chaos for him. Trying to find his bearings, he looked forward to prosecuting the GSK case.

After about thirty minutes, the four DAs walked back into the room. I didn't know Dudley well enough to read her mannerisms, but DA Schubert looked calm and at ease. That was a good sign. As they all stood at the front of the room, Schubert announced, "We all agree to seek the death penalty against Joseph DeAngelo. It was unanimous."

Amy and I looked at each other and nodded. We had asked Loretta Maggiore and Ken and Keith Smith to be available for a phone call over the noon hour. We rushed back to our office and called Loretta first.

After we told her our decision, she immediately promised, "I'm going to make sure I live long enough to see Brian get justice."

We then got on a conference call with Katie's brothers. When we told them the DAs' decision, they both remained silent for a moment before they thanked us and told us, "We'll be with you all the way."

We went to court that afternoon to formally and publicly announce that we would seek the death penalty in the *People vs. Joseph James DeAngelo Jr.* The defendant stood there with his mouth still slightly open, expressing no reaction to the announcement, which seemed a bit incongruous with the high-stakes meeting earlier that morning behind closed doors.

Seeking to proceed with capital prosecution, we now needed to move the case forward to its ultimate conclusion. Time was our enemy. Our victims grew older with each passing day, witnesses and investigators would get infirm and die, and time never stopped. We needed to preserve the evidence.

— — —

The day after the court appearance, Sergeant Clark and Detective Peters drove the entire GSK prosecution team to each of the crime scenes in Sacramento. Driving through the Cho, Kenny stopped the van in front of a house whose windows and front doors were covered with metal bars, and we all got out. I was not far from where Homicide Sergeant Jim Barnes and Billy had first told me about the EAR six years earlier. Clark pointed to Phyllis's house where she had been sexually assaulted back in 1976.

Not far from her house and the other crime scenes in Rancho Cordova, we saw the cement canals that crisscrossed the neighborhoods, allowing the EAR to escape quietly and quickly on a bicycle underneath street level. I pointed out to Cheryl and Debbie, "These canals cut across multiple streets. It would take a police vehicle many more minutes to arrive on the other side. After a rape, he would slip down there, hop on a stolen bike and be far away in a matter of minutes."

We then walked to where Benny Pickett first witnessed the prowler and heard the Maggiores walking their dog. We retraced the same path they took as they ended up in the backyard of a house on La Gloria Way. David was just a teenager hanging out on the second floor of his home in February 1978 when he heard a gunshot. Looking out his second-story window, he witnessed Brian and Katie's execution. Walking up to the house, we saw a man in his fifties standing in front of the garage. It was David, who still lived in the house he grew up in. Sergeant Clark had previously interviewed him, and they spoke casually for a few minutes.

David took us to his backyard and pointed over to the adjacent yard where the Maggiores were murdered. His voice trembled with emotion even after forty years. I looked over the fence into Nicholas Ottlinger's yard. It looked the same as it had on February 2, 1978. Time had stood still in that backyard. Mr. Ottlinger was now elderly and rarely left his house, but we desperately needed to get him on the witness stand to preserve his testimony.

We spent the rest of the day driving to all the crime scene locations in Sacramento before wishing the rest of the team a safe trip back home. We would soon meet up in Southern California.

— — — — —

Summer 2019

In early June 2019, Sergeant Clark, Detective Peters, and I flew to Santa Barbara to visit all the GSK crime scenes in the American Riviera. We were staying just outside of downtown and went to the same bar where I had shared a drink with Paul Holes about a year earlier. A thick layer of fog stubbornly hung over the Santa Barbara Coast the next morning as nearly the entire prosecution team gathered at Queen Anne Lane. Since this was her county, Kelly Duncan walked us through the property. We walked down the long driveway that led to Catherine and Anthony's house. They had been lucky to escape DeAngelo's clutches—one had run into the streets naked and screaming, while the other had hidden by lying on the ground in a fetal position under some bushes.

Standing in the driveway, I could see where FBI Agent Stan Los had stood when he saw Catherine screaming and DeAngelo pedaling away on a bicycle. We walked by the side of the house to the area where investigators found DeAngelo's shoe impressions; detectives would later find the same prints outside Offerman's condo. The team made its way over to the open field next to the victims' house. I had only seen it in aerial and crime-scene photos. I needed to see San Jose Creek, which DeAngelo had used, like the concrete canals of Rancho Cordova, as his secret route to his crime scenes. As I stood on the edge of the field and looked down into the creek, filled with thick brush and a canopy of trees that shielded light from the bed, an ominous feeling still emanated from the spot. I could picture DeAngelo emerging from the darkness, a demon in a mask, carrying the instruments of death. I could still feel the evil he left imprinted on this place. In college, I once spent a night in an apartment where the previous resident had been stabbed to death in the kitchen. You could see the indentations from the weapon in the linoleum floor. Later that night, I heard chairs being moved in the kitchen. I ran out and turned on the lights. No one was there, but the chairs had been moved.

Ventura prosecutor Cheryl Temple walked over to me. I talked about the pieces of ligature found in the creek bed that matched the strings used to tie Robert Offerman and Debra Manning before they were murdered.

Everything fit. Next, we drove over to the Offerman condo, less than a mile away. The building's exterior looked perfectly normal, its chocolate brown paint helping it blend into its surroundings. Neatly trimmed patches of green grass sat underneath large trees that dotted the complex. Concrete paths weaved in and out around the complex. Debbie Lloyd from Orange County mentioned to me that the area reminded her of the neighborhood where Manuela Witthuhn and Janelle Cruz had been murdered in Irvine. Forty years before, gunshots had rung out in the night, but on this June morning, everything seemed quiet and peaceful. A few steps from the condo, a grove of avocado trees led down to a different section of San Jose Creek.

From there, we headed to the big red barn house, where DeAngelo murdered Cheri Domingo and Greg Sanchez. Quiet streets curved gently through the quaint neighborhood. The coastal fog had burned off, and the home's brick walls, perfectly manicured front yard, and the large front windows looked inviting under the late morning sun. Kelly Duncan pointed out that the barn-shaped garage, which was red back in 1981, had since been repainted a neutral gray that hid any memory of its bloody past.

With Cheryl leading the way, we drove south to the Ventura crime scene. The Smiths' house sat partway up a hill that overlooked the valley. A redbrick retaining wall framing the front of the house matched the red tile roof. We walked to the side of the house, where we saw a drainage canal and an open hillside from which a stealthy intruder could walk up to the backyard and gain access. A lady walking her dog glanced curiously at our group—a dozen people milling about, peering at and taking pictures of an ordinary-looking house. Thirty-eight years prior, patrol cars with flashing lights had filled the street as Dr. Claus Peter Speth arrived on scene to collect two crucial rape kits from Charlene.

After a quick two days in Santa Barbara and Ventura, we flew back to Sacramento to resume the never-ending work on the GSK case. Several months earlier, I had been promoted to supervise one of the most elite units in the office, the Gang, Hate Crime, and Major Narcotics Team. Although the prosecutors under me possessed at least a decade's worth of experience, I still needed to provide them with guidance and advice. Just as Norgaard reviewed all the homicide reports for charging decisions, I did the same for the crimes related to my unit. A constant stream of detectives came in and out of my office throughout the day. I made sure to arrive at work by 6 a.m., reserving those precious few hours before the rush arrived. In the evenings, after dinner with my family, I quickly pulled out my laptop and got to work. As a child, I had studied English at the dinner table with my dad, who was doing homework to get his associate's degree. Forty years later, I was still sitting at the dinner table.

— — —

With the kids home for summer vacation, my wife planned a trip to Mendocino. The rugged coastline up north provides some of the most spectacular scenes on Earth. The salty air, the crisp mornings, and the long fingers of fog caressing the trees calm the mind and soothe the soul. It was good to get away, and Jenny wanted me to disconnect from work. On a five-mile hike through the woods that ended with a trail down to the beach, we reached the summit before the descent. Just then, my phone began to buzz. Cell-phone service here was spotty at best, but somehow, someway, my phone picked up a single bar of cell service. My wife looked at me, almost daring me to grab my phone, but I wasn't going to fall into this trap. I smiled and kept hiking. Half a mile later, I sneaked a peek at my phone and saw that Debbie Lloyd from Orange County had called. We were headed home the next day; the return call could wait.

"The new owners are tearing down the Harringtons' house in Dana Point. We need to take more pictures of it before that happens, sometime in the next ninety days," Debbie warned me when we chatted the next day.

"I have an idea. Let's fly drones over the house and even inside. We could perhaps try to retrace his possible path to and from Patty and Keith's house. Let's do the same thing for the Witthuhn and Cruz crime scenes," I told her. Debbie loved the idea, and I worked on setting it up for September. At that time, the Sacramento County Sheriff's Department was just starting to build up their Drone Unit, employing seven drones to use at crime scenes. The lead instructor, Doug Weidman, had retired after serving twenty years as a deputy with the department. He owned a private company flying drones for farmers and others who needed to film locations from the air. Once I told Doug that we needed drone videos of the Golden State Killer crime scenes, he wanted to start working immediately, saying, "It hurt to hear that DeAngelo wore the badge, and anything I can do as a former cop to make up for it, count me in." He commanded a thirty-four-foot mobile home as his drone mission control. He reached out to Sacramento Sheriff's Deputy Joe Gordon, who had just started working part-time in the Drone Unit.

I put Doug in touch with Debbie and with Orange County DA Lead Investigator Erica Hutchcraft, who served for years as an officer with the Irvine Police Department before switching over to the District Attorney's Office. With short blond hair and a relentless work ethic, she rivaled Sergeant Kenny Clark in her vast knowledge of the GSK case, particularly his crimes in Southern California. She had worked on all the Orange County cases long before anyone wrote a book or went on the TV program *48 Hours*. Debbie and Erica coordinated with Doug and Joe Gordon to map out the drones' flight plans to film the crime scenes.

In early September, Doug and Deputy Gordon drove down in the mobile drone command center to Doheny State Beach in Dana Point, located just a few miles away from the Harringtons' former home. They parked the RV in a shopping center parking lot down the street, close enough to be able to monitor the drone remotely. Having gotten the new homeowner's permission to film the outside of the house, Debbie, Erica, and I settled inside the RV to watch the live feed from the drone as it flew over the Harringtons' home. Under Doug's control, the drone flew from the streets up through the dirt paths and heavy bushes, trying to recreate the GSK's possible paths to the house. It touched down in their backyard and showed the view of the ocean before it turned back toward the rear patio door and then up around the house. Watching the drone footage gave us a realistic first-person point of view of how the killer may have walked to the patio door.

As we watched the video, I commented, "There are just too many crime scenes spread across the state to do a jury view, but this is the next best thing."

"We should do this for all the crime scenes. It brings everything to life," Debbie suggested.

After we finished filming, the team gathered at the Harringtons' house and entered the backyard. The blue waters of the Pacific Ocean glistened like a shiny, undulating curtain, and a gentle breeze rustled our hair. Matt Murphy stopped by to chat for a few minutes. It was good to catch up with him. Less than three months later, Murph left the Orange County District Attorney's Office and started his own law firm. He continued to appear as a special consultant providing legal commentary on the television show *20/20*.

We then headed over to film the Witthuhn and Cruz crime scenes in Irvine. Deputy Gordon told me that they had almost had to cancel the filming earlier that morning. President Trump flew into Los Angeles that same day, and the FAA had placed a temporary restricted flight ban over a thirty-five-mile radius. By some miracle, the sites in Irvine fell less than a half mile outside the restricted zone, and so we were safe to fly the drones.

Operating out of the mobile home, Doug flew the drones over each crime scene, covering the front and back of the residence and up to the fence line from the park, showing where the GSK had hopped over fences to enter and leave the crime scenes. Joe and Doug also mounted a drone to the hood of their car and drove down the street to show how he might have driven through the neighborhood searching for victims. At the Cruz residence, we walked from her front door to the adjacent park. As we strolled along a hedge-flanked pedestrian walkway, Erica pointed out that a person standing at the access point of the path could easily surveil the front of Janelle's residence while blending into the background. They could then quickly escape through the park and out onto the surrounding streets that intersected with the freeway. This presented the perfect place from which to stalk someone. Mounting a drone on a handheld flycam, a device that allows a video camera to take smooth and stable shots while in motion, Doug retraced those very same footsteps from the house through the hedge-flanked walkway and out through the park, providing another first-person perspective through the killer's eyes.

With the filming in Orange County completed, we made plans to record all of the crime scenes with a drone in the near future. We returned to

Sacramento and provided a copy of all the videos to the defense attorneys. A few weeks later, I received a phone call from Public Defender Joe Cress. He told me that he had been on vacation in Orange County and decided one day to check out the Witthuhn and Cruz residences. At each location, he saw a drone flying overhead that seemed to follow him as he walked through the park and around the two residences. He grew concerned that he was somehow under surveillance. When he watched the videos that we sent over, he realized that he had happened to be there while we were filming and was captured on video. We had a good laugh about the incredible coincidence.

— — —

Since DeAngelo's arrest, every victim invariably asked us the same question: Did we find any of the trophies that DeAngelo took from his victims—the wedding bands, earrings, class rings, photographs, and other personal mementos? We couldn't provide an answer as the case remained active and litigation pending, but by the end of the summer, the answer to that question took a strange twist.

Detective Peters received a phone call from Ernesto,* a former coworker of DeAngelo's at Save Mart. After his official retirement, the defendant continued to work part-time as a mechanic for the company. Ernesto worked in the same department, and the two had struck up a friendship. The news of DeAngelo's arrest as the East Area Rapist/Golden State Killer had shocked him. After reading about it in the news, Ernesto recalled a comment DeAngelo had made many years earlier: Before his house was built in Citrus Heights, he had created a secret compartment somewhere underneath the property.

I had always felt that DeAngelo kept some of the jewelry or other property he stole as "trophies," using them to relish in his sick crimes. But we didn't find anything during the initial search of the house after his arrest in April 2018. Interviews with family members, friends, and coworkers failed to unearth the location of any trophies. However, this new development provided us with a new possibility. Detective Peters wrote a "piggyback" warrant, which gave us the authority to reenter the house and conduct another search. In the meantime, I located a person who utilized ground-penetrating subsurface technology to locate pipes and underground structures before utility companies start digging. DeAngelo's house, which had been put up for sale, sat empty as we scheduled the execution of the warrant and the search.

Warrant in hand, I arrived at the house around 10 a.m. and waited outside for Kenny, Rob, and the Sheriff's Department Homicide team. As I walked up, a white van displaying the slogan "Call Before You Drill" pulled up. The driver, Tom,* shook my hand and introduced himself. We instructed him to back his van into DeAngelo's garage to avoid arousing suspicion from the neighbors. Sporting a long ponytail, jeans, and a black company T-shirt, Tom never once asked why we were conducting a search at the house, or why a dozen plainclothes homicide detectives were milling about. I suspected that he had conducted an Internet search of the property and recognized its notoriety. I told him we were searching for a possible compartment or safe that may be hidden somewhere underneath the property so that he would know what to look for.

Tom's equipment utilized ground penetrating radar (GPR), which can locate objects in the ground even if it's buried beneath thick concrete. GPR reflects high-frequency electromagnetic waves into the ground, interpreting the waves to determine the locations of objects underground. He pulled out a plastic box located two inches above the ground, with four wheels and vertical handles connected to a small monitor. It looked like a plastic lawnmower. He started in the living room, then moved to the family room, kitchen, and each bedroom, rolling the device back and forth, covering every inch of the house as if he were vacuuming the floor.

After finding nothing of real import under the house, Tom extended his search to the garage, the front of the house, and the backyard. He swept every inch of the property, including a little shed in the back that DeAngelo had converted into a playhouse for his teenage granddaughter. The backyard represented our last and best chance at finding the alleged hidden safe. Tom even walked up the steep embankment that separated the house from his neighbor's property.

Although the weather in Sacramento begins to cool down in September, the air that day felt hot and humid. It was our last heat wave of the year, and the sun beat down on us. After searching the entire backyard, Tom kept returning to an area located to the right side of the house. He paused over a particular spot and kept moving the device back and forth. I watched him intently. Had he found something? Was there a safe buried underground that held all the trophies? I couldn't help but imagine DeAngelo coming out here every night, standing in the dark over the hidden trove beneath his feet, closing his eyes and reliving all his sadistic crimes.

Tom pulled out two metal rods bent at 90 degrees on each end. He held one in each hand and started walking around the place that his machine had zeroed in on. The group of detectives gathered around him. We all watched in silence. Each time he came to the location of interest, the rods started to move and cross each other. He then spray-painted the ground where the rods reacted to something underground. He continued scanning the spray-painted area with the metal rods as we all looked on.

I walked over and asked, "What are the rods telling you? Is there something right there?"

Without even looking at me, he replied, "Yes."

"Yes? Is there something there?"

Still walking around with the metal rods, he intoned, "Yes, there's a disturbance in the force right there."

In that moment, standing in the blistering sun, I thought to myself, *The "force?" Is this fucking* Star Wars *we're talking about here?* Before I could answer my own question, Tom explained, "When you dig up the ground, you disturb the dirt and composition of that area. So even if you refill the hole with dirt, the ground-penetrating radar and these divining rods detect that disturbance." Perhaps DeAngelo had dug a hole at that location, buried something deep down, and then refilled it with dirt.

Tom stood back and pointed to the ground. Picking up their shovels and pickaxes, the team members started digging. I could feel the excitement pulsing through me like the force. As depicted in the movies, I imagined the blade of the shovel striking metal and the detectives pulling the treasure trove out of the ground while everyone cheered. This had to be the location of the hidden trophies because the force told us. They worked for over an hour under the unforgiving sun. As they got deeper and deeper, the ground got harder and harder. No matter how deep they dug, however, they found nothing but more dirt. Hope began to fade with each shovel of dirt and each passing minute. My heart began to sink as I paced back and forth between the blistering sun and the shade. There was nothing there.

I was crushed. I desperately wanted to find the wedding bands, earrings, and class rings he had stolen from the victims. I wanted to bring them a measure of closure. For a moment, I got a taste of how Carol Daly, Paul Holes, Kenny Clark, and the countless other investigators felt as they hit one dead end after another over the four-decade hunt for the GSK. Although our search ultimately came up empty, we owed an obligation to each and every victim to explore all possible leads in locating their stolen property. DeAngelo never once said a word about what he did with the stolen mementos. But just like we never gave up on finding his true identity, we will never give up on the search for those trophies.

As Tom conducted his search, I walked around DeAngelo's residence. Like the homes he broke into throughout Sacramento, his house only had one floor. After his arrest, the residence remained mostly empty and unoccupied. I saw empty boxes of Diet Dr Pepper stacked on the kitchen floor. In the garage, we found equipment that DeAngelo had used to reload his ammo with gunpowder. I asked Kenny to collect the items for evidence. Of particular interest were several cartons of books on the kitchen counter. One of DeAngelo's daughters studied psychology, and from the books strewn about in the house, we saw that she had a particular interest in killers. The books of note included Anthony Bruno's *The Iceman: The True Story of a Cold-blooded Killer* and Dominick Dunne and O. J. Simpson's *If I Did It: Confessions of the Killer*. She had also read Ian Halperin's *Unmasked: The Final Years of Michael Jackson*. Ironically, her father, unbeknownst to her, had famously worn a mask while committing his many heinous crimes. We locked up the house after our search and continued forward.

As summer turned to fall, I grew more restless to move the case along. We needed to preserve the evidence with court testimony; we needed to start the preliminary hearing.

11
“I Admit”

Fall/Winter 2019

Age, memory, and lost evidence present some of the greatest challenges for prosecuting cold cases successfully. On February 2, 1978, as the East Area Rapist was murdering Brian and Katie Maggiore, Nicholas Ottlinger heard gunshots coming from his backyard and ducked down. He heard Katie's scream and ultimately found her body. When questioned by detectives, Ottlinger told them that he had never seen before the pretied shoelaces found next to Brian's body. Forty years later, Ottlinger, a crucial witness, was eighty-eight years old and spent most of his days alone.

All the detectives who originally investigated the East Area Rapist were now in their sixties to eighties and long since retired. One of the detectives who investigated the Orange County crimes was in his nineties and deaf. Finally, many of the survivors struggled with health problems and advanced age. We needed to preserve the evidence and move the case forward, but the defense attorneys expressed no interest in speeding up the case. Time was their friend.

In California, the prosecution can move to the criminal trial stage using one of only two procedures: a grand-jury indictment; or a preliminary hearing, or "prelim." The first procedure requires us to present evidence before a grand jury, which would ultimately indict or charge DeAngelo. During such proceedings, the defense attorney is absent, and prosecutors essentially play both roles, presenting both the incriminating and exculpatory evidence. Even the defendant is absent from the hearing. Without the need to wait for the defense to announce it was ready, this procedure would move us quickly towards setting a trial date. Orange County typically utilizes a grand jury to indict on their big homicide cases. During the initial meeting in Los Angeles about the trial venue, OC prosecutor Baytieh had advocated for its use.

But going to a grand jury also had its potential pitfalls: While it afforded a quicker means to obtain a trial date, the defense could still seek a continuance of the trial, claiming that it was unprepared to proceed due to the massive scope of the case. So instead of delaying the case on the front end, they would simply do it on the back end. And because the defendant and their attorneys are excluded from the proceedings, any grand-jury witness testimony is inadmissible at trial because the defense will not have had the "right to confront" via cross-examination. If an investigator or witness passes away before trial, their testimony is lost forever. Moreover, with a grand jury, if the prosecutor fails to admit exculpatory evidence, the charges can later be thrown out and the conviction reversed. While it presented some benefits, the grand-jury process was rife with significant perils.

In cases with elderly victims or those with terminal illness, prosecutors can conduct "conditional exams" before a judge. Both the defense attorneys and their clients attend these proceedings, with counsel afforded the opportunity to fully cross-examine. Having complied with the "right to confront," the video testimony can later be played to the jury. However, the law prohibits conditional examinations in death-penalty cases. As we discussed how best to preserve the evidence and move the case closer to trial, Debbie brought up using a grand jury once more. But after I explained my concerns, she agreed that we should proceed by way of a preliminary hearing.

The second process, the prelim, requires us to present evidence and call witnesses to testify in front of a judge. However, the defendant and their attorneys are present in the courtroom, engaging fully in the litigation of the case—in effect, a minitrial. At the conclusion of the prelim, the judge determines if sufficient probable cause or evidence exists to hold the defendant over to trial. This is a fairly low standard of proof, and we had more than enough evidence. Importantly, the prelim would be the only sure way of preserving the testimony of our elderly witnesses.

Getting the defense to agree to schedule a preliminary hearing presented our greatest challenge. If given the choice, they would never set a date, so we needed to drag them into the courtroom. During a conference call with the prosecution team, we aimed for a hearing date in the spring, which would give us enough time to organize the minitrial, which we expected would take perhaps six months or longer to conduct. I took a deep breath as I thought about the logistical nightmare of flying witnesses from around the state into Sacramento. We would methodically present the evidence in chronological order from the Ransacker series through the EAR and then the murders in Southern California.

At the next court appearance in January, I would make the pitch and argue for setting the prelim. The public defenders would vehemently object, but Judge White now presided over the case in Department 61 after Judge Sweet transferred to another assignment as part of the natural rotation of judges. An experienced judge who loved to grind away at his job, he relished presiding over trials and appreciated lawyers who possessed the same mentality. I knew he represented our best chance of setting a prelim date over the defense's objection. I spoke with Judge's White's clerk, making sure he would be there in January.

— — —

I graduated from McGeorge School of Law in 1998. During my time there, I competed on the mock trial team under the tutelage of Professors Joe Taylor and Jay Leach, who showed me how to build the foundation of a great case in the courtroom. A former homicide prosecutor and chief at the Sacramento DA's Office, Taylor later transferred to the Ventura DA's Office as its second-in-command before being appointed head Public Defender of Riverside County. Having served on both sides of the courtroom, he told me, "Your greatest asset is your credibility. Your word means everything." Pausing for a moment for dramatic effect, he then gave the tiniest of smiles and said, "Thien, it's easy to give your word and even easier to give it away. So always keep your word. If you do what you say you'll do, everyone will follow your lead—the jury, the judge, even the defense attorney and the community."

When Taylor retired as McGeorge's Advocacy Director, Leach hired Cary Bricker, a former hard-charging public defender in the most prestigious federal district in America, the Southern District of New York. They fell in love, married, and built the trial-advocacy program at McGeorge into a powerhouse. They asked me to return to my alma mater as a mock trial coach, teaching law students the art of advocacy and participating in competitions around the country. For over sixteen years, I partnered with fellow Sacramento Deputy DA Keith Hill to coach students, who won numerous awards and competitions across the country. Over 40 percent of the attorneys in my office were our former students. While Keith took a break from coaching to battle brain cancer, I continued coaching, and in early November 2019, I led a team of students to New York City to compete at Fordham Law School's Kelly Competition.

While we enjoyed New York City, I did notice a lot of people coughing and sneezing, especially in crowded places like Chelsea Market. I take my flu shot religiously every fall and had done so again. On my flight home, I felt more lethargic than usual. By the time we landed in Sacramento, I felt lightheaded and congested. I spent the next week in bed with a high fever and congestion before returning to work. At the time, I had no idea of the coming storms.

— — —

We scheduled the next court appearance for January 22, 2020, in Department 61, where we had been for the last year and a half. We planned to petition Judge White to set a preliminary hearing date. As the judicial officer who signed the original arrest warrant and every subsequent search warrant in the case, he knew more about the Golden State Killer than any judge. I wanted the case to be preassigned to him, but he was stuck in Department 61 rather than a trial department in the main courthouse.

Nearly two years after his arrest, the case arrived at a critical crossroads. We desperately needed to move the case along and preserve the evidence before witnesses passed away. The defense wanted to put off setting a hearing date indefinitely. Another continuance for the sake of a continuance would be an absolute disaster. For an entire week, I worked on my arguments and counterarguments for setting the prelim, repeatedly testing them with my colleagues from Southern California. Responsible for running the day-to-day operations of the Ventura DA's Office, Cheryl Temple always found time to indulge in strategy sessions with me. We both agreed that our urgent need to move the case forward was directly related to DeAngelo's successful efforts to evade capture over the last four decades. He should not now benefit from any further delay. "He's already had a forty-year continuance," Cheryl emphasized.

I spent many of my commutes home talking to Debbie Lloyd, who wondered aloud if the judge would cave to the defense's request. Whenever a defense attorney claims that they would provide ineffective assistance of counsel, judges often back off for fear of creating a reversible error, meaning a mistake made during a case that makes it likely to be overturned in the appellate courts. Debbie pointed out that the survivors were upset, and rightfully so. He'd evaded capture for so long and gotten the chance to enjoy his life, while the victims' lives were ruined, and many of them never got the chance to grow old.

Except for Contra Costa County, the prosecution team arrived in Sacramento the morning of January 22. Jim Mulgrew, our research specialist from Orange County, came too. He had argued the Rodney Alcala case before the California Supreme Court, going toe-to-toe with the defense while satisfying the justices' questions. He prevailed, saving the hard-earned conviction that Murph had obtained at trial. I ran through the arguments while Jim played the role of the defense attorney. He argued that the right to be represented by a lawyer was meaningless unless that lawyer was prepared. With the sheer volume of police reports and evidence, no lawyer could competently prepare for a hearing. Justice rushed was justice denied. We argued back and forth, jousting counter arguments with each other. As the saying goes, "iron sharpens iron," and I enjoyed the intellectual challenge and competition that Jim provided. Listening to Mulgrew play public defender, I was thankful he would be on my side of the courtroom that afternoon.

We arrived in court thirty minutes early, coming in through the back corridor to avoid the throng of cameras and media setting up in the hallway. Once inside, I got set up at the counsel's table and started pacing the courtroom. Cheryl, Debbie, and Jim sat in the row right behind me. After a few minutes, Ann Tran and Mailyn Chuong brought the victims in. Jane Carson, who had flown in from the East Coast to join us, took a seat in the second row behind me. I walked over and explained to her the purpose of our court appearance. She was ready to testify right then and there. I could tell she was in a fighting mood.

When she asked me if DeAngelo was going to do his feeble old man routine again. I told her, "Probably. He's a manipulator. They sent me videos of him in his jail cell, and he has no impairments there. This is all a show for him." Her eyes narrowed as she stared at the empty cage.

Phyllis and Kris walked in and sat down on the other side of the courtroom, right behind the cage, with a direct view of where DeAngelo would enter and stand during the proceedings. I went over to greet them. Sitting right in between them was Gay Hardwick, a victim of the East Area Rapist when she lived in Stockton with her boyfriend, Bob. The couple would later marry and remain together to this day. The facts of Gay's assault mirrored Linda's in Citrus Heights and Mia's in Contra Costa. Over the course of the previous two years, she had grown frustrated with the lack of communication and help from San Joaquin County District Attorney Tori Verber. We always provided our survivors updates on their cases both before and after court appearances, mostly through the victims' advocates. But DA Verber did none of that. Phyllis and Kris became friends with Gay, forwarding our updates to her, and we eventually "adopted" Gay as one of our victims. I take great pride in our profession and the people that work in it, but seeing a survivor ignored by their DA infuriates me. Two years later, DA Verber would lose her reelection bid as claims that she had failed to protect victims dogged her campaign.

While talking to some of the victims, I saw Public Defender Diane Howard come into the courtroom. With her retirement pending, she was playing a less prominent role in the case as the primary responsibilities transferred to Joe Cress and Alice Michel. When I commented to her that she had gotten to court earlier than usual, she gave me a wink and a smile and said, "I love the cameras, and so I like to get the best spot in the courtroom." And she did exactly that by occupying the seat right next to the cage where DeAngelo would be standing.

After the bailiff opened the courtroom doors, the media rushed in to set up their cameras and microphones. With everyone in place, they brought DeAngelo into the cage. He looked gaunt and pale, having lost significant weight while in custody. According to my contacts in the jail, his consumption of junk food and soda had slowed to a trickle. He spent nearly every waking minute pacing in his cell like a caged animal. The surveillance videos the jail staff sent me showed a ghostlike figure walking in a triangle from his bunk bed to the door to the wall and back to the bed again for hours. It was hypnotic watching him.

Judge White called the case and turned to me. I stood up right at the counsel's table to begin my argument:

"The People at this time are requesting that the court set the matter for a preliminary hearing. The defense has filed a motion in opposition, citing a variety of reasons to support its proposition, among which the defense argues that the scope of the case, specifically the defenses and the voluminous amount of discovery in the case, warrant a continuance on the matter.

"But I would like to put some things into perspective," I continued, my voice beginning to rise. "It was the defendant who decided to embark upon a crime spree that spanned eleven different counties; it was the defendant who purposely evaded capture for forty years and delayed the commencement of this case; and it was the defendant who was allowed to enjoy his life before his capture. It is ironic today that the defendant is seeking to indefinitely delay the preliminary hearing, because he happened to be a prolific criminal, who happened to generate a tremendous amount of discovery and reports."

I often present my opponent's arguments preemptively so that I can attack them before they even have an opportunity to set it up. Controlling the narrative, I continued to hammer away. "His attorneys are claiming they don't have the time to prepare for the preliminary hearing. Time is their ally and time is their friend, but we are running out of time. There is a clear necessity to set the matter for a preliminary hearing, as the vast majority of the witnesses in this case are elderly. Under Marsy's Law [California legislation that protects victims' rights], the victims, the victims' families, the witnesses, and the People are all entitled to have their day in court and to present the evidence in this case. Any further delay would deny us due process, deny the victims justice, and deny accountability for the defendant's crimes."

Both Public Defender Alice Michel and Joe Cress stood outside the cage next to DeAngelo. Flanked by deputies, the GSK stood motionless, his mouth half open, staring blankly at Judge White. Michel stepped forward to present her argument.

"We have discussed how long we think, given our staffing, that it would take us to complete a review of the evidence that we've been provided to date, and we anticipate we will be able to complete a review by the end of the year, after which we will be able to discuss setting up a preliminary hearing date." Just as expected, the public defenders' position was to delay as long as they could and avoid setting, or committing to set, a preliminary hearing date. They wanted to wait another eleven months, and then and only then, maybe see if they might be able to discuss picking a date.

Judge White stepped in. Never afraid to make a tough decision, he said, "I don't dispute the concerns that are being raised by the defense. The People, however, are entitled to bring this to a preliminary hearing. I'm not going to delay the setting of that hearing to a date requested by the defense. I'm going to set the preliminary hearing for May 12 in Department 9 at 8:30. That will be the order. Mr. DeAngelo, do you waive time to the hearing on May 12th?"

To set a preliminary hearing, a defendant must first plead "not guilty" and select a hearing date. The law requires that the proceeding occur within ten to sixty days of the "not guilty" plea. May 12 exceeded that time period, and that required his consent to "waive time." When Judge White asked him the question, the defendant gave no response, instead staring straight ahead vacantly. Cress walked to the front of the cage and explained the process to him.

The judge asked him the same question again, but he stood mute until Cress instructed, "Say it, say it out loud." For the first and only time in court that day, DeAngelo nodded his head up and down and muttered, "Yes." With the utterance of that simple word, court ended, and we accomplished our primary goal: to move the case forward. But we faced other troubles brewing on the horizon.

— — —

A week after the court appearance, Cress and Michel sent a letter to the prosecution team offering to "plead Mr. DeAngelo to all charges in the complaint and admit all of the enhancements and special circumstance allegations in the complaint." They would do so if we took the death penalty off the table. While this represented a serious offer by the defense, this case was much broader and bigger than the complaint, which is what DeAngelo's lawyers had focused on. The offer did not address the uncharged victims, and we were going to reject any resolution that did not consider them.

The public defenders leaked the offer to the media in a feeble attempt to influence our position. They even had one of their investigators send the information to some uncharged victims in Contra Costa County. We remained steady in our position that any resolution that failed to address all the survivors did not merit further discussion.

— — — — —

Spring/Summer 2020

As spring approached, we continued to focus on the prelim. But while we had our heads buried in the work, events on the other side of the world soon landed on our doorstep. As I sat at the dinner table outlining a witness's direct examination, my wife called out, "Come over here. Have you seen this on the news? People are getting some sort of flu in China, and no one knows how bad it is."

Watching the broadcast, I brushed it off. "Its probably just some seasonal thing. Besides, I had the flu already after coming back from New York. I'm fine." Jenny just shook her head at me as I went back to work at the dinner table. As we soon found out, I was very wrong.

"The victims all want a meeting," Victim Advocate Ann Tran told us. Amy and I were curious about the exact purpose of the gathering.

"The uncharged victims want to make sure that they are not left behind as we move forward with the preliminary hearing and the case," Advocate Mailyn Chuong explained.

"Let's set it up. They will absolutely not be left behind, and we want to reassure them of that," I said.

"Gay Hardwick, the San Joaquin County victim, is beyond frustrated with her DA. Should we invite her as well?" Ann asked.

"Absolutely, they should all be there," I responded.

We scheduled the meeting for March 12, 2020, in our main conference room, where we had conducted the death-penalty presentation the previous year. Ann and Mailyn escorted over fifty people into the room, including Phyllis, Kris, Gay, and Linda, along with their families and friends. The GSK prosecution team attended the meeting as some of the victims from the other counties were present as well.

Jennifer Carole, Lyman Smith's daughter, sat near the front. Cheryl Temple mostly communicated with her during the case since she was a Ventura victim. After DeAngelo's arrest, Jennifer moved to Sacramento and rented a home so she could attend all the court appearances. She often posted on social media about the hearings. Amy and I routinely read her stories as well as those of other bloggers who followed the case. We wanted to keep a pulse on the general public's sentiment, especially that of victims.

With a moral compass focused on fairness, Jennifer never hesitated to speak her mind. Although her father's murder constituted one of the main charges in the case, she felt strongly that the survivors with uncharged incidents equally deserved justice, which I completely agreed with. I felt we should charge every case we could, but I was not the district attorney. Jennifer encouraged Phyllis, Kris, and Gay to voice their concerns.

Amy started the meeting by updating everyone on the latest developments and our expected timeline for litigation. When she was done, I wanted to spend some time listening. We often hear, but it's even more imperative that we genuinely listen. Kris raised her hand. She had heard that the defense was offering a plea deal in which DeAngelo would admit to all to the charged offenses in the complaint. "There are several of us, including myself, with uncharged cases. We want to make sure that we don't get left behind."

She had been only fifteen years old when the EAR sexually assaulted her. That horrific evening upended her entire life, setting her on a dark path. It had taken her many years to arrive at this point. Finding her voice, Kris stood up and advocated not only for herself, but also for many others whose charges we could not file because of the inadequacies of the law. I sat and absorbed all that Kris said and did not say. Her voice quavered, but her spirit remained steady.

"We deserve justice too, and we've waited a long time for it," Kris continued. I saw Phyllis sitting on the edge of her seat, nodding her head. I knew where her heart was.

I came back to the front of the conference room and said, "I wish we could charge every single case, but the law won't let us. I know that regardless of whether we can charge your case or not, we will get justice for you. Not everyone may be called to the witness stand, but everyone will be heard. At some point, DeAngelo will have to sit down and face each of you. We will make sure that he has no place to hide or to run. Justice will be yours."

Ventura Chief Deputy Cheryl Temple walked to the front of the room and spoke to Jennifer and the rest of the survivors. She reassured everyone that all the prosecutors would fight for all of them. No one would be left behind. Many of these survivors were teenagers or in their twenties when the EAR assaulted them, and all of them suffered immensely over the years. Many lost their way, and many others wondered how their lives would have turned out if the EAR had never crossed their paths. His arrest nearly two years ago, while answering the burning question of who had raped them, opened up other painful parts of their hearts and lives that had been closed. That chapter of their lives had been written not by them, but by the monster known as the East Area Rapist. But in this moment, Kris, Phyllis, Gay, and so many other survivors were writing a new chapter for themselves. They had found their voice, and we heard them loud and clear. Soon enough, so would Joseph DeAngelo.

— — —

The very next day, President Donald Trump declared a national emergency in response to the COVID-19 pandemic, and California Governor Gavin Newsom ordered all public schools from kindergarten through high school closed. More than 5.7 million students were sent home indefinitely. One week later, California issued a shelter-in-place order, enforceable as a misdemeanor crime with $1,000 fine or six months in jail. The world seemed to literally shut down.

Just before the order went into effect, I drove to our local warehouse store, Costco, to stock up on toilet paper, latex gloves, sanitizers, masks and nonperishable food items. The line to get in was out the door. Once inside, I found empty shelves and people walking around aimlessly looking to buy something, anything. With the impending shelter-in-place order and the empty shelves at Costco, I headed to the local Asian supermarket, where I found everything we needed for the next several weeks.

In the early days of the pandemic, we knew so little about the virus. How deadly was it? How contagious? Could you get it from touching a countertop or being in the same room with an infected person? For several days, the courts shut down, and people under arrest remained in custody without the ability to see a judge. Slowly, courtrooms opened again, but court appearances were made remotely, with attorneys appearing over Zoom. This became the new norm.

Cheryl called me one early morning in late March as I went for a walk. I had to get out of the house. We talked about being barricaded at home with our kids and spouses. The first time we heard the term "social distancing," we both searched the Internet for the definition. We agreed that with the shelter-in-place order and the rapidly increasing infection rate, the preliminary hearing in May would have to be delayed. However, we were dancing on the edge of a razor. Bringing a witness to court, especially someone elderly with a compromised immune system, might expose them to a deadly virus; on the other hand, any further delay in the case could result in a loss of witnesses who suddenly became ill from the coronavirus. Ultimately, the COVID-19 pandemic would infect over 700 million people and kill over 7 million around the world. But in those first few months, we had no choice but to put one foot in front of the other. In addition to facing a global pandemic, I would soon face other challenges.

In the midst of the virus spreading around the world, I received some good news at work. DA Schubert promoted me to her executive team, naming me the Assistant Chief over Community Outreach, Community Prosecution, our Post-Conviction Unit, and Media Relations. With this position, I would be the public-facing representative of the office and the community liaison. Having spent the bulk of my career in trial, this assignment sent me in a completely different direction, hosting town-hall meetings and talking to community members about social justice, homelessness, and crime. It felt completely foreign to me. Nonetheless, I approached it with the same level of obsessive preparation I always had. However, I made sure to remember Professor Taylor's advice from many years ago. I reminded myself that as long as I was authentic and kept my word, everything would work out.

As the rate of anti-Asian hate crimes escalated at astronomical rates in the ensuing months, I worked to bridge the gap of mistrust of law enforcement and go after offenders. Rates of theft, domestic violence, child abuse, and violent crimes increased as our streets became ghost towns.

In the wake of George Floyd's murder in May 2020 in Minneapolis, protests roiled the country, and the racial reckoning that had long simmered beneath the surface of American society boiled over, inevitably and unstoppably. I watched helplessly as rioting and looting engulfed cities across the country. On the evening of May 30, rioters looted and destroyed over 197 businesses throughout Sacramento, resulting in over $10 million in damages. A group of protestors split off from the main group and marched to the District Attorney's Office, where they tried to set the building on fire and caused nearly $30,000 in damages. I watched in horror via a live security camera and felt an utter sense of powerlessness.

When morning came, I was tasked with two main responsibilities: identify the masked individuals who had vandalized our office and help reconnect our office with our constituents. We reviewed cameras from across Sacramento and executed electronic search warrants to identify the suspects, whom I eventually charged with multiple felonies. At the same time, I worked to let our residents know that justice and safety were rights that belonged to them as well. I soon realized that while my actions in the courtroom directly impacted the lives of those affected by that particular crime, my new duties in the community affected an entire spectrum of society. For example, Asian American elders were being bullied and beaten and killed, while Asian Americans of all ages were being berated and blamed for the coronavirus and many other societal ills that had nothing to do with them. As the highest ranking Asian American prosecutor in the office, I felt a responsibility to stem the tide of anti-Asian hate while building trust among all groups.

While I charged headfirst into my new position, we continued our progress on the GSK case. Several of us on the prosecution team saw an opportunity to fulfill our promise to the victims. After reading through all the rape reports, speaking to the survivors, and seeing the absolute destruction he had wrought in so many different communities, my initial gut reaction was that he deserved the death penalty, and we should not deviate from that path. But I also recalled the promise we had made to Phyllis, Kris, Gay, and the other survivors. We needed to make sure that their voices would be heard and that they would not be left behind. One day, DeAngelo would have to face each and every one of them.

Cheryl despised DeAngelo's depravity as much as any of us. She was one of the finest prosecutors and trial lawyers I'd ever worked with, and I trusted her judgment. She also believed that DeAngelo deserved death, but if we could keep our word, we should seize that opportunity. We both strongly agreed that DeAngelo must admit to all the uncharged crimes. It was the chance for all the victims, charged and uncharged, to get justice. As we went back and forth about the parameters of a plea, we felt that affording all the victims the chance to give an impact statement at the sentencing would fulfill the promise we had made.

I called Debbie separately as I needed to get an idea of her thoughts before setting up a meeting with the rest of the prosecution team. As the one constant on the Orange County team, Debbie held a certain level of sway over her office. The relationship with the OC DA's Office had started off rocky, but over the last year, I had grown to trust Debbie and her office. As the decision to seek death needed to be unanimous, so too did the decision to change course. Like Cheryl, Debbie prioritized the need to ensure that the uncharged victims be able to express themselves. Debbie also worried that with COVID rates skyrocketing, a preliminary hearing seemed less certain to happen. The danger of losing witnesses to a pandemic whose scope and fury we did not yet fully understand represented a real concern for us all.

In April 2020, the GSK prosecution team gathered on Zoom to explore a comprehensive resolution of the case. We decided to set an in-person meeting with the public defenders, but we first needed to inform them in very clear terms the parameters of our position. We wrote them a message, stating, "To all of us, this has the hallmarks of a death case. Frankly, if we tried this case, we'd get death. In regard to factors in aggravation, we anticipated introducing crimes of violence committed against sixty-two additional, separate victims. These crimes are provable, beyond a reasonable doubt; but were not chargeable in the complaint simply due to the passage of time. These other victims are very much a part of this case. Indeed, their existence is one of the reasons this defendant's crimes warranted seeking death to begin with."

From the outset, we wanted to make clear our core belief that all the victims deserved justice. We also noted, "This is not a negotiation. Rather, this is a clarification . . . to what we believe comprises the scope of this case."

Out of respect to the victims, we did not want them to find out in the media or through third parties the possibility of any resolution. We wanted them to hear it from us first. As such, we told the public defenders, "We have an ethical duty to consider your offer in light of our duty to our victims. However, this discussion is to remain confidential, with no leaks, references, or mention of this discussion to anyone outside the immediate defense team. There can be no mention of this discussion to members of the public. Any such leaks will end any further discussion."

The governor forbade large gatherings of people without social distancing and the use of face masks. Since the start of the pandemic, my office, along with many workplaces across California and the world, became barren. Almost everyone worked remotely, from home or exotic locales, while appearing on Zoom calls with an artificial background that masked our true location. Sacramento was a ghost town. A scattering of people wandered in empty streets as silence filled the air.

After hand-delivering the message to the defense, we set up an in-person meeting. We could not do so indoors according to the orders issued by the governor. In between the courthouse and my office sat a large parking lot for people on jury duty. In the first two months following the shelter-in-place order, all in-person trials ceased, and the parking lot sat empty. In the middle of April 2020, I decided it would be our rendezvous point.

I parked my car in the middle of the lot and sat on my hood to wait for everyone to arrive. Cheryl Temple walked over, then Amy Holliday. David Alavezos from Tulare County arrived along with Kelly Duncan from Santa Barbara. We began to form a circle as Debbie and Pat Dixon from Orange County stepped in. From the west, I saw Public Defenders Joe Cress and Alice Michel approach on foot. Joe carried a small notepad.

The roads were empty, the sidewalks quiet. Not a soul stirred anywhere. During COVID, the animals came back to take over the places they had given up to us. I could hear the birds chirping as a gentle breeze kissed the leaves on the trees across the street. A stranger walking by the lot would have seen a strange sight, people standing six feet apart in a circle talking. A meeting of this importance should be held in person, not over Zoom.

I kicked off the meeting. "Joe and Alice, your offer is serious and genuine. But we need to clarify a few things." I looked over to Cheryl, which was part of our prearranged plan.

"We want to be clear: We are not negotiating, since ethical rules preclude us from using the death penalty to negotiate a better deal," Cheryl started to say as both public defenders nodded their heads in agreement. "To be clear," she continued, "DeAngelo would plead to all the charged offenses and be sentenced to the maximum sentence, all fully consecutive to each other." This meant the sentences would be stacked to be served one after the other.

Joe responded, "Yes, that is correct."

Both Debbie and Pat Dixon from Orange County then emphasized that the charged offenses did not accurately and fully reflect the full scope of his crimes. There were sixty-two additional victims that could not be ignored. Since most of the uncharged incidents occurred in Sacramento and Contra Costa Counties, I stepped back into the conversation. "This case is much broader and bigger than the four corners of the complaint. Those uncharged victims need justice too. Although he cannot be sentenced to the uncharged incidents, those survivors need to hear him admit that he raped them. Each victim, charged or uncharged, will be giving an impact statement at sentencing. They will all get their day in court."

Both public defenders voiced aloud their concern that DeAngelo might not be able to remember the particular facts or recall committing each and every one of the uncharged cases. I looked at them both and said firmly, "He does remember, he needs to remember, and he will remember, because we are willing to give you a reasonable amount of time to sit down and review the discovery with him to ensure that he will admit culpability to all his crimes."

They both nodded their heads in silence. We also mentioned that DeAngelo would waive his appellate rights, which meant he could not turn around after pleading, claim his rights were violated, and appeal the deal trying to undo it. The case would be final, providing true closure. The defense confirmed that this would be a part of the resolution. To their true credit, both defense attorneys represented their client with the utmost integrity while also acknowledging the humanity of the victims. This was the fairest resolution possible, recognizing the unprecedented times we were in. If the Golden State Killer had been arrested in the 1980s, 1990s, or even at the turn of the millennium, when our defendant and witnesses and victims were younger, I doubt a resolution would have happened. But we were in the middle of a pandemic with no end in sight, with aging victims, witnesses, and a defendant in his seventies. A resolution that gave every single one of DeAngelo's victims a seat at the table of justice was the right resolution for the right moment in history.

After the elected district attorneys for all the respective counties conferred and agreed to the resolution, we needed to coordinate the victim notification. We felt strongly that they needed to hear about the resolution from us directly. Amy and I made a joint call to Loretta Maggiore before we called Ken and Keith Smith. Loretta felt relieved to know that she would keep her promise to see the day when justice was delivered to her late son. Both Ken and Keith trusted our judgment and thanked us profusely. Perhaps some of the weight could finally be lifted from their shoulders.

We then split the list of survivors to call, with each of us responsible for notifying certain victims. As we moved down the list of survivors, we learned that they had already heard from other victims about the resolution. Word traveled quickly. They all felt a tremendous amount of relief. Phyllis, Kris, Gay, and Jane felt especially grateful that DeAngelo would admit to their assault and that they would get to speak at the sentencing. After forty years, they would finally get their day in court. Two years earlier, we had ripped the mask off the monster, exposing his gnarly and decrepit face and hollow, dead eyes. Now, I felt a great sense of relief that we could finally fulfill our promise. DeAngelo and the world would soon hear their voices.

After the court scheduled the preliminary hearing, Presiding Judge Russell Hom preassigned the People vs. the Golden State Killer to Superior Court Judge Michael Bowman for all purposes. A former prosecutor early his career, Bowman later opened his own practice and became one of the premier defense attorneys in Sacramento. For nearly two decades, he defended murder cases and drive-by shootings. Almost six-foot-four, he could charm any jury. If one of your relatives got in trouble, Bowman was on the short list to hire. Once the governor appointed him to the bench, he worked well with both sides.

For the last several years, we had asked Judge Bowman to swear in our new attorneys after they passed the Bar. He always started off his speech by telling them, "You can paint a thousand pictures and never be a painter. But if you tell one lie, you will be painted as a liar." Like Professor Taylor, he believed that a lawyer's greatest asset was their credibility. Getting Judge Bowman assigned to the case was a good draw.

Having secured a plea agreement, we had several weeks to work out all the logistical details, which in that moment seemed daunting. We scheduled the plea for the end of June. We needed to find a courtroom big enough to hold over two hundred people, in the middle of a global pandemic. Amy and I thought about the Golden One Arena, where the NBA Sacramento Kings played basketball, but it was too big and impersonal. We looked at the large auditoriums at Cal Expo, the location of the California State Fair, but it seemed too rustic. We even visited an airport hangar at Mather Air Force Base in Rancho Cordova. I thought the location would be poetic since the genesis of the GSK started in the Cho and would end in the Cho. However, the location lacked proper air conditioning, which was unacceptable for the end of June when temperatures could reach the upper nineties.

We finally settled on the ballroom at California State University, Sacramento. Not too big and not too small, not too fancy and not too rustic, the ballroom represented the Goldilocks of locations. But we had to get the approval of the Sheriff's Department. I reached out to Lieutenant Ed Yee, who had served in the department for over twenty-five years. Rising up through the ranks rather quickly, Ed ran Central Station, located in

South Sacramento, for several years. That area included the predominantly Asian, Latine, and Black neighborhoods of the city. I worked with him on gang cases as well as other crimes. Nothing ever surprised or rattled Ed, who dealt with every situation in a very practical manner. His attitude was always "Let's figure it out," rather than saying no reflexively.

By May 2020, he ran security at the courthouse. Nothing happened there without his knowledge since his deputies escorted the inmates, protected the judges, and dealt with all the operational issues in the building. But in this situation, for the first time ever in Sacramento's history, we wanted to move legal proceedings outside of the courthouse.

I told Ed, "The GSK is going to plea on June 29th, and we need a courtroom to fit over two hundred people." His eyes widened.

"We don't have any courtrooms that can fit that many people, especially with the COVID restrictions," he remarked. "We need to maintain social distancing. Where are you looking to hold it?"

"If we find a big and secured place offsite, would you be open to holding it there?" I asked.

"Judge Bowman needs to approve it," he immediately responded, but then figured out what I was doing. "Ah, but you want my buy-in first. Where are you looking?"

I told him, "We've been looking everywhere—Golden One, the Memorial Auditorium, Cal Expo where they hold the state fair, and even a hangar out at Mather. But the best place is the ballroom at Sac State."

While Lieutenant Ed Lee handled all the security inside the courthouse, the SWAT Team ran operational control over DeAngelo's transport to and from an offsite courtroom, including physical custody of his person. We needed their buy-in as well. For that, I reached out by phone to Jim Barnes, who was now the undersheriff. Eight years earlier, while driving to a homicide crime scene in the Cho with then Sergeant Barnes and Billy, I first learned of the East Area Rapist. The universe gave me a chance to close that loop. After telling Barnes that the EAR was pleading guilty and admitting to all the charged and uncharged cases, I added, "I need a favor though . . ."

I told him we had reserved the ballroom at Sacramento State to accommodate the two-hundred-plus people in attendance while maintaining social distancing. The county's highest-profile inmate would be transported offsite for court proceedings and then returned to the jail afterward. We needed department approval.

"We'll find a way to get it done," he reassured me.

Before hanging up, I reminded Jim of our conversation in his truck eight years earlier when I first learned of the East Area Rapist. He remembered it and marveled at how life always managed to find its way to the right place.

— — —

The case of the *People of the State of California vs. Joseph James DeAngelo Jr.* was to come before the Sacramento County Superior Court on June 29, 2020. Although the GSK had appeared in regular court facilities half a dozen times since his arrest, this would be his first hearing under lockdown. For several months, the country and the world had been grappling with the global COVID-19 outbreak, whose scope stretched beyond anything humanity had seen in a century. Under my supervision, the prosecution team moved forward with the new reality, adjusting our logistics on the fly as the lockdown and distancing restrictions wreaked havoc on the criminal-justice system. We barricaded ourselves at home and masked religiously and drenched our hands repeatedly in sanitizer at work. Every one of us was terrified of becoming infected or bringing it home to our loved ones. The face covers may have protected us from the virus, but they came with an unsettling measure of anonymity. Masks shielded our faces from examination and judgment. We could hide behind them.

My core team consisted of some of the top prosecutors from across California. We secured the ballroom at Sacramento State University as a makeshift location in which to have DeAngelo enter his plea. No one had ever attempted to do what we set out to accomplish: remove a high-profile inmate from jail and transport him offsite to a temporary courtroom, all the while observing social distancing. The improvised setting had to accommodate as many as 200 people; existing court facilities could barely fit a couple dozen people who had to stay six feet apart from each other.

By law, all state courtroom proceedings are open to the public, including the media. The judge for the plea, the Honorable Michael Bowman, had recently approved our request to go outside of a traditional courtroom. After checking in with Lieutenant Ed Lee as to the Sheriff's Department's position, the judge recognized the historical nature of the case, the unprecedented times we were in, and the need for all the victims to personally witness the promise of justice finally being fulfilled. Thanks to his decision, throngs of media would be in attendance, and they would film and beam the events around the world. About a week before DeAngelo was to enter his plea, I had a vision: The infamous GSK walked into the courtroom, his face obscured by an N95 mask. I thought, *The judge, jury, media, and a number of survivors of his vicious attacks would be present, and the mask would protect him from showing his face to the world.* Some of the survivors had expressed to me their wish to see their tormentor clearly for the first time. I couldn't stand the thought of not being able to help them seek that measure of closure.

Then, an idea: Make the GSK wear a clear face shield. I ordered one online and it arrived the next day, in time for a meeting Judge Bowman had called to finalize the logistics for the plea hearing. In my younger days as a trial lawyer, I would walk into courtrooms breathing fire and brimstone, employing only one strategy: attack, always attack. I never gave an inch, constantly moving forward and contesting every issue as I tried to pummel my opponent into submission. While this approach was mostly successful, it induced animosity from opposing counsels. It came from a place of fear within me: I was afraid to miss a fact, to concede on a crucial issue, to look or sound weak. As I grew older and tried more cases, I realized that outcomes did not always hinge on every tiny issue or ruling, that not all battles needed to be fought. That taking a step back might provide an opportunity to take two steps forward, and a quiet word sometimes spoke louder than a strident yell. But sometimes, you needed to get loud and angry to convey that something mattered to you.

In the courtroom, I've used anger in many different ways. I have learned that it is like salt. It alone is not food, yet it adds flavor and fullness to any dish. Fury alone does not make for a compelling argument, but it can augment meaning and importance. As details about the plea hearing were decided, I steered the conversation to three important issues. With a calm voice, I said, "Judge, when the defendant pleads to the charged offenses, he needs to say 'guilty.' That specific word needs to come out of his mouth. Some of his victims have waited forty-plus years to hear him say it."

Judge Bowman looked over to DeAngelo's defense attorney. "What do you think?"

"That's fine with us," responded Public Defender Joe Cress.

"And when he admits to committing the uncharged crimes," I continued, my voice getting louder, "he should actually say the words, 'I admit.' He shouldn't hide behind bland words like 'yes' or 'correct.' This day is about the survivors and victims."

Again, the judge asked the defense, "What do you think?"

Once more, Cress replied, "That's fine with us, Judge."

Now it was time for me to get angry, to show the judge that this issue mattered to the People of the State of California. "Judge, when the defendant carried out his crimes, he wore a mask. When he committed his burglaries, his rapes, and his murders up and down the State of California, he wore a mask!" My voice grew steadily louder as the indignation rolled off my tongue. "His police badge and uniform. His wife and his daughters. His unobtrusive life as a retired mechanic living in a tranquil suburb. Just more masks for him to hide behind, to conceal his true identity as a monster."

I pulled out the clear face shield I had ordered. "And so, when he finally comes to court to accept responsibility in front of the victims and survivors whose lives he tore apart without regard, he shouldn't be allowed to hide behind a mask like he has done all his life. He should wear this." I let the silence punctuate the point I made.

In a voice as velvety as whiskey aged in oak barrels, Judge Bowman turned to the defense and said, "I think that sounds perfectly reasonable, don't you?"

Joe Cress paused for a moment. I could see the wheels turning, the various scenarios flashing in his mind. He didn't like my request, but he wanted the plea deal to go through. He could tell by my voice and body language that this issue meant a great deal to us. "We are fine with it, judge."

— — —

An old-time prosecutor once told me, "Young man, always get to the courtroom before your opponent. You want to mark your territory. Get your files all set up on the table and soak up the entire room because that's your home. You own it and you run it. Everyone else there is just a guest, especially the defendants and their attorneys." I always took that advice to heart and made it a practice to be the first to arrive in court. In preparation for the plea, all parties agreed to meet the Friday before the hearing to view the courtroom. I scheduled the judge and defense attorneys to arrive at 1:30 p.m.; my team and I were there at 10 a.m. to meet the Sheriff's security team.

Our staff set up the stage at the front of the ballroom, about three feet higher than the floor, facing the audience. An elevated platform at the back of the room would accommodate the media. The prosecutors occupied chairs in the audience to the left of the stage, allowing us quick access to a podium from which the respective county prosecutors would speak, depending on the charge. The judge's bench sat at the center of the stage, next to the podium. The defense table was also on the dais—I wanted the GSK visible to everyone. But the team had placed the defense table facing the judge and perpendicular to the audience. That would put DeAngelo's left side toward the victims, with the defense attorney sitting next to him, blocking the view of the survivors. He wouldn't have to face those whom he hurt. Grabbing the table, I immediately told the crew to rearrange it so that the defense table faced the audience. They would see the GSK's face, he would see theirs, and there would be nowhere he could hide from his shame or their anger.

Sergeant Dan Donelli oversaw the department's SWAT unit. Standing over six-foot-three, he looked like Sean Connery playing James Bond, except bigger. Donelli handled every aspect of security for the defendant, including the transport of DeAngelo from the jail to the site, where he sat in the ballroom, and his return to jail. The SWAT team placed DeAngelo in one of three unmarked vans with tinted windows. The vehicles all left the jail simultaneously and headed in different directions while drones observed overhead. While some might have thought this was overkill, the last thing anyone wanted was for something to happen to DeAngelo as the world watched. If someone attempted to or succeeded in breaking the Golden State Killer out of custody, they would vault to instant worldwide notoriety. We weren't about to let that happen.

Once at the ballroom, the security team placed DeAngelo in a bulletproof vest and delivered him to a secure room. There, he met with his attorneys and waited until called to court. A sniper sat on an elevated platform above the ballroom, and everyone entering the facility went through metal-detector screening.

I asked to speak with Sergeant Donelli. "Dan, I would like the defendant to sit right here at counsel's table, where he would directly face the audience, for security purposes. Are you good with that?"

"Whatever you want," Donelli responded quickly. Pointing to how the table had been arranged, I further emphasized to him that we were doing this for "security purposes." He looked at me inquisitively. He wanted to ask me something but refrained. My voice grew even louder. "We are doing this for fucking security purposes, right??"

"Oh yes, yes, we are placing the tables that way for security purposes."

"Great, thank you," I replied.

Judge Bowman arrived at Sacramento State right at 1:30 p.m. He walked onto the stage, strolled over to the bench, and sat down. The defense team arrived at the same time. Public Defenders Alice Michel and Joe Cress stepped onto the stage and looked at their table. I stood a few feet away from them, casually trying to hide my purposeful stares. They started whispering to each other and pointing at the table.

Cress spoke up first. "Judge, why is the defense's table placed facing the audience like this?"

Standing at the podium, the judge looked over to the table for the first time. "Why is the table set that way?"

On cue, Sergeant Donelli answered in a loud, authoritative voice, "For security."

Judge Bowman nodded and said, "That makes sense."

I had gotten what I'd wanted, to make DeAngelo face his victims.

The night before the plea, I tossed and turned in bed, waking up several times to look at my phone before closing my eyes again. An early summer heat wave made the night unbearable; morning couldn't come quickly enough. From the moment we had arrested Joseph DeAngelo two years before, the case of the *People of the State of California vs. Joseph James DeAngelo Jr.* had completely consumed every aspect of my life. As we prepared to write the final chapters of this case, the faces and names of all the victims came rushing back in my mind. They had endured decades of nightmares, drug abuse, failed relationships, mental breakdowns, and more. They had prayed for this day, dreamed of it. Some victims had passed before we were able to find him and bring him to this makeshift courtroom.

Moreover, three generations of officers had chased dead ends and rabbit holes as they investigated every conceivable type of suspect—drifters, drug users, railroad and telephone workers, real-estate developers, university administrators, and more. The pursuit left behind alcoholism, divorces, and broken people dealing with the haunted memories of what they had seen and learned. So many people had waited for this moment. I felt a responsibility to them all. The whole team did.

On the morning of June 29, the prosecution team, along with the district attorneys from the different counties involved in the case, arrived on a chartered bus and entered the ballroom through a back entrance. DeAngelo would soon be arriving through the same door. I could feel the nervous, electric anticipation in the air. The prosecutors wondered whether he would actually go through with his guilty plea or refuse to do so at the last minute. I made a wager with Orange County Prosecutor Debbie Lloyd, who thought that DeAngelo might change his mind and plead not guilty. Laughing uneasily, she said, "I can totally see him playing us one last time."

But I had inside information. Being in Sacramento, I was talking face-to-face with his defense attorneys, reading their body language and listening to the tone of their voices. I knew there was no going back. Like a tsunami, the growing and rising momentum would be too much to resist. They even brought back DeAngelo's original public defender, Diane Howard, out of retirement. With her Louis Vuitton bags and flamboyant jackets, Howard was dubbed the "GSK whisperer." She had the ability to calm him down at key moments—his arraignment, or when detectives stripped him and took pictures of his penis. She was likely doing the same now as the moment for him to finally admit guilt before the world drew near.

Retired Sacramento County Undersheriff Carol Daly was in attendance, and as I approached her to say hello, I saw tears in her eyes. After the Sheriff's Department assigned her to investigate the East Area Rapist series in 1976, Carol brought her unique blend of compassion, competence, and persistence to the case for three decades before retiring in 2005. She leaned in and whispered, "We've waited, these victims have waited so long for this." With a squeeze of my hand, she said, "Thank you."

"Carol, it should be *you* that we thank." She then walked over to some of the survivors that arrived. As I took my seat in the prosecutor's section, Jane Carson and Kris Pedretti arrived in the ballroom. Gay and Bob Hardwick soon arrived together, followed by Linda O'Dell and Trish. I walked over to Kris, who told me that Phyllis wouldn't make it as she was recovering from her cancer treatment. As the first rape victim of the EAR, Phyllis struggled for many years with the trauma. Now, cancer kept her away from the very place she'd waited so long to be: the plea of her rapist. The cruelties of life rarely gave Phyllis a moment of peace, but we hoped today would be one of them.

— — —

A few minutes before 9:00 a.m., the metal door leading from the private back hallways opened. Everyone grew quiet and turned their heads as members of the SWAT team escorted DeAngelo into the courtroom. A murmur rolled through the crowd of 200 as flashbulbs sent pulses of white light. Handcuffed and outfitted with a belly chain—a physical restraint device used to control a prisoner's movement—DeAngelo wore a short-sleeve orange jumpsuit. He was rolled into the courtroom slumped in a wheelchair. Best of all, he wore the clear face shield. DeAngelo was a "mouth breather," gulping air like a fish flopped on its side on a dock. His gaunt, angular face and dead, hollowed-out eyes were clearly visible through the mask. There was no hiding on this day.

Judge Bowman took his seat at his bench framed by the flags of the United States and California. "Welcome to Department 24. Due to the ongoing COVID-19 pandemic and the need for social distancing, this matter is being held remotely as to accommodate the public rights as well as the victims' rights, the victims' family's rights to be present. The court has granted access to the press as well. This matter is being livestreamed. We have taken the temperature of all individuals present. I am asking all individuals to wear their mask, with the exception of the attorneys while speaking on the record. I would remind everybody we are still in court, so no talking in the audience. . . . My understanding is there is a change of plea and disposition in this matter."

Just like on *Law & Order,* when a defendant pleads guilty in court, the prosecutor must give an allocution, a recitation of the facts that satisfies all the elements of the crime. It is our opportunity to reveal the truth and to shine a light on the evil that men do, as "justice is truth in action." We went through the allocution in the order of the charges listed on the complaint, with prosecutors from each county detailing the crimes committed in their respective jurisdictions. As I read aloud the facts of Brian and Katie's murder, her brothers stood up from their chairs in solemn silence to represent the young couple, forever frozen in their youth. Katie's frightful scream that night as she ran down the side of the house to escape the EAR will echo through eternity. Forty-two years later, Brian and Katie could finally rest in peace.

The sexual-assault survivors had repeatedly expressed their displeasure at being referred to as "Jane Does" in the complaint. They wanted the defendant and the world to know their names; they no longer wanted to hide in shame, shrouded in anonymity. I presented their request to be referred to by their first names on the complaint and at the hearing, but DA Schubert overruled my suggestion. Before the plea, they had all agreed to stand up during the allocution of their individual incidents. They demanded to confront DeAngelo, to show how they'd turned pain into power and tragedy into triumph.

As we read Trish's allocution, I saw her rise slowly. Tiny and frail, she straightened her back and looked right at DeAngelo. On that hot summer night many years ago, he had punched her and dragged her bloody body outside her house. Now he sat chained to a chair, and soon enough, the deputies would drag his feeble body to prison. She was the one standing now, not he. I saw the twinkle in her eyes as DeAngelo uttered the word: "Guilty."

Then Linda stood up. Four decades ago, she moved to Sacramento from the Midwest to start a new life with her new husband. DeAngelo tied, tortured, and separated Linda from her husband before raping her. Today he would see her face once more and finally face the consequences of his crimes. He took her wedding ring that night, but today she would take his freedom. She watched with satisfaction as her tormentor murmured through clenched teeth, "Guilty."

There were a number of the GSK's crimes on which the statute of limitations had expired and thus could not be charged against him. His rape of Phyllis fell under that category, but that did not stop her from participating fully in the court proceedings. She was always in the front row for every court appearance, and the first to reach out her hand to me when I walked into the courtroom. I knew that it broke her heart not to be there for DeAngelo's plea, but she was fighting cancer and needed to save her strength. And with a compromised immune system, she could not risk exposure to COVID.

When the allocution of Phyllis's assault was read aloud, something amazing happened. Every survivor in the audience stood up to represent her. I felt chills run up and down my spine. Forever tied together by trauma, people who were once strangers rose in unison to reclaim what the Golden State Killer had taken from Phyllis and from each of them. As DeAngelo said, "I admit," a quiet murmur rolled through the audience. At that moment, although I missed Phyllis's warm smile and kind eyes, we undoubtedly felt her presence among us.

Over forty years earlier, Kris was at home alone when she heard someone inside her house rushing toward her. She was only fifteen years old. Like many of the other survivors, she struggled both in quiet and loud ways in the years after her assault. Along with Gay, she led a group of victims of the EAR/GSK's expired and uncharged crimes, fighting to be recognized and demanding that justice belonged to them as well. As part of the plea, which removed the death penalty, DeAngelo was required to admit to all the uncharged offenses that he had committed. Certainty would be theirs; he could no longer hide behind his denials or silence. As Carol Daly said, "Kris had waited all these years for this." The years of torment and the long, winding roads filled with pain all led to this place, this moment. Kris stared directly at DeAngelo, her heart beating louder and louder as he uttered the words, "I admit."

DeAngelo raped Jane while her three-year-old son lay nearby. At the time, Jane served as a reserve captain in the United States Air Force. She pushed forward with her life and focused on her career and family. She wrote a book about her ordeal. She traveled the world. She divorced, remarried, and started a new life on the East Coast, far away from the pain. On the surface, Jane exuded strength and perseverance, but over the years, as her rapist evaded capture, her anger only grew. After we caught DeAngelo, she took many opportunities to bash him publicly. In court and before the television cameras, Jane called him a coward and an animal. I admired the fire and brimstone Jane rained down upon DeAngelo. I also knew that anger is a secondary emotion; it is never the first emotion we feel. As human beings, we first experience hurt and pain, which give rise to the anger. In the early morning hours of October 5, 1976, DeAngelo had deprived Jane of her dignity, robbing her of the power and control that was rightfully hers. On this glorious early summer morning, Jane took that control back.

Before court started that morning, she embraced me warmly before stepping back and asking, "Do you want to see what's on the back of my shirt?" A mischievous grin spread across her face as she gave me a wink.

"Oh no," I said. "Do I need to be worried? What do you have?" She turned around. The back of her orange T-shirt read:

Victim
Survivor
Thriver
East Area Rapist
Golden State Killer
See You in Court

"That's a cool shirt, Jane! Please don't do anything crazy," I smiled at her. Jane's only response was that same grin and wink.

As we began reciting the allocution for Jane's case, she stood up and stared straight at DeAngelo, daggers shooting from her eyes. However, she wasn't done. Jane walked slowly toward him until mere feet separated them. With the back of her T-shirt to the cameras at the rear of the room, she moved closer, one deliberate step in front of the other, closely watched by the judge, the bailiff, and the audience. She was now face-to-face with her nefarious attacker. DeAngelo refused to look directly at her. Thoughts raced through my mind: *Oh my God, what is Jane doing? Is she going to say something to him? Is she going to jump the stage and hit him?*

As she inched closer and closer, she could see the whites of his dead eyes and hear his labored breathing. She moved methodically, a lioness following her prey. The hunter had become the hunted. DeAngelo had nowhere to run and nowhere to hide. As we continued reading the allocution, the audience and cameras panned in, watching Jane's every move. Deputy Oscar Munoz, a veteran courthouse bailiff, walked over and stood in front of the stage between Jane and DeAngelo, his hands resting gently on his gun belt. Undeterred, Jane kept advancing. Having witnessed countless trials, Deputy Munoz had seen people lose control and become violent in the courtroom. He could have grabbed her arm and pulled her away; instead, he looked at Jane with gentle empathy.

Without turning her gaze away from her rapist, Jane quietly said to the bailiff, "I just want him to look me in the eyes. Just one time, I want him to look at me."

Deputy Munoz replied in a soft voice, "He will never look at you. He's a coward, and he'll never look you in the eyes." Undeterred, Jane remained steady and continued to glare at DeAngelo while examining every line and wrinkle, every twitch and every blink behind that clear face shield.

As the adrenaline of the moment subsided, I knew that Jane would not attack DeAngelo physically or move closer. She wanted to send him a message: I am in control now. I am strong. You are weak and insignificant. As we finished, she returned to her seat with a slight grin on her face that matched the one she had given me earlier. On this day, DeAngelo sat down at the banquet of his consequences.

12
Voices for Victims

August 2020

We scheduled the sentencing of Joseph James DeAngelo for the week of August 19, 2020, with the reading of victim impact statements set for Tuesday through Thursday in Department 1 of the Sacramento Superior Court. Judge Bowman would impose DeAngelo's sentence on Friday, August 21, at the Sacramento State Ballroom, where his plea took place. We carefully choreographed the impact statements, starting with the Sacramento victims on Tuesday, followed by the survivors from other counties on Wednesday, and concluding with the family members of all the murder victims on Thursday.

As I did the night before DeAngelo's plea, I tossed and turned in bed and stared at the ceiling, unable to keep my eyes closed. I felt the heavy responsibility of the upcoming week's court proceedings, in which each survivor, after forty years of living the same nightmare, finally woke up to confront the demon of their dreams. It was their right, their day, their moment. I desperately wanted the proceedings to run perfectly and seamlessly for them. Phyllis, busy fighting cancer, wasn't able to attend the plea in June, and I was looking forward to seeing her at the sentencing and listening to her impact statement. But on Monday night, I learned that she would not be able to attend; her sister would read her statement. I was heartbroken.

As we settled into our seats at the counsel's table on Tuesday morning, I saw DeAngelo shuffle into the courtroom wearing a white sweater over his orange jumpsuit and a regular mask covering his face. His face and body looked even more gaunt than last we'd seen him. The deputies belly-chained him to his seat, but this skeletal shell of a monster had nowhere left to run, not on this day or any of his days left on this planet.

Once Judge Bowman took the bench, we started with the very first impact statement.[1] Karen Veilleux, Phyllis's sister, walked up to the podium and read Phyllis's heartfelt words.

> On June 17, 1976, I went to bed not knowing that in just a few hours, my life as I knew it would change. I was a normal young woman of twenty-two, happy and carefree. The only dark spot in my young life was the death of my mother eighteen months earlier. I was vivacious, fun-loving, a little shy, and I loved life. My father was in Massachusetts visiting his sister, and I was alone in the house.
>
> Early on the morning of June 18, 1976, Joseph DeAngelo, henceforth called the devil incarnate, broke into my home, blindfolded me, tied me up, threatened my life with a knife, and raped me. Life as I knew it irrevocably changed that day. That once happy girl became fearful, suspicious, hypervigilant. My sense of safety was shattered. The ringing of the telephone invoked terror, [I was] afraid I would hear his voice again when he called to taunt me, as he did in January of 1978. Noises in the night disturbed what little sleep I could manage. I had an alarm system installed in my home and suffered greatly if I ever had to spend a night alone. Years of living like this have adversely affected my health.
>
> In 1976, women were treated more like suspects than victims when it came to rape. My sense of importance in this world diminished with this treatment. When I found out that this devil had been captured, I felt relieved, but his capture brought about a rush of memories of the rape, wondering what he did with the things he stole from me, what would happen next.
>
> The roles have now reversed. His victims and their families are now free, and his freedom of forty-plus years is now revoked.

1 The impact statements have been edited for clarity and length.

> He deserves to spend the rest of his miserable life imprisoned, no more freedom for him.
>
> I am not what happened to me, I am what I choose to become.

Phyllis had waited over forty years to write those words and to have the world hear them. But most of all, she'd waited to cast each and every one of those words toward the wretched soul who sat chained in that courtroom. DeAngelo just sat there, staring straight ahead with the same vacant look.

— — —

I remember meeting with Trish for the first time, two years before. Her hands trembled as we talked and I could tell then that the trauma she had carried around for over four decades weighed her down like a heavy anchor. She asked her daughter, Patti Cosper, to read her statement as she sat a few feet away in the audience:

> Your Honor, it's been four decades, plus four years, since Joseph DeAngelo attacked me at my parents' house. It happened during the Labor Day weekend, September 4, 1976. I was loading a basket full of clean laundry into my car. He came up behind me out of nowhere on that Saturday night. That night forever changed me.
>
> I was twenty-nine years old, about the same age as DeAngelo. I was separated from my husband, learning to live on my own after a long marriage. My daughter was seven years old, and my sons ten and fourteen. I had a good job with the state and was enjoying my newfound freedom and independence. But my world was different after the attack. I never felt safe for many years. It was hard for me to trust people. I was always looking over my shoulder, expecting someone to jump out and hurt me.
>
> I wonder why he picked me to be one of his rape victims. I'll never know if he came upon me by accident, or if he carefully planned out his attack beforehand. Who was he? Did he know me?

Did he know I would be at my parents' house that night? Will he follow me from now on?

He punched me in the face and broke my nose. I had a concussion from falling backward and hitting my head on the driveway. I saw stars. I lost consciousness. He shook me until it soon became clear that he and his knife had complete control over me for the next two hours, the trauma of which I am being treated for at this time. I could not escape. I did what I had to do to stay alive. He stole my car and my purse, which meant he knew my own address from my license and registration. Because of that, I moved out of my apartment so he couldn't find me and my children.

I was somehow able to get on with my work and being a single mom. I went back to work with the remnants of a black eye and a slightly swollen nose. The lump on my nose never went away. I learned to accept that it was just part of my face. My coworkers would ask how I got the black eye, and I would just say 'I was mugged.' That's what we told our children, too. What really happened became a dark secret that I kept buried, except for telling a few close friends. It just wasn't something I wanted to think about, much less talk about.

I longed for things to go back to how they were. I pretended life was fine, but it wasn't. It was exhausting. It was hard to find joy. My mind was never at peace. I turned to alcohol and drugs to help blot it all out and numb my pain. How I felt about men changed after that night. I no longer cared if I was seen as attractive. I didn't trust them anymore.

I am blessed to have married my husband thirty-two years ago. He is on my healing journey with me. So is my family, except for my parents, who have since passed away. My mom didn't want to move, so I continued to visit them there. I celebrated Christmas and other holidays at their house as if nothing ever happened. Sometimes there was no place to sit except on the organ bench he tied me to before he drank my dad's beer and left. I was always afraid that my dad would kill someone he thought could be my attacker. He was out looking for him with other people in the east area of Sacramento.

I was diagnosed with complex PTSD soon after DeAngelo's arrest in April 2018. His arrest was a total shock. It stirred up all the painful memories of the past I had learned to block out. I was with my daughter when the news scrolled on my phone. She already knew what happened to me back in 1976, but it was a complete surprise to my sons. The news and its aftermath prompted me to have a mental breakdown, and I was hospitalized, [Welfare and Institutions Code] 5150, for three days in June of that year. I was emotionally exhausted, unstable, and not able to deal with reality. I had trouble sleeping after I found out they caught him. I had vivid nightmares. I was prescribed different medications to deal with my anxiety and depression. I'm now getting therapy from a woman who specializes in treating this type of trauma.

Some people are wired wrong, and DeAngelo is one of them. Luck finally ran out for this messed-up human being, at least a poor excuse for one. It is my hope that you punish him to the full extent of the law for the horrific crimes he committed. He admitted that he caused all the suffering and misery to so many victims over the past forty-plus years. He truly is an evil monster with no soul. Did his little penis drive him to be so angry all the time? Did he study criminology so he could carry out his evil deeds as a bad cop without getting caught?

In closing, I want DeAngelo to end up in a place he deserves. I don't buy his act that he's on his last legs. The last years of his pitiful life ought to be spent in the worst prison in existence today. I have a favor to ask, though. When you hand down his sentence, please do not address him as "sir" anymore.

— — —

Before court, I saw Jane Carson in the hallway. I half-jokingly asked her if she planned to wear any special T-shirt for the sentencing. She smiled and gave me a little wink. "I have a little surprise for DeAngelo!" she admitted. All I could do was give her a gentle smile and shake my head.

With her usual fire and brimstone, Jane came out guns blazing, addressing DeAngelo directly.

> Yes, DeAngelo, it's been forty-four years. On Oct 5, 1976, when you broke into my home in the early hours just after my husband had left for work and shoved your knife into my neck, bound my wrists, blindfolded me, and then gagged me with cloth. Do you remember that? You also did the same to my precious three-year-old son. How dare you? Then you repeatedly threatened to kill us. The fear escalated when you started tearing sheets. I had no idea what you were planning to do with all that cloth. Maybe strangle us?
>
> Yes, I was frozen in fear beyond description. My attention was not on the rape—your penis was so tiny—but fully on where you put my son when you moved him from the bed. Where did you put him, and what would you do to him?
>
> I even wrote a book called *Frozen in Fear* detailing my journey after my assault. I tried to escape my fear with alcohol, but medicating myself didn't work. I may have been one of your victims, DeAngelo, but now I'm a survivor-thriver and have led a great life. I put my fears aside and finished my nursing degree at Cal State the year of your attack and then spent thirty years in the air force, achieving the rank of colonel. Yes, evil one, I turned my pain into power and my mess into a message by facilitating groups of women who had been sexually assaulted and volunteering at our crisis center—all very worthwhile activities. Who knows what I might have accomplished had my life not been interrupted by your vicious attack?
>
> If it wasn't for the trauma I endured, I wouldn't be the person I am today. I am proud of what I've accomplished. I'm blessed

beyond words. I see that your eyes are closing. Yes, my wounds may have healed, but my scars do remain.

Oh, by the way, DeAngelo, do you remember the roast you had cooking in the oven the day you were arrested? Too bad you didn't get a chance to enjoy it. Many of your victims will be enjoying a delicious roast every April 24th in remembrance of your capture. The only roast you'll experience is when you roast in hell, because that's where you're going."

Jane paused and looked periodically behind her into the audience. I knew Jane was up to something, just like at the plea. Jane continued her impact statement:

"I want to thank all of my supporters here today. I also want to especially thank a friend that has accompanied me here today. And that friend is Bonnie."

Jane then told Bonnie, "Take your mask off . . ." before continuing with her statement:

"If Bonnie were able to speak, Joe, she would want you to know that as a teenager fifty years ago, she broke her engagement to you when she realized that you had become manipulative and abusive. When you thought you could kidnap her and force her to marry you, even with a gun pointed at her face, you could not make her choose you. She was done with you. I can see that 'I hate you, Bonnie' was a result of your frustration because you lost control over her. But she bears none of that responsibility for your violent choices, and we consider her one of us—a sister, survivor, thriver of your malicious attacks. When you are wheeled away to begin your sentence, you will return in Bonnie's eye to that insignificant place of being gone from her life forever. Amen."

Jane wanted to force a reaction from DeAngelo. When she brought Bonnie to the podium, I immediately looked over to the defendant. He tried to remain stoic, staring straight ahead, but he gulped, and his breathing, the up-and-down movement of his chest, quickened as Bonnie's name was heard in the courtroom. Jane accomplished her mission.

— — —

Kris was only fifteen years old when DeAngelo viciously attacked her. In the two years since we first met, I could see the light grow brighter in her eyes and hear the certainty grow louder in her voice. With her husband, Steve, sitting nearby in support, Kris walked up to the podium.

> Your Honor, my name is Kris Pedretti. Thank you for allowing me to share the impact that the night Joseph James DeAngelo raped me had on my life. As the evening began on December 18, 1976, I was a normal fifteen-year-old kid. I loved going to school, having sleepovers, going to church.
>
> It was a week away from Christmas, and the house was decorated. I was Christmas shopping for my friends and family. My world was predictable, and it was safe. But by the time that night came to an end, my world was forever changed. My safety was shattered as a masked man, DeAngelo, wielding a knife, assaulted me, telling me I would be killed if I didn't do what he demanded.
>
> He raped me repeatedly, moving me in and out of the house after each time he raped me. He tormented me and told me over and over again he would kill me. I believed him. At three different times that night, I thought I was going to die. That night, I sang "Jesus Loves Me" in my head as I waited to die.
>
> The next morning, December 19, I woke up knowing I would never be a child again. Although I was grateful to be alive, I felt that, somehow, I had died. I was forced to begin an endless journey alone to try to survive in a world where nothing was as it was mere hours before. I couldn't make sense of any of it. Try to act normal, I told myself. What was normal? I certainly didn't feel normal; nothing felt normal. So much had changed in such a short time. I no longer fit in where I did before. I was not a normal teenager anymore. The next year, because I no longer fit in, I changed schools three times, moved to a new city, quit going to church.
>
> I struggled for the next forty-one years—panic attacks, failed relationships, frequent job changes, few friends. I think it is incredibly ironic that DeAngelo only had daughters and a granddaughter,

no sons or grandsons. If I were able to address DeAngelo, I would ask him to imagine his daughters and granddaughter at fifteen years old, then to imagine them going through the horror that he put me through. How would he have reacted? How would he be able to watch powerlessly as those he loved struggled to make sense of what they did to deserve such a devastating act of hate? I wonder if he even has the capacity to feel what this would have done to them, how it would permeate the core of their very being.

I understand that no amount of therapy can bring back those years to me the way they were supposed to be. He stole my formative years. I lost my youth, my innocence, my faith, and my trust. Who would I have grown up to be? Sadly, I will never know.

As I look at him today, I see a pathetic coward in a deplorable shell of barely human material. He tried to conceal his soulless being from others by becoming a husband, a father, and a grandfather. He used and manipulated his own family so that he could look like a regular guy as he enjoyed his dark life once they all went to bed, feeling safe in their make-believe world.

If I could speak directly to DeAngelo I would say to him: Your secrets have been exposed. Your double life is over. The world—and I mean the entire world—knows who you are and what you did. You will forever be known as a despicable coward who hid behind a mask of evil. The shame is yours to keep as it eats away at whatever soul you have left.

He is finally getting what he deserved all along. I want him to comprehend that there is not a prayer strong enough to save him. For decades he lived free in the same neighborhood that I lived in, as well as many others. He was free while each of his victims and their families lived in pain, often nearby. Who knows how many times we passed each other in a grocery store or at a restaurant, oblivious to the fact that this rapist and murderer was only a few feet away?

Through this experience, I have learned how utterly important it is to be able to express out loud in some manner, whether verbally

> or in writing, that the shame and guilt belongs to the rapist, not the victim. Now is the time for me to start my new journey. I have received overwhelming support from so many people; it's time for me to pay it forward. I hope to provide support to others as so many have done for me. It truly changed my life.

— — —

Every time we saw Linda O'Dell, she would not stop thanking us. She stepped up to the podium and spoke from her heart.

"I survived. First, I am not the same person that I was in my thirties, forties, and fifties. Today, I forgive you, and kindness is a sign of strength, not weakness. This is for me, not for you. I am practicing what my Lord and Savior did for me."

— — —

From the day that Gay raised her hand and asked for a DA to represent her, our office adopted her as one of our survivors. A gentle soul with a quiet voice, she made sure DeAngelo heard her loud and clear.

> I'm Gay Hardwick, formerly of Stockton. While living there, in the first home my husband and I purchased together, on March 18, 1978, where we had such hope for our future together, Joseph DeAngelo attacked us while we were sleeping. He kidnapped me from my bed, raped me repeatedly, sodomized me, and forced oral copulation. He stole the precious few pieces of jewelry that I owned, which were gold rings given to me by my brother and parents to commemorate my graduation from college the year before. He ate from my refrigerator and drank two beers while I lay bound and blindfolded, unclothed, freezing on the hardwood floor in front of an open door in the cold March night air. He ransacked our home, and in between, he tormented me with threats of imminent death for me and my loved one should I make a sound or resist in any way.

The aftermath of this attack has been with me for forty-two years. That's a very long life sentence for someone who had done nothing to deserve such hatred, violence, and desecration of my body.

To illustrate the lasting impact of this event, I have three clean sheets of paper here, representing three lives. All three have unlimited potential in this world. These paper lives might serve to hold the written formula of a lifesaving scientific breakthrough, a beautiful poem, a soul-moving watercolor painting. Certainly, they would carry words of love, comfort, encouragement, and shared memories to their families, both the younger and the older generations.

This life (paper #1) was never touched by Joe DeAngelo. To this day it has remained in pristine condition, able to sweep itself clean and select new endeavors as it has freely chosen. It has served the world to its fullest capacity and still has much to give and do.

This life (paper #2) was murdered by Joe DeAngelo. It is a life violently taken by him in his effort to preserve himself, while satisfying his evil, perverted, sadistic urges. This life might have contributed so much to our world and brought love, comfort, and shared memories to its grieving family members. But instead, this life so full of potential was turned into a broken dream, stolen from us all by this monster, leaving a void the size of this soul in the lives of many others.

This paper (paper # 3) represents my life. On March 17, 1978, it looked like this, ready to take on my hopes and aspirations. At the age of twenty-four, I was working as a marketing director and broker for a real-estate development firm. I had a lucrative income of my own, I was independent, and I had a bright future. I was deciding whether I might go on to get my MBA or go to law school. I was in love with a young attorney, my man from Kentucky, and the future seemed limitless.

But then, on March 18, Joe DeAngelo broke into our home, and using his tactical police training, he was able to awaken us from a deep sleep with a blinding light in our eyes. Under threats of immediate death from his .357 Magnum pointed at our heads, we were bound and blindfolded. You already know the rest of the story. I survived the repeated attacks on my body, the hours of terror, the understanding during those hours that there was a purely evil presence in our home, a diabolical, depraved, mumbling, and weeping being in human form.

Finally, he was gone, and though I had been certain that I and my loved one would die, we did not. However, our lives were never the same. This life, my life, would never again be like paper #1. This life was now full of creases and wrinkles, and no matter how hard I tried to iron them all away, press them, smooth the lines, make it function, my life would never be the same again. There is no way my paper life (paper #3) could ever again be like paper #1. So, what are these creases and lines, you may ask, why, after forty-two years, can't I just get over it?

Besides the sociological impacts that contributed to my PTSD, there are the very real physiological and psychological changes brought about by the trauma from Joe DeAngelo's attacks. There are the feelings of needing to always be hyperalert to danger, nightmares, sleeplessness, flashbacks, social anxiety, inability to be or stay alone. Becoming a Black Hawk helicopter parent. I remember an incident, two decades after my attack, when I thought I was fully recovered. My husband and four children were in Monterey on vacation, but I had returned to attend a mandatory evening class for my credentialing program. I was actually looking forward to some personal time alone, had purchased Chinese takeout, and was ready for a well-earned quiet evening in our home. But as I sat down on the couch in my pj's to enjoy my food and watch a movie, my eye strayed to the kitchen counter, where there was a roll of duct tape sitting and measured lengths set out ready for use. My triggered response to this was the certainty in my mind that there was someone in the house ready to bind me with these tapes. I didn't know where they had come from, and I ran to my car in terror, in my pj's, and fled to my dad's house, shaking, trembling, and where I spent the night in his care, in my childhood bed, while my takeout was left to spoil in our family room where I left it. Two decades later!

As it turned out, I would later learn that while I had left earlier on vacation with three of our kids, my husband had come along later, staying to coach a junior basketball team for one of our kids. Not yet having uniforms, he had used the duct tape to fashion numbers for their T-shirts, and what I had seen were the remnants of his efforts.

Other things such as trust issues, body-image issues, lost opportunities that I just didn't have the energy to pursue any longer, such as law school or graduate work, are also a part of this wrinkled life. I left my career because I could no longer cope with the stress and anxiety of traveling and being exposed to so many strangers on a daily basis in order to do my job. I stayed home for ten years, where I felt safer. Finally, at the age of forty-two, I entered a teacher credentialing program and became an elementary-school teacher. At least I wasn't afraid of children.

I've written a good life on it, a happy family on my page, and have been married to a saint of a man for forty-one years this week. Through it all, he has supported me emotionally, physically, financially, and in every other imaginable way through our life together.

Around 2012, nearing the end of my teaching career, I was suddenly contacted by Paul Holes, who was an investigator with Contra Costa County. This was when I learned about the murders that had been committed, and their connection to the East Area Rapist attacks. Then came the arrest. No one from my jurisdiction had the decency to let me know that Joe DeAngelo had been arrested. My two adult daughters found out from the news media and called me—again, another traumatic development. Every contact with my local officials up to the announcement of the plea deal had been initiated by me. Not an email or phone call, unless in response to my own efforts to stay informed. For the past two years I've had to advocate for myself.

I have one final paper to share with you. This one was also once a clean, crisp, blank page, full of possibilities that may have benefited the world. But it has been reduced to pulp, and it represents Joe DeAngelo's life as it is today, a toxic, steaming, evil mass of human waste, best kept sealed tightly. There is no excuse for this. So, I get that he may have been an abused child, and as a boy witnessed his sister being raped. But what kind of human sees something like that and decides, "Oh, boy! That's what I wanna be when I grow up!" I, and many others like me, were traumatized within an inch of our lives, and we did not decide to become serial rapists and murderers.

For two years now, I've witnessed DeAngelo choose to devolve, dissolve, and decompose, through his sheer will, into this seemingly puny coward before us today. He has bargained for and obtained the removal of the death penalty, though if there was ever anyone more deserving of death, I can't imagine who.

We survivors can continue to smooth out our lives, and as my fellow survivor Trish quoted recently, "try to make the rest of our years, the best of our years."

— — —

A junior in high school when he lost his sister, Ken Smith remembered Katie fondly every time he spoke about her. Even with the passage of time, I could still hear the pain in his voice as he talked about her loss.

Your Honor, my family and I and many other families are all here to see the terror and evil that DeAngelo brought to so many finally come to an end. We can all start to put this horrible ordeal into its final stage of healing.

He robbed my sister Katie and my brother-in-law, Brian, of their young lives. He took away their chance to have a family of their own. He took my brother Keith's family's chance to know and love their aunt and uncle. He took away my wife's and children's and grandchildren's chance to know and love them. His mistake was, he has no idea how much Katie and Brian were loved. They've remained alive in all our hearts.

I learned something else. My sister Katie had just turned twenty just four days before he killed her in cold blood. And in those twenty short years, she touched so many others, not just our family, with her love and kindness. I've found out that so many others have kept her in their hearts the whole forty-two years since he took her life. So, you see, Katie and Brian were special, and we all loved them so much. You have hurt our family and so many other families so much, but now that part is over. You no longer live in the shadows; we all know who you are.

So, he can stop his silly little act of being weak and feeble and pay for what he did. He's not important. We'll remember Katie and Brian for the rest of our lives, but after he is sentenced, he will be a nobody. He's not worth any more of my family's time.

People like to say that now we can have closure. To me, closure means there's an end. There's no closure for us, as nothing changes. It doesn't bring Katie or Brian back. I guess it does bring closure for him, as it is the end for him. He can't hurt anyone again.

— — —

Sitting in her living room, Loretta Maggiore told me that she would live to see the day that Brian's killer was brought to justice. In poor health, she could not personally attend the hearing, but watched from afar on television and asked me to personally relay one simple and final message to the Golden State Killer in court.

"Your Honor, we do have one final message from Loretta Maggiore, who is Brian Maggiore's mother. She said that she has nothing good to say about Joseph DeAngelo, and so, she will say nothing at all to him."

With that, Judge Bowman said, "Thank you, Mr. Ho. That concludes Sacramento's cases for today."

Next, family members and friends of Claude Snelling, Robert Offerman, Debra Manning, Lyman and Charlene Smith, Cheri Domingo and Greg

Sanchez, Manuela Witthuhn, Patrice and Keith Harrington, and Janelle Cruz read their impact statements. We then recessed for the day before returning in the morning to the ballroom at Sacramento State.

As prosecutors, we often bear the metaphorical burden of absorbing the sins of the world and then shepherding our survivors through their trauma. For two long years, through the drama and infighting, through discarded and lost evidence, through DeAngelo's shenanigans, and through the grueling days and long nights, we had carried out one of the largest criminal prosecutions in the history of California to this moment. Our victims stood at the podium of justice and made their voices heard. For the first time in over two years, I slept through the entire night. I dreamed of Brian and Katie that evening; I couldn't see their faces, only their backs as they stood in the sun. They had been with me for over two years. When I woke up, I thought to myself, *They're moving on to wherever they were headed that night in February 1978.*

— — —

After arriving at the ballroom, I walked over to my seat to the left of the stage. The defendant's plea hearing in June had taken most of the day, but in contrast, the actual sentencing itself would not take long. It would be comprised of three major components: first, the elected district attorneys with charged crimes would each provide a brief statement; second, the defendant and his attorneys were afforded the opportunity to speak; and finally, Judge Bowman would impose DeAngelo's punishment.

I got Billy Satchell a seat in the audience to watch the sentencing. The East Area Rapist represented the bogeyman of his childhood in the Cho, and he wanted to see the case to its ultimate conclusion. Throngs of media were there to cover the proceedings from beginning to end. After Judge Bowman entered and sat down, the door to the back hallway opened, and the defense attorneys filed in—Joe Cress, Alice Michel, and Diane Howard, returned from retirement to attend. The SWAT Team then rolled DeAngelo into the ballroom in a wheelchair. He wore a regular face mask. Having already forced DeAngelo to wear a clear face mask all day long during the plea, I did not demand the same requirement. Today's focus on was not on him, but on the victims seeing the punishment imposed.

Judge Bowman read the charges and turned to the district attorneys assembled in the audience. Contra Costa County District Attorney Diana Becton spoke first.[2]

"Over four decades. That is a long time to wait for justice to be served. Finally, we have arrived at that day, the day when those who have waited so very long will hear that Joseph DeAngelo will now serve the rest of his life behind bars. The bogeyman, the man whose horrific and unspeakable crimes devastated the lives of so many people, lives that will never be the same, lives forever changed. I want to underscore the strength of our victims and their families, the courage that they displayed over the years, and their courage this week to come forward and share, in open court with all of us, the pain and the agony that they had endured over the years. After today's sentencing, Mr. DeAngelo will never threaten our victims again, and he will never harm another soul."

Orange County DA Todd Spitzer then walked to the podium and gave a powerful statement.

"Yesterday marked forty years to the day that a stranger walked into Patty and Keith Harrington's Dana Point home and robbed those three-month newlyweds of their lives. Yesterday, Keith's two brothers testified about their youngest brother. Manuela Witthuhn spent twenty-eight years on this earth, never knowing the joy of motherhood. Janelle Cruz, eighteen years old, her life was ended before she realized her dream of graduating from college, before she could pick out a wedding dress—natural things that we all live for.

"As he was destroying your lives, he got to be on his boat, blowing out birthday candles, and holding his granddaughter, but all the time, in the back of his mind, he knew, he knew we would get him. I honestly believe that this beast deserves the ultimate punishment of death, but we met with our victims. We knew the age of the case, we knew how long it took to solve, and we knew that this was the right thing to do so you could be all here today in your lifetime."

---

2 The district attorneys' statements have been edited for clarity and length.

Santa Barbara County DA Joyce Dudley approached the podium next to speak on behalf of her victims.

"Yesterday, I listened to Debbi Domingo's powerful words about not being able to enter her home or know the details of what happened. What you need to know is what you already know; in life you loved them, and they loved you. And now that this case is finally over, perhaps what you need to concentrate on is the details of that love. Focus on the things that made them lovable and allow yourself to let those memories make you smile again. I believe it is possible to get healing and comfort from that knowledge, because knowing that you are loved, and that you were loved, is truly the most powerful knowledge of all."

Tulare County DA Tim Ward, in his easy and affable manner, walked to the stage and told us:

"Your Honor, when your gavel falls today, the sentence will be final, and this case will soon be viewed through the prism of history. As we have seen and heard this week, the defendant slowly ceases to be the focal point of that story. Instead, my prayer going forward is that the legacy that remains will focus on the triumph and the resiliency displayed by the survivors that we have heard from this week. Though these despicable horrors began in Tulare County, we will not be defined by evil. Instead, our entire community stands silently alongside the Snelling and the McGowen families, all the families here today, and the families across the state. In searching for some positive message to remember, I say this: As science and technology evolve, a space for evil like this to operate gets smaller and smaller. DNA will never forget. By God's grace, the doors of justice will open for other families. That voice of hope is the true legacy that shall remain, and it shall not be silent, ever."

From the beginning of the search for the Golden State Killer, Ventura County staff walked alongside us through all the valleys and summits. District Attorney Greg Totten spoke of the constant battle between light and darkness, good and evil.

"As we have witnessed during these victim-impact statements, this is a case about light and darkness. The victims and survivors who testify before this court are people of light. By their courage, they shine a very bright light on the magnitude of crimes before the court, painting a picture of the immense impact these horrific crimes had on their lives. In a sense, they've also brought to light their loved ones. And in doing so, they have honored their memories as people of purpose, people of character, as people who would have made a difference in this world. We must also confront the terrible darkness of the defendant, who sits before the court, stoic, void of humanity and lacking any remorse, and utterly unredeemable. Even now here in the courtroom, he turns away from the light and will not look at his accusers, for fear that the truth of their testimony penetrate the deep darkness of his soul."

As the host district attorney of the People vs. the Golden State Killer case, Sacramento County DA Anne Marie Schubert took the stage last, reminding the audience of the long road we had traveled.

"It's been 16,417 days since Joseph DeAngelo began his reign of terror—44 years, 11 months, and 11 days. For those in Sacramento, it's been 16,136 days since the first rape of Phyllis—44 years, 2 months, and 4 days. It's been 42 years since Brian and Katie were taken from this world. It's been 12,529 days since Janelle, that beautiful light, was taken."

Addressing the survivors, she advised:

"The greatest revenge is to live your lives. Paint your children and grandchildren with hearts and rainbows. Water ski again, knowing that the monster of your childhood or your younger years is gone forever and will die alone in prison."

Turning her attention to DeAngelo, she said:

"To the defendant, your name will fade from the headlines. I think some of the most powerful words we heard from this week were from Kris [Pedretti], who said, 'Mr. DeAngelo, there is no prayer strong enough to save you.'"

After Schubert spoke, Judge Bowman took a brief recess to change court reporters. However, the real reason for the short break involved DeAngelo. Public Defender Joe Cress had informed us before court that the Golden State Killer might make a statement to all the victims and survivors. To facilitate that, the SWAT Team would have to remove the belly chain, allowing him to stand up during his comments. The courtroom would have to be cleared of civilians to do so.

After a ten-minute recess, we resumed the hearing. As the room sat in silence, Joe Cress announced, "Mr. DeAngelo would like to make a brief statement." A murmur spread across the room as DeAngelo stood up. He looked particularly thin and bony. With his right hand, he removed his mask, rocked back and forth, and peered down at his mask. He looked up again and pauses for several seconds before uttering:

"I have listened to all your statements, each one of them, and I am truly sorry to everyone I've hurt. Thank you, Your Honor."

After DeAngelo sat down, Judge Bowman weighed in with his eloquent comments.

"The court is not saying that Mr. DeAngelo does not deserve to have the death penalty imposed. It merely means that the court feels that it would never come to pass. All the parties should be commended with reaching this resolution for the results of this trial, and a plea of guilty is the same. Mr. DeAngelo will spend the rest of his natural life and ultimately meet his death behind the walls of the state penitentiary. Mr. DeAngelo, I've listened for the last three days to the people that you've terrorized and their friends and their families. Their impact statements will always be with me. I was moved by their courage, their grace, their strength—all qualities that you clearly lack. I know whatever words I say today will pale in comparison to the words of the survivors that have spoken.

"I've listened to the survivors, and I've watched you, but I could not help but wonder what you were thinking? Are you capable of comprehending the pain and anguish that you have caused? When a person commits monstrous acts, they need to be locked away so they can never harm another innocent person. It is my sincere hope that with the opportunity to be heard these last few days, and the sentence to be imposed, the survivors will find some resolution, will find some peace, and hopefully find some justice, however imperfect. Mr. DeAngelo, you are now remanded to the custody of the Sacramento Sheriff to be delivered to the custody of the Director of Corrections and Rehabilitation to serve the remainder of your life in prison. We are adjourned."

— — —

I sat throughout the sentencing, absorbing every word spoken and every tear shed, at times lost in my thoughts as my mind wandered to all the different dark places, all the dead bodies, all the broken souls, and all the relentless investigators who never gave up. We had gathered forty-five years' worth of loss and hope, shame and redemption, despair and determination, death and life in one place. As I took a deep breath, I looked across the room and saw the entire GSK prosecution team sitting with their backs straight, their heads held high, knowing that we had kept our word to all the victims. In the back of the room, I saw Sergeant Kenny Clark with his arms folded and Rob Peters with his bowtie and wide grin. DA Chief Deputy Grippi and Homicide Chief Rod Norgaard sat a few rows behind me. I recall eavesdropping on their conversation over two years ago and hearing the word, "EAR." There was former Undersheriff Carol Daly, the guilt and weight of all those years finally lifted from her shoulders. Jane Carson stood proudly, ready to rain more fire and brimstone upon DeAngelo. Gay sat next to her husband, Bob, holding his hand. In another area of the ballroom, Linda and Trish were surrounded by their families.

And then, I saw Kris sitting to the side with Phyllis. Wearing round glasses just above her mask, Phyllis sat quietly in her chair. Although I could not see it underneath the mask, the twinkle in her eye told me she was smiling. For forty years, she had waited for this moment. No matter how "imperfect," justice belonged to Phyllis on that hot August day. A few months later, Phyllis Zitka passed away. If we had pushed forward with a death-penalty trial, she would have never lived to see justice delivered.

Years have passed since that day, and in the years to come, when I think of the case, I no longer think about DeAngelo's heinous crimes or the details of his life or some novel legal strategy. Instead, my lasting memory and image of the People vs. the Golden State Killer is Phyllis in our make-shift courtroom, at peace, holding the providence of justice in the hollow of her hands.

Epilogue

Delving into a criminal case is like peering into a magic mirror. It reflects the essence of our existence—a look into our soul. It allows us to understand who we are because we see our own reflection. The struggles and successes, the deep lines etched by pain and wisdom, eyes and hearts filled with anger and determination, still bright with the strength of the human spirit. In the end, we choose what we want to see.

In every homicide case that I have tried, I always share with the jury a simple observation: The human being is capable of such great beauty, and the human animal is capable of such great depravity. We can paint the Sistine Chapel or compose a symphony, and we can also use a knife to carve human flesh. A police officer, sworn to protect and preserve, can terrorize entire communities and become one of the most prolific and sadistic serial killers in our nation's history, as DeAngelo did.

As I write these very words, I am sitting under a summer night's sky, my eyes turned toward the wide-open expanse. Shooting stars flash across the velvety firmament. I look back at the GSK case and ask myself these same questions: How can we simultaneously create life and utterly destroy it? In life, we choose to feed either the human animal or the human spirit; to choose death or life, hate or love.

We are greater than the sum of our individual parts—more than what our genes tell us we should be, and more than the circumstances life deals us. While monsters like DeAngelo can try to excuse their heinous acts by blaming their childhood trauma, survivor Gay Hardwick explained it best in her impact statement when she said, "I get that he may have been an abused child, and as a boy witnessed his sister being raped. But what kind of human sees something like that, and decides, Oh, boy! That's what I want to be when I grow up. I, and many others like me, were traumatized within an inch of our lives, and we did not decide to become serial rapists and murderers. . . . There is no excuse for this." The choice is always ours to make.

The three generations of officers who pursued the Golden State Killer and the prosecutors who fought inside and outside the courtroom chose service over self. The victims and survivors who suffered under the blistering pain of trauma chose resiliency and love over despair and hopelessness. DeAngelo's choices led him behind bars for the rest of his life.

How fitting that Katie Maggiore's brother, Ken Smith, was a correctional officer at Corcoran State Prison, where DeAngelo now spends his days alone in a cold cement cell. I receive periodic updates on his status. Upon DeAngelo's sentencing, I sent a package to the Department of Corrections containing all the victims' impact statements along with videos of him in his jail cell, moving without any limitation just hours before and after he pretended to be an invalid at his court appearances. I advised them of his penchant for manipulation and warned them against his future attempts at malingering to obtain favorable housing status.

Victims, Survivors, and Thrivers

A few months after the sentencing, I felt my phone buzz and saw Victim Advocate Mailyn Chuong's name scroll across the screen. When I picked up, she got right to the point. "I wanted to let you know that Phyllis just passed away."

I sat in silence for a moment, lost in my thoughts. "Thanks for letting me know. At least she got to see DeAngelo sentenced before she passed. You know, if we had continued to seek the death penalty, Phyllis wouldn't have lived to see the trial," I answered.

In her final days, Phyllis was surround by the love of her sister and her husband, Kris, and Carol Daly, who tended to her every need. In her final hours, Phyllis turned to Carol, who sat at her bedside, and asked, "After you were assigned to the case, why didn't you go back and reinterview me? I needed you back then." Gripped in the throes of cancer, Phyllis still felt the pain from four decades earlier.

Carol leaned in and whispered, "What matters most is I'm here now." As Carol administered one last dose of morphine, Phyllis chose to let go, and her gentle spirit slipped away.

In her honor, Kris and Gay chose to start a nonprofit called Phyllis's Garden, which conducts victim-centered trainings for law enforcement. They work to change officers' focus to treating victims as patients, and not a piece of evidence. Even today, many victims of sexual assault are interviewed in sterile and spartan police-station rooms, sometimes in the same location used to interview the perpetrators. Law enforcement often lacks the funding to create inviting places for survivors to speak about their trauma. Phyllis's Garden raises money to create "soft interview rooms," which provide soothing lighting and décor and comfortable furniture. Devices that record statements and interviews are made more discreet, reducing personal discomfort. Blankets, tissues, toys for children, and refreshments are available to assist individuals in navigating these challenging moments. According to Kris and Gay, "Those who have experienced trauma are more likely to recall details and return for further interviews in an environment that feels safe, comfortable, and supportive."

Through their nonprofit, Kris and Gay have created over half a dozen soft interview rooms. A portion of the publisher's and my proceeds from this book will go to support Phyllis's Garden so they can continue to build more rooms and aid victims, survivors, and thrivers. The donation will be made in Phyllis's name and in honor of all those who have transformed their pain into purpose and amplified the voices of victims.

Jane Carson spends her summers in Maine and the rest of the year in the South, enjoying a wonderful life with her husband. She continues to speak about the Golden State Killer and assist victims and survivors of violent sexual offenses.

Trish and Linda still live in the Sacramento area and continue their journey of healing, surrounded by the love of their families.

Law Enforcement

Carol Daly enjoys her garden and dotes on her grandchildren. During the case, the victims would gather in her expansive backyard for support, and Carol continues to work with Kris, Gay, and many of the other survivors. When it comes to helping victims find their voices, she never retired.

Sergeant Michelle Hendricks went on to lead the Sheriff's Department's Sexual Assault Investigative Team, holding predators accountable and obtaining justice for victims. After she mentored another generation of Michelle Hendrickses, she then transferred to my office, where she now works in our newly formed Cold Case, Science and Technology Unit. Kevin Papineau returned to working homicide cases and now partners with Michelle to solve cold cases.

After thirty-plus years in our office, Monica Czajkowski retired from the Sacramento DA's Office. She shuns any attention or adulation for her tenacious work—it was she who zeroed in on DeAngelo and alerted everyone to him. Her triumphant moment was made on the foundation built by our colleagues at the FBI and genealogist Barbara Rae-Venter, who continues to consult on cold cases. Sacramento DA Lieutenant Kirk Campbell returned to run our team of investigators on the Homicide and CST units. Walking by his office in the early afternoon, you can still see him counting his pistachios and solving crimes.

Just before DeAngelo's arrest in April 2018, Paul Holes retired from law enforcement. However, that has not stopped him from contributing to investigations around the country. He wrote the bestselling book *Unmasked: My Life Solving America's Cold Cases,* which detailed his efforts to identify the GSK and myriad other criminals. He has produced multiple television shows and podcasts and appears at countless events annually, bringing much-needed attention to the field of criminology and to the relentless determination of law enforcement.

Homicide Detective Sergeant Kenny Clark retired from the Sheriff's Department after an illustrious career and now lives a quiet life with his wife. He spends his time listening to the ocean waves that drown out all the death he has witnessed. Detective Rob Peters, still sporting those black-rimmed glasses and bow tie, was promoted to sergeant and continues to investigate violent crimes. He still flashes his signature grin every time I see him.

The Public Defenders

Diane Howard returned to her retirement, traveling the world and living the life she worked for. As DeAngelo's whisperer, she continues to receive telephone calls and letters from him in prison.

Alice Michel received a promotion to the executive team at the Public Defender's Office. After receiving the same promotion, Joe Cress left the office when the governor appointed him as a judge on the Sacramento Superior Court.

The Judges

Judge Michael Sweet returned to trying cases in the main courthouse as he gets closer to retirement. On the other hand, Judge Steve White will never retire; he continues to preside over trials and "grind" away. Detectives and DAs still bring him complicated search warrants to review.

After DeAngelo's sentencing, the entire bench elected Judge Michael Bowman as the Presiding Judge of the Superior Court for a two-year term. Upon completion of his term, he returned to presiding over serious cases, including sexual assaults, homicides, and death-penalty cases.

The District Attorneys

After many years of service, both DA Greg Totten of Ventura County and DA Joyce Dudley of Santa Barbara County retired from office. Tulare County DA Tim Ward, Contra Costa County DA Diana Becton, and Orange County DA Todd Spitzer remain in their respective offices. I see them periodically at conferences and greet them with warm handshakes.

In 2022, Sacramento DA Anne Marie Schubert decided to run for California Attorney General as an independent. She came in fourth place among five major candidates, garnering 7 percent of the vote. She then opened a consulting firm, providing political advice.

Golden State Killer Prosecution Team

In the years after the People vs. the Golden State Killer case, those of us on the prosecution team went our separate ways. Some returned back to our old jobs, others sailed off into retirement, and a few of us found new challenges. Although we all returned to our lives, our shared experience will connect us forever.

David Alavezos stayed in Tulare County as the Chief Deputy, prosecuting murder case after murder case—the Judge White of prosecutors. Marguerite Rizzo returned to her job overseeing the L.A. County DA's Forensic Science section, providing guidance on investigative genetic genealogy for prosecutors throughout the country.

Kelly Duncan came back to Santa Barbara as its Assistant Chief under the new DA. She lives on several acres nestled among the rolling hills of the American Riviera. In the evenings, you can find her sitting on the porch watching the sunset and enjoying a glass of wine. When we see each other at the annual prosecutor's conference, we laugh and reminisce through the rose-colored glasses of our memories.

Cheryl Temple was one of the finest prosecutors I ever worked with. After DA Totten retired, she briefly served as the interim district attorney of Ventura County before leaving the position. She now spends her time raising her wonderful sons. Beyond driving her children to sporting activities and being the best mom they could ask for, Cheryl continues to expound on legal strategy and the nuances of the law while advising DA's offices throughout the state on high-profile prosecutions. At least once a year, we talk on the phone and catch up. Invariably, our conversation returns to the GSK and the amazing team we worked with.

Pat Dixon came home to Newport Beach, in Orange County, where he continues to wear his impeccable suits. DA Todd Spitzer promoted him to run the Homicide and Gang teams in the OC. Ever the gentleman, Pat reaches out to me once or twice a year on legal issues that our offices face.

Although retired from an illustrious career at the Orange County DA's Office, Jim Mulgrew worked from time to time in their Post-Conviction Unit, defending verdicts won by his office. If I ever need legal research or a precedent to support my argument, I turn to Jim.

Debbie Lloyd continued to work as a retired annuitant for Orange County. Although she took time off, she still helped the office periodically with needed projects. Having spent her career in that office, Debbie found it hard to leave. She loved the work, the people, and the place. Our phone calls became less frequent, but her voice still sounds familiar when we do talk.

Sacramento Chief Deputy Steve Grippi retired and traveled the world. Instead of putting out fires in the office, he now spends his days playing golf. Homicide Chief Rod Norgaard took over for Grippi before retiring himself. He grew out his goatee but still wakes up every morning around four to walk his dog. I call him up for advice every so often, and we meet up for sushi every couple of months.

I endorsed Amy Holliday when she ran for judge. After she came in first place during the primary, the governor appointed her to the bench four months before her term was to officially start. Fair to both sides, her heart still beats strongly for the victims of violent crimes.

In the months after DeAngelo's sentencing, I slept more than I had ever slept in my life. I went on long walks with Jenny on the trails near our home, meandering among the Heritage Oaks that dot the hillside and listening to the gurgling stream. I spent most of my professional life inside the walls of a courtroom, trying case after case, eating all the sins of the world, bleeding and breathing every aspect of the trial. But after all the battles in the courtroom, I thought to myself, How many more summits did I need to climb? How many more opponents must I defeat in the ring? How many more autopsies and funerals must I see?

I returned to my job as Assistant Chief DA and focused on healing the community's wounds, past and present. Instead of speaking to a judge or jury, I listened to the people of my community. I wanted to sit in John O'Mara's red chair one day and rub my chin like Norgaard as detectives pitched homicide cases for me to file. I thought my dream job was Homicide Chief, but life sometimes takes you in different directions.

When DA Schubert ran for California Attorney General in 2022, the position of Sacramento DA opened up. As the gatekeeper to our justice system, I felt that the position of district attorney held such high importance within our society. Like other elected officials, whether countywide, statewide, or federal, the position affects the very fabric of our everyday lives in ways both small and grand. Two other people were running for the position, but both, I felt, lacked my experience in the courtroom, the classroom, and the community. I had never once run for anything, not even student council, yet here I was, considering running for the highest law-enforcement position in the county.

While I was debating a run for DA, Schubert walked into my office. She supported someone else in the office to succeed her; there was conjecture that her choice was made to advance her own political agenda. The conversation was short. She looked at me and said, "You need to wait your turn." Those words particularly stung. As an Asian American, I am well aware of the "model minority" stereotype that we make good workers but not good leaders. We are often viewed as too weak to lead, and many of us are told we need to be "more forceful and dynamic." But when we show strength and confidence, we are called stubborn, strident, inflexible, or worse yet, "a supreme dictator."

After being told to wait my turn, I thought to myself, Why do I even want this job? Years earlier, I had looked with disapproval at the drama and politics that swirled around the DA position. But something changed in me. Working in the community, I saw the need for a leader that builds bridges rather than burns them; that listens rather than dictates; that keeps their word rather than gives it away. Moreover, I also witnessed firsthand the impact of poor leadership. A bunker mentality, an absentee-landlord approach to leading, a lack of transparency, poor staff retention, the lack of a cohesive long-term plan for addressing public safety, and bridges burned both inside and outside the office. We needed a new start and a new vision, one rooted in the best traditions of the past but with a focus on the future.

Before making the decision, I talked to my wife, because when you run for office, your family does as well. On vacation in Orange County, walking along the beach near the Wedge, Jenny told me, "Thien, the community needs you, and the office needs you. You need to run." Four years earlier, she had given me the same permission to pursue the Golden State Killer case.

The road ahead was going to be difficult. Schubert not only endorsed someone else, but she actively worked against me. She attempted to strip me of my position on the executive team out of retribution for not waiting my turn and for derailing her succession schemes. Schubert even reassigned me to an isolated desk position because she feared my work within our community, relenting only after I threatened to file a lawsuit.

Despite it all, I walked precincts, knocked on doors, and talked to everyday people. Most of all, I listened to what the constituents were saying. After months of campaigning, in June 2022, the people of Sacramento elected me as the thirty-third district attorney in the county's history.

After I was sworn into office on January 3, 2023, I walked into Billy Satchell's office one morning. He was sitting in John O'Mara's red chair, rocking back and forth. Homicide detectives from the Sheriff's Department had just left his office after discussing the filing of murder charges. After

Norgaard retired, I promoted Billy to the Homicide Chief position. Five years earlier, I had rushed into his office one April morning to tell him we had found the East Area Rapist. On this particular morning, I told him instead about an idea that had come to me one night in a dream, an idea full of symbolism and meaning.

When I was a young lawyer interviewing for a job at the Sacramento DA's Office, I sat in the lobby outside the Executive Offices, or "Mahogany Row" as people called it. On the wall hung the photos of every district attorney in Sacramento County dating back to 1850, when William Wallace was the first. Schubert removed those pictures and threw them in a closet when she got elected. After taking office, I put them back up on the wall. My color photograph, taken after I was sworn into office, now sat above the top row of pictures. One day, after I retire, a black-and-white picture of me will join the rows of photos below.

I re-displayed the photographs on the wall for several reasons: First, to remind me, and everyone who comes afterward, that one day we all will be nothing more than a picture on a wall, a memory, a story; the institution will move on without us. But it also affirms that we will go on in the memories and hearts of those whom we serve. We are part of a long line of prosecutors imbued with the sole and collective purpose of finding the truth and rendering justice.

Second, it was to recognize that in the 153-year history of Sacramento County, none of the people on that wall looked like me or shared my life's experience. Not one other Asian American, African American, or Latine person, not one immigrant, not one person who learned how to speak English by watching cartoons. My hope is that by seeing my image on that wall alongside my predecessors, future prosecutors of all backgrounds will picture themselves next to us and know that anything is possible, that any dream can be realized, and any vision can come to pass—even one where a young refugee child became a DA who had the great honor and privilege of prosecuting the People vs. the Golden State Killer.

Acknowledgments

At the time of this writing, the Sacramento County District Attorney's Office employs over 180 prosecutors and nearly 500 employees. To run this operation, I rely upon the steady leadership of Chief Deputy Scott Triplett, Assistant Chiefs Bret Wasley and Tan Thinh, and the rest of our executive team. Our mission is to bring justice and build trust in our community, to hold the powerful accountable, and to give voice to the voiceless, and I do so with Assistant Chief Rochelle Hao Beardsley and Supervising District Attorney Sonia Martinez Satchell by my side. They are the engine that powers the push for change, and their communications team ensures our message resonates. Doug Elmets is the wordsmith who helps craft my communications with the public.

People from around the world watched the plea, impact statements, and sentencing of Joseph DeAngelo in June/August 2020. The order of the proceedings, the placement of the participants, and its visual impact required detailed planning and execution. Our media team, led by Rochelle and Public Information Officer Shelly Orio; and Rhett Thompson and Steve Pagagiannis of the Forensic Media Services team pulled it all off seamlessly.

Writing a book requires a village of collaborators. As a first-time author, I relied heavily upon my publisher, Third State Books, led by co-founders Stephanie Lim and Charles Kim. I trusted their mission of providing a platform for authentic Asian American stories and perspectives in a publishing industry that often ignores us. I leaned into the sage wisdom of my editor, Charles, who lifted my prose to new heights. Prerna Chaudhary and Emily Tom helped tremendously in keeping us organized, and the folks at Books Forward were instrumental in getting my story out into the media.

Our criminal-justice system is at the intersection of every aspect of society, leaving no corner untouched. To navigate the political pitfalls as the highest law-enforcement official in California's capital, I rely on my trusted political adviser, Jeff Gozzo, and his right-hand person, Valeria Hernandez.

Generations of law enforcement relentlessly pursued the Visalia Ransacker/East Area Rapist/Original Night Stalker/Golden State Killer. Many of them did not make the pages of this book, but their contributions will forever be remembered, including Sacramento County Sheriff's Department Detectives Dick Shelby and Ray Biondi, Sacramento Police

Detective Pete Willover, and former Orange County Sheriff's Department Detective Larry Poole. Your determination made all the difference. Additionally, Sacramento Sheriff Jim Cooper grew up in Rancho Cordova during the EAR's reign of terror in the 1970s and remembers the pervasive fear that paralyzed his community. His agency continues to partner with my office to solve cold cases.

To all the victims who never got to celebrate another birthday or anniversary or see another sunrise, to all the survivors and thrivers, and to all the families deeply affected by these crimes, thank you for your courage and resilience and the choice you made to uplift the human spirit. And to Phyllis, Jane, Trish, Linda, Gay, and Kris, thank you very much for authorizing me to tell your stories with the public. Your insights and contributions could never be measured in full.

I am my parents' son. I received the gifts of my father's insight and my mother's passion. Their courage and selflessness echo throughout my life, and to them I am forever grateful.

Lastly, my wife, Jenny, and our three children form the very foundation of my life. Without their unwavering support and love, the sun would shine less brightly, the birds would sing less often, and life would be less meaningful.

Selected Index

Compiled by Prerna Chaudhary and Emily Tom

P

Q

R

S

T

U

V

About Thien Ho

Thien Ho was elected Sacramento District Attorney in 2022. Over a twenty-five-year legal career, he has prosecuted hundreds of high-profile sexual assault, gang, and homicide cases and led the Sacramento County DA's Office's Gang and Hate Crime Unit. In 2017, he received Prosecutor of the Year honors from both the National Asian Pacific Islander Prosecutors Association and the Sacramento DA's Office. He is best known for successfully prosecuting Joseph DeAngelo, a.k.a. the Golden State Killer. Ho lives in Sacramento with his family.

Founded in 2023, Third State Books brings innovative Asian American and Pacific Islander voices, stories, and issues to audiences who cherish them. A cornerstone of our ethos is to effect narrative change by owning our own stories. Our name, "Third State," refers to our unique experience as immigrants and the children of immigrants, bringing the best of America and of our cultures of origin to occupy a distinctive space and identity all our own. Through fiction and nonfiction, for adults and children, Third State Books publishes stories that fully represent authentic Asian American experiences to universal audiences.

Third State Books is a proudly independent publishing house distributed worldwide by Publishers Group West, a division of Ingram Content Group.

Please visit us at thirdstatebooks.com and engage with us on social media @thirdstatebooks.